DUE

Changing Health Care
for an Aging Society

Changing Health Care for an Aging Society

Planning for the
Social Health Maintenance Organization

Walter N. Leutz
Brandeis University Health Policy Center

Jay N. Greenberg
Brandeis University Health Policy Center

Ruby Abrahams
Brandeis University Health Policy Center

Jeffrey Prottas
Brandeis University Health Policy Center

Larry M. Diamond
Brandeis University Center on Aging

Leonard Gruenberg
Brandeis University Health Policy Center

Lexington Books
D.C. Heath and Company/Lexington, Massachusetts/Toronto

Library of Congress Cataloging in Publication Data
Main entry under title:

Changing health care for an aging society.

Includes index.
1. Aged—Medical care—United States. 2. Health
maintenance organizations—United States. 3. Aged—
Medical care—United States—Cost control. I. Leutz,
Walter N. II. Title: Social/HMO. [DNLM: 1. Health
Maintenance Organizations—organization & administration—
United States. 2. Health Planning—organization &
administration—United States. 3. Health Services for
the Aged—organization & administration—United States.
4. Social Work—organization & administration—United
States. WT 30 C456]

RA413.7.A4C43 1985   362.1'0425   84–29987
ISBN 0–669–10139–7 (alk. paper)

Second printing, December 1985

Published simultaneously in Canada
Printed in the United States of America on acid-free paper
International Standard Book Number: 0–669–10139–7
Library of Congress Catalog Card Number: 84–29987

To Dennis, John, Mitch, Sam, and Joanne

Contents

Tables and Figures

Tables

Figures

Foreword

In the Deficit Reduction Act of 1984 (P.L. 98-36) Congress directed the Secretary of Health and Human Services to "demonstrate the concept of a social health maintenance organization as described in Project No. 18-P-9-7604 . . . of Brandeis University." This unusual action reflects strong national interest in finding new delivery systems for the elderly that have the potential to be cost-effective as well as comprehensive. More important, it indicates that national leaders recognize the inevitable and growing mismatch between the need for care resulting from demographic trends and the ability of the public sector to provide the necessary resources. This imbalance demands new approaches and ideas.

The graying of America through the first few decades of the twenty-first century is both inevitable and well-known. Less well known by the general public today, but unlikely to remain that way for much longer, is the impending financial crisis in Medicare. Over the next few years, there will be significant pressure to reduce Medicare benefits. Concurrent with this will be recognition of the rapidly increasing need among the elderly for long-term care. The driving factor is not the increasing number of those now age 65, but rather those over age 80, an age group that will be growing at a much faster rate. The number of individuals who experience catastrophic costs for long-term care services will grow, and it is unlikely that any one level of government will step forward to take on a financial responsibility of such overwhelming dimensions.

It is against this background that the social health maintenance organization (SHMO) was conceived. The concept of a SHMO wove together two lines of thinking of the staff and faculty at Brandeis's Heller Graduate School. First, those concerned with service delivery saw the potential to improve both efficiency and effectiveness by integrating the broad array of health and social services needed by the elderly into a single system of care. Second, those of us concerned with finance saw the importance of providing individuals with financial protection by pooling the risk of long-term care. The SHMO incorporates both lines of thinking. It combines current expenditures by Medicare, Medicaid, and individuals as revenue sources, and it uses this pooled financing to pay for both acute and chronic care. If this consolidated model of financing and service delivery is successful in providing expensive institutional care more efficiently and appropriately, the

SHMO has the potential to both reduce future Medicare and Medicaid expenditures and buffer catastrophic out-of-pocket costs for chronically ill individuals.

Back in 1979 the SHMO was only one of several possible solutions to long-term care problems proposed by Brandeis in an earlier book in this series (Callahan and Wallack 1981). Of all the options explored, it was our desired approach, and we sought the necessary funding to further develop and test the idea. In 1980 we received a grant from the Health Care Financing Administration to develop the specifics of the model and conduct a national search for provider sponsors committed to quality care for the elderly. We also began a search for foundation funding, since HCFA did not agree to underwrite planning and development costs at sites. Because our objective was to test the SHMO concept and not the ability of providers to establish an integrated delivery system, we selected providers with proven track records at managing efficient programs. Certainly, in the long run it will be the ability and character of the providers as much as the soundness of our idea that will decide the worthiness of the SHMO.

The four demonstration sites that have completed planning and development are very different types of organizations, but they are similar in their uniformly high quality and their commitment to improving care for elders. The sponsors are: Metropolitan Jewish Geriatric Center in Brooklyn, New York; Ebenezer Society and Group Health, Inc., in Minneapolis, Minnesota; Kaiser Center for Health Research in Portland, Oregon; and Senior Care Action Network (SCAN) in Long Beach, California. The executives and boards of directors of these organizations are to be commended for their courage in sponsoring the SHMO demonstration. It was a high-risk venture when they signed on, and the risks and costs have mounted rather than diminished with time. Of course, the demonstration would not have been possible without the many foundations that have supported the project.

The urgency of trying new approaches to our long-term care crisis led the U.S. Congress to legislate the SHMO Demonstration. Seldom does a small demonstration receive such high-level attention or secure its survival through a specific act of Congress. The action reflects congressional recognition of the need to explore efficient delivery system alternatives that tap new sources of private financing. To not experiment now with the SHMO and other promising approaches may lead only to more expensive and inefficient public responses in years to come. The only way to keep our government and our elderly citizens from being overwhelmed by a crisis in long-term care is to have the foresight and the courage to explore new directions.

This book analyzes the issues and obstacles that were addressed in transforming this far-reaching concept into an operational program. If research and evaluation show that the programs are successful, the book will be an invaluable resource for future SHMO sponsors.

Stanley S. Wallack
Director
Health Policy Center
Brandeis University
Waltham, Massachusetts

Acknowledgments

This chronicle of the Social Health Maintenance Organization (SHMO) planning and developing process would not have been possible without the efforts of the many who made the project happen. Listing their names here seems a small acknowledgment for the time and efforts of staff throughout a long planning period; for the chances taken by the project's advocates in sponsoring agencies, the government, and foundations; and for the openness of our colleagues in all settings who shared their time, materials, and insights during the development of this book.

Our first thanks go appropriately to the Health Care Financing Administration (HCFA)—both for partially funding the Brandeis staff and especially for providing two excellent project officers, Sidney Trieger and Thomas Kickham. Two years ago, they saddled us with writing a project report on the "issues and choices" facing providers thinking of developing a SHMO, and that report led directly to this book. Others at HCFA who have been very helpful over the years are William Clark, Ron Deacon, Alan Friedlob, Trudi Galblum, Gerald Riley, Nancy Rowe, Donald Sherwood, and John Sirmon.

Working with the staff and supporters of each of the demonstration sites has been a rich experience for all of us at Brandeis, both professionally and personally. They are a talented and diverse group that has managed to stay together through difficult times—and still have fun. The demonstration has been fortunate enough to have four skillful, thoughtful, and dedicated site directors: Sam Ervin at Senior Care Action Network (SCAN), Merwyn Greenlick at the Kaiser Center for Health Research, Dennis Kodner at Elderplan, and John Selstad at Medicare Partners.

Beyond these leaders, singling out individual contributions, affiliations, and titles of the site staff, board members, public officials, and others who played key roles would be needlessly cumbersome. We know and they know the roles they played. Rather, we simply list them, with thanks to each for his or her unique contribution.

For Elderplan, we thank Issac Assael, Joan Cassamassino, Carmen Cintron, Eli Feldman, Emily Glazer, Betty Greenfield, Melvyn Hecht, Debra Kuppersmith, Seymour Levine, Paul Salisbury, Martin Sandhaus, Kenneth Scileppi, Doris Simon, Carole Snyder, Marc Wecksler, and Judy Zimbalist.

For Medicare Partners, we thank Carol Austin, Linda Berglin, Ann Carter, Jane Gendron, David Grube, Bob Held, Kay Jones, Kevin Kenney, Joelyn Malone, Jeanette Metz, Harold Norby, Brian Osberg, Bob Power, Victor Sandler, Leonard Schaeffer, Cindy Threlkeld, Betsey Walton, Patricia Willems, Ted Wise, and Janet Woodhull.

For SCAN, we thank Jay Beeler, Don Comstock, Chau Dang, Hue Dang, Dorothy Graham, Mary Griffin, Noel Gould, Julie Hanief, James Hillman, Robert Holmes, Allan Ide, Robert Kane, Ross Kaplan, Joe Kocon, Henry Lamb, Ray Lyons, Michael Markley, William McMorran, Sheela Mehta, Richard Rytting, Elizabeth San Filippo, Carol Schrey, James Serles, Constance Swanson, Irene Wallet, and Merwyn Williams.

For Kaiser, we thank Mike Anderson, Geri Bailey, Ted Columbo, Susan Dietsche, Lynette Doane, Marna Flaherty, Richard Froh, Marvin Goldberg, Tom Hussey, John Hutchison, Sara Lamb, James McConnell, Lucy Nonnenkamp, Paul Powers, Hazel Stewart, Daniel Wagster, and David Zeps.

None of these sites would have been more than a dream without a truly remarkable level of support from private foundations and corporations. A total of over $3 million in grants and another $2 million in loans has been given to the sites and Brandeis by twenty-three separate backers. They are Altcare Foundation, Atlantic Richfield Foundation, Bank America, Florence V. Burden Foundation, Bush Foundation, California Community Foundation, Commonwealth Fund, Ebenezer Foundation, Edwards Memorial Trust, Caldwell B. Esselstyn Foundation, Fingerhut Family Foundation, First Interstate Bank Foundation, John A. Hartford Family Foundation, Robert Wood Johnson Foundation, Henry J. Kaiser Family Foundation, Morgan Guarantee Trust Company, New York Community Trust, Northwest Area Foundation, PEW Memorial Trust, Retirement Research Foundation, St. Mary Medical Center, S.H. & Helen Scheuer Family Foundation, and United Hospital Fund.

Finally, thanks to our colleagues at the Heller School at Brandeis— especially Stanley Wallack and Robert Morris for early work on the SHMO concept, Stuart Altman for his support and guidance at key times, and Joanne Bluestone for two years of leadership and direction. And two special acknowledgments to Ana Lino and Mary Tess Crotty, who stuck with the manuscript through its two lives, even when they wondered where it would all lead.

Changing Health Care for an Aging Society

1
Introduction and Overview

The Social Health Maintenance Organization (SHMO) is an integrated approach to acute and long-term care for the elderly. It is intended not only to reduce costs, but also to improve appropriateness and quality of care. It tries to achieve these goals by combining the services of the now-fragmented health and long-term care systems into a single SHMO entity. The entity will enroll a broad cross-section of the local elderly population through voluntary open enrollment procedures, and it will be financed on a prepaid, capitated basis with provider risk sharing. Payments will come from Medicare, Medicaid, and private premiums.

Like all new ideas, the SHMO is a product of its times. Its goal is to respond to current problems, and its solutions to these problems are built on existing models. But like all exciting new ideas, the SHMO synthesizes and extends current thinking. It is a model for a new type of financing and delivery system, and it puts forward new solutions that show some promise of transcending the limits of current approaches.

The limits can be pushed only so far, however. In practice, the implementation of the SHMO model has been bound by current reality—both in terms of knowledge and practice, and in terms of how far policymakers and providers should be or are willing to go in taking chances on an untested model. New policies and altered practices are being created in the Demonstration, but it is unreasonable to expect that a system transformation can move smoothly into place all at once.

This introductory chapter sets forth this larger context for thinking about the SHMO as a concept and explores its potential. It analyzes the concept's origin in the current system and then shows how the model could address current problems and improve outcomes. At the same time the analysis does not gloss over potential pitfalls. It is appropriate that the Brandeis staff—as creators of the SHMO concept—be introspective as the Demonstration begins (Greenberg and Leutz 1984).

This chapter also highlights and "maps" the six subsequent chapters, which analyze the practical issues and options that were faced by Brandeis, provider sponsors, and public policymakers as all worked to create operational SHMOs. Included are the choices the Demonstration made on the variety of detailed implementation issues that had to be solved in each of the areas covered in the chapters: organizational arrangements, service delivery design, resource allocation, enrolling a membership, capitation finance, and the management of financial risk.

It is clear that the Demonstration has been limited by a plethora of real-world constraints of knowledge and policy and that the initial SHMOs—like all new ventures—do not exploit the full potential of the concept. It is also clear, however, that some significant achievements have been made and something new and exciting is about to take place.

Current Problems and Solutions in Health Care for the Elderly

Social policies are designed to address perceived social problems. If policies are to be effective, it is important that the right problems be identified. There is little worse than a cogent analysis and ambitious program for the wrong problem. Too often the problem definition in health care is focused simply on the immediate issue of rising costs rather than on underlying causes. This leads to short-term "solutions" of the "cut-and-shift" variety—cut public reimbursement rates and shift costs to providers, individuals, and other third-party payers—without ever addressing underlying problems.

The rationale for the SHMO grows out of an analysis that sees three underlying problems in current health care systems for the elderly: (1) the absence of appropriate insurance mechanisms for chronic care; (2) the lack of efficient and effective delivery systems, again, especially in chronic care but also including a lack of coordination between acute and chronic care; and (3) reimbursement arrangements that do not encourage providers to work together efficiently. The three problems are of course interrelated, and it is one of the advantages of the SHMO that it aims to make progress on all three fronts at once. Furthermore, the three problems are not at all unrelated to costs, especially public costs. In fact, one cannot control or use resources most efficiently without addressing these underlying problems.

The Need for Long-Term Care Insurance

The financing of long-term care contrasts with the financing of hospital care for the elderly, for which insurance coverage is considered adequate. In 1977, public insurance (Medicare) paid 84 percent of the acute hospital costs for those age 65 and over; private insurance covered nearly 8 percent; and direct payments by individuals and Medicaid accounted for less than 3 percent each (Fischer, 1980). In the same year, Medicare paid only 2 percent of nursing home costs, and private insurance covered about 1 percent. Medicaid paid nearly 48 percent of nursing home costs, and nursing home residents and their families paid more than 48 percent out-of-pocket (GAO 1979). The actual out-of-pocket costs for the two services reflect the contrast: less than $500 million for hospitals, more than $5 billion for nursing homes. These are catastrophic costs for many of the elderly, and such spending often leads to their impoverishment. About half of the people Medicaid supports in nursing homes were not initially poor and went on Medicaid only after "spending down" to eligibility levels (GAO 1979). While some would call Medicaid an insurance program, the open-ended deductible stretches the meaning of the term.

An insurance mechanism in long-term care would serve both the elderly and the Medicaid program: Non-poor individuals could avoid this cause of poverty, and Medicaid could greatly reduce its nursing home caseload. Chronic impairment is also a type of risk that is appropriate for insurance in that there is a very high variance in costs: Only 20 percent of the elderly will ever enter a nursing home, and less than 5 percent are residents at any one time (Keeler, Kane, and Solomon 1981). Thus, a few people will incur very high expenses. This point suggests a need for an insurance approach rather than simply an increase in personal savings. While options such as IRAs for long-term care (Fullerton 1981) and home-equity conversions (Scholen and Chen 1980) will increase available income, they will not negate the need for insurance.

Although a few private insurance firms are now offering policies, availability is restricted geographically; reimbursement is mainly for institutional care; and a variety of benefit limits, exclusions for preexisting conditions, and waiting periods usually apply (Meiners 1982). Most important, the coverage of community-based and in-home chronic care is extremely limited. The best private policies cover home care but for much more limited periods and lower benefit levels. United Equitable, for example, pays for twenty-four months of skilled nursing home care at $60 per day, but only thirty days of home care at $7.50 per day (Meiners 1982). Since most people would prefer to stay in the home and avoid a nursing home, long-term care insurance will not attract its broadest possible market until home- and cummunity-based services are covered. Also, it will be potentially less cost-effective since, like the public system, it contains a bias toward expensive institutional settings.

Service Delivery Problems

The argument that the service delivery system is a major problem in health care for the elderly stems from two factors: the underdevelopment of home- and community-based chronic care services, and the fragmented arrangements for managing the care of clients across the full range of acute and chronic care services. The underdeveloped system of home- and community-based services in long-term care contrasts sharply with the large institutional system. The difference stems largely from the biased reimbursement system—especially in Medicaid's usual practice of making chronic care payments only for nursing home settings. Noninstitutional services have only occasionally been supported by Medicaid, and several other public programs (such as Title XX and Title VI of the Older Americans Act) have been insufficient to create an adequate and coordinated noninstitutional system (Cohen 1983). No single organization is responsible for the care of clients across the whole system, access is haphazard, and the system has a strong institutional bias (Eustis, Greenberg, and Patten 1984).

The separation of the acute and chronic care systems—at both the institutional and the professional levels—also works against the interdependent nature of the services being given. Many hospital patients could be more appropriately cared for in nursing homes if beds were convenient, available, and properly staffed, and many hospitalizations from nursing homes could be avoided if the homes offered better primary medical care services (Master et al. 1980).

Such efficient practices make sense as goals, but they have been extremely hard to achieve under prevailing reimbursement arrangements. Both the government and the private insurance industry are fearful of reimbursing for a broader range of services because of the possibility of increased costs due to the "add-on" effect. That is, it is widely acknowledged that many applicants to nursing homes could be more appropriately cared for in home and community settings, and demonstration programs have shown that such care can be arranged. However, there are legitimate fears that the "add-on" effect of the costs of new cases—the creation of new cases in the community who would not have entered nursing homes—will predominate over savings from the "substitution" effect of fewer people entering nursing homes (GAO 1982). While demonstration programs have shown some service delivery success, they have shed little light on how much expanded coverage would cost. They have not provided a picture of how many potential users of services are in the community, and they have not developed the technology to manage the flow of users by means of eligibility criteria, access guides, resource allocation protocols, and other methods.

Some of the fears of the add-on effect are based on the fact that support from family and friends is the dominant mode of long-term care for chronically impaired elders. The Health Interview Survey (1979) indicates that 73 percent of disabled community elderly relied exclusively on family and friends for their assistance. Another 16 percent received help from both informal and formal care givers (Soldo 1983). There are perhaps twice as many impaired elders being supported at home by spouses and children (9 percent of the elderly) as there are in nursing homes (5 percent) (Mindel

1979; Nelson 1982; Callahan et al. 1980). The fear is that formal programs of in-home services would supplant some of these informal supports, and again, demonstration programs have not documented techniques to encourage and maintain informal support in tandem with formal services.

In summary, the service delivery problem is closely related to the insurance problem, and the solution of the former will facilitate work on the latter. For insurance of community-based chronic care to be offered, a service delivery system must be demonstrated that can (1) integrate home- and community-based services with institutional services; (2) coordinate the population's access to the system; (3) manage the care of patients across all levels of care; (4) predict and control system costs; (5) maintain informal support; and (6) provide quality care.

Reimbursement, Provider Incentives, and Provider Behavior

The third problem with current health care systems for the elderly is that diverse reimbursement systems give the major participants in the system— physicians, nursing homes, hospitals, and individual patients—a grab bag of incentives. Some incentives encourage effectiveness, but few of the participants face incentives that promote efficiency. First, physicians are given the power and autonomy to be effective in acute care, since what they order is largely paid for through Medicare and private supplementation insurance. This situation hardly encourages efficiency, however, especially in the use of expensive hospital resources. Once patients are no longer in the acute care system (that is, their needs no longer qualify them for Medicare and private insurance coverage), physicians lose much of their power to be effective, since they can no longer allocate resources for patient care. Physicians cannot simply "prescribe" the services of custodial homes, home care agencies, and related public programs and expect that their orders will be carried out, as they can with acute care. Rather, all of these programs administer their own admissions criteria and procedures, and they rely on different sets of funding sources than do physicians and hospitals.

Turning to the second participant in the system—the nursing home— the incentives for providers are again biased against greater efficiency. On the one side, the relationship of nursing homes to acute care is rough where it should be smooth. As long as nursing home beds are in short supply and reimbursement is made on a fixed per diem basis, nursing homes have no incentive to take difficult postacute cases from hospitals, since they are not paid extra for the extra work. On the other side, the frequent transfer of acutely ill patients to the hospital from the nursing home is encouraged. Either Medicare or Medicaid, or both, will pay for the hospital, and it is easier for the physician to visit the patient in the hospital anyway. On the noninstitutional side, there is very little in the system to divert some patients from nursing homes into home- and community-based chronic care. Medicaid agencies in many states are now testing wider eligibility and coverage for these services through waivers under section 2176 of the 1981 Omnibus Budget Reconciliation Act, but their initial projects have been cautious (Greenberg 1983b). Also, 2176-type programs will not address the acute/chronic separation (Wallack and Greenberg 1983).

Hospitals are the third significant provider participant in the system, and incentives here have recently moved toward larger system perspectives because of the diagnosis-related group (DRG) reimbursement system. DRGs should encourage hospitals to find faster paths out of hospitals into nursing homes, home health care, and rehabilitation hospitals. DRG-based payments are not, however, likely to discourage the reverse flow. Hospitals will undoubtedly form new kinds of relationships with these other levels of care under the stimulus of DRGs, but it is not yet possible to tell whether this will lead to cost savings and greater system efficiency.

The final participant in the system—the beneficiary–patient—must negotiate this maze. On the acute care side, preventive and routine maintenance care are discouraged through the Medicare part B deductible and copayment requirements. Entering the hospital carries new disincentives with the recently increased coinsurance there. Leaving the hospital for a nursing home continues to present real financial risks for patients, given the good chance that Medicare and insurance will not pay the bill. For individuals who need chronic care, the options and incentives are fewer and more extreme. Those with financial resources can purchase in-home services—*if* they can find them. Those without resources who want to stay at home must rely on family and a limited range of free public programs—*if* they can find them. The institutional alternative is open to both groups of people, but the high costs and stringent Medicaid spend-down requirements make institutional care financially unattractive for all but the richest and the poorest, and those who can "beat the system" by divesting assets.

The Potential of the SHMO Model

The SHMO model attempts to address all of these current system problems through a strategy of consolidation, which is based on the precedent of the Health Maintenance Organization (HMO). The HMO's consolidated approach is a powerful model for managing the acute care system, and its proponents point to improvements in efficiency and benefit coverage, with no compromise on quality as compared with the fee-for-service system. Questions about "savings" due to favorable selection are acknowledged, but the arguments for the HMO system's efficiency are still compelling (Luft 1978; Manning et al 1984).

The SHMO expands and extends the HMO's consolidation strategy by including institutional and noninstitutional long-term care services in conjunction with acute care. In doing so it builds on the successes (and aims to lessen some of the shortcomings) of long-term care demonstration projects. Such projects have shown that many functionally impaired individuals can be cared for more appropriately in the community and at home than in nursing homes, and that both acute and long-term care services can be delivered more effectively when they are coordinated with one another (Shen and Zawadski 1981; Master et al. 1980; Abrahams and Leutz 1983; Wecksler, Durmaskin, and Kodner 1983).

This fully consolidated model gives the SHMO the potential to be an extremely powerful intervention. Five dimensions of the model are key to that power. First, a full range of acute and chronic care provider agencies will establish formal relationships with each other to assume joint responsibility for outcomes in the entire system. In theory, they will be motivated to work toward system goals rather than the individual agency goals that they pursue under the fragmented fee-for-service system.

Second, consolidation of services and professionals will allow a redefinition of divisions of labor and the development of techniques for coordination. Professionals will be able to develop norms of practice for coordinated care across the full range of services.

Third, the SHMO will serve a cross-section of the elderly population. Including both functionally impaired and able-bodied elderly allows the development of an insurance "risk pool" to mutualize the costs of new long-term care benefits. Additionally, by voluntarily agreeing to join, the member agrees to have his or her care managed. The SHMO takes on the responsibility to manage care, including such decisions as who receives long-term care services, how much they receive, and what is expected of informal caregivers.

Fourth, the SHMO will be financed on a prepaid, capitation basis by both members and third parties, and these payments will be "pooled" at the level of the SHMO entity. That is, premium structures and levels will be worked out in advance, and the SHMO will combine all payments to pay for all services. Prepayment and pooling mean that the SHMO will not face the current system's financial barriers to innovation in service delivery. Rather, financial incentives can be restructured within the SHMO itself in a manner that is consistent with total system goals.

Finally, the SHMO assumes financial risk for service costs. That is, it is expected to live within the budgeted capitated payments, and it faces the prospect of either gain or loss based on performance. If the system can be organized to give no incentive for making inefficient decisions, risk is a facilitating ingredient in making cost-effectiveness a criterion in decision making.

In almost every area of development, the SHMO poses new issues. It brings together two formerly separate research streams—those in acute and chronic care. At the very least, the SHMO is a bigger and more complex HMO—an HMO plus long-term care. Alternatively, some of the planning teams have found that creating SHMOs not only involves changes in scale, complexity, number of actors, and so on, but also calls for and facilitates qualitative changes in policies and practice. The following sections reflect on the potential of the model in the five dimensions described above. An overview of the broad issues and options in each area is introduced to indicate the potential of the model, and then the choices made in the initial phase of the Demonstration will be summarized. Included in the summary will be references to corresponding sections in later chapters.

Organizational Consolidation

In order to understand the SHMO it is appropriate to start at the institutional level. Here the model is quite flexible so long as a basic goal is achieved (that is, the responsibility for integrating the full range of acute and long-term care services is assumed by an identifiable agency or a group of agencies acting in concert). Achieving consolidation on the organizational level is essential to creating an integrated service delivery system and a consolidated system of financing.

There are at least two good reasons for providers to try integrated systems. First, it allows them to control uncertainty more effectively by making more of the key variables internal to the organization. Vertical integration is a well-established business strategy that allows internal prices and controls to be instituted over broader portions of the system. It also allows strong units to help weaker ones through difficult times, a feature that is attractive in today's uncertain world of health care financing. Second, integration makes sense in service delivery. Health services are interdependent, and services can sometimes substitute for one another at the interfaces of levels of care and professional practice. Coordination and continuity of services can be more easily managed in an integrated system, but these are not the only advantages. Efficiency can also be improved, since internal incentives can be structured toward using the less costly form of care where there is more than one choice.

But it is one thing to recognize the advantages of integration and another thing to create a truly integrated system for the SHMO. The provider agencies and groups that come together in a SHMO need to surrender some of their current autonomy by sharing power and authority with their new partners. They need to decide jointly how to develop the new product line, divide revenue and risk, and perhaps create and control new corporate entities. It is likely that each partner will have to make changes in existing programs to accommodate both the other partner(s) and the new program. It is not easy for established organizations to give up very much of their autonomy and independence on issues such as these.

Sponsors and partners must also be concerned about possible negative directions the SHMO might take and find satisfactory ways to maintain control over its development. How can a small long-term care sponsor keep from being overwhelmed by the larger SHMO budget? Might a SHMO end up competing with a parent HMO? How can a relatively small experimental program like the SHMO be successfully integrated into a large, established program like an HMO?

These issues of balancing autonomy and interdependence in the creation of an integrated SHMO system are examined in chapter 2. The issues are addressed at the levels of both structure and internal control.[1] Structural factors examined include whether or not to become a sponsor for a SHMO, how sponsors select partner providers, and how the partners can structure their formal relationships. The form of association can take a variety of legal routes, including partnerships, joint ventures, new corporations, simple contracts, and the like. Internal control issues examined include the definition of expectations and performance standards, providing incentives to meet standards, and monitoring the performance of the various parties. The key mechanisms in such control systems at an agency level are internal financial arrangements among the participating parties, and these require further comment here prior to a description of the actual sites.

Since premiums to the SHMO are prepaid by individuals and third parties, the participating provider agencies and groups are paid by the SHMO entity, not the "outside world," as in the fee-for-service system. The program can, therefore, structure internal payments so there are incentives to achieve particular goals. SHMO planners face two important problems in structuring performance expectations and incentives: first, assigning responsibility for outcomes, and second, deciding on the appropriate magnitude for incentives.

The most sensible way to structure financial incentives is to give providers some responsibility for costs where they have control over outcomes (Leighton 1979; Zelten 1981). Thus, HMOs traditionally give physicians some "risk" (such as bonuses for exceeding targets, penalties for falling short) for hospital utilization, since they largely control admissions. Since the SHMO creates new kinds of interdependencies among providers, there are many utilization decisions that will be *jointly* controlled; for example the decision to transfer patients between the hospital and nursing home or between the nursing home and home care will often be made by both physicians and case managers.

It follows that risk for such service costs should be shared among the providers who share control. However, it is a challenge not only to define the breadth of providers' responsibilities but also to devise internal payment mechanisms that make providers *feel* they are responsible. Also, there is little or no precedent on which to base performance standards. In both cases the precedent of HMOs is not really applicable, since the SHMO is a new, broader, and better integrated system. It might be a real mistake to enshrine a set of performance standards that do not produce maximum efficiency in the model.

Furthermore, there is reason to be concerned about the magnitude of internal incentive systems. If the individual provider agencies stand to lose significant amounts of money, they can be expected to act in a manner that protects them against such losses. They might try to shift costs to their partners by overestimating their own costs, which would lead to higher system costs. They might be tempted to compromise on quality of services. Thus, it may well make sense to keep initial incentive arrangements modest until experience is gained.

The five sponsors that were designated to test the SHMO model in the Demonstration illustrate the variety of arrangements possible on the structural and control levels. The sponsors were chosen after a developmental process at Brandeis and a wide search by Brandeis staff that reached scores of providers across the nation. Agencies contacted included HMOs, hospitals, medical centers, long-term care agencies, and governmental units. The sponsors eventually chosen include a hospital, an HMO, and three long-term care agencies. All of their funds for planning and development have been raised from private foundations or donated by sponsors.[2] A brief overview of the organization of the sites follows. A more detailed discussion of the early development process, site selection, and the sites themselves is found in chapter 2.

Mercy Hospital, Springfield, Massachusetts. Mercy Hospital was an original applicant with Brandeis in connection with the demonstration proposal to the Health Care Finance Administration (HCFA). Mercy's interest in being a sponsor stemmed from its large elderly census and its plans to expand into long-term care services. However, Mercy had to withdraw as a site about a year after planning began when it became clear that the hospital could not develop a viable medical component for the project, largely because of opposition from affiliated physicians. Uncertainties about marketability and support from the state Medicaid system also played a part (Popko and Laskey 1982).

Metropolitan Jewish Geriatric Center (MJGC), Brooklyn, New York. MJGC owns two large nursing homes and operates a variety of community-based programs. The center saw the SHMO as a way to extend and consolidate its services to the elderly (Kodner 1981). For medical services MJGC created a new geriatric medical group in conjunction with Cornell Medical College. Hospital services will be purchased from two community hospitals, and long-term care will be provided by MJGC. To pull the participants together, MJGC formed a closely controlled nonprofit corporation called Elderplan, Inc., which will be licensed in New York State as an HMO. Elderplan will make incentive payments to the medical group for meeting performance targets in the medical and hospital areas, but the two will also share risk for "bottom-line" (total system) profits and losses. Since MJGC's development effort has required the formation of several new entities, it has been expensive. However, the focus of all parties toward the SHMO may make this a very powerful model.

Kaiser Permanente Medical Care Program, Portland, Oregon. Kaiser–Portland is a large, established HMO that was an original site in the HMO Medicare demonstration (Galblum and Trieger 1982; Greenlick et al. 1983). Participation in both that demonstration and the SHMO was motivated in part by the Kaiser system's large and growing elderly membership and the attractions of prepaid Medicare reimbursement. Given Kaiser's size and experience, Kaiser officials decided to develop the SHMO's long-term care services within the agency rather than take on a formal partner. Issues of internal control may well be more difficult to work out at Kaiser than the structural issues will be. Since the SHMO is a small, new program being grafted on to a large and established system, Kaiser will need to reorganize elements of the system to make sure its far-flung staff works in concert with the project. Since Kaiser is a self-contained system, this task will need to be accomplished through administrative and organizational means rather than external incentives.

Ebenezer Society, Minneapolis, Minnesota. Ebenezer Society is a comprehensive long-term provider with a range of services similar to MJGC's. However, because of Ebenezer's more limited corporate goals concerning expansion, and because of the already competitive HMO market in the Twin Cities, Ebenezer was favorably disposed to follow Brandeis's interest in the model of a mature long-term organization linking with a mature HMO. Its chosen partner was the Group Health Plan, Inc. (since renamed Group Health, Inc.), the largest and oldest HMO in the area. The partners solved incentive and service delivery issues early in the effort. Between them they already controlled all the services required in the model, and they decided to share financial risk on the bottom line. That is, each partner would be reimbursed for its costs and would then divide remaining profits or losses. More difficult to devise was a way to structure their relationship so as to allow integration around SHMO business but allow each partner's other business to remain independent. The solution was a formal partnership with a series of formal understandings concerning limits of liability and restraints on associated behavior. The name for their joint venture, Medicare Partners, follows from the form.

Senior Care Action Network (SCAN), Long Beach, California. SCAN is the third long-term care sponsor, but it is a very different agency from both MJGC and Ebenezer. It is a brokerage-model, case-management agency that provides no direct services of its own. Rather, it relies on an extensive network of referral relationships with existing community providers both in the long-term and acute care sectors. Still, SCAN's corporate goal for the SHMO was not unlike MJGC's, and SCAN made the same key decision: establishing a new HMO (SCAN Health Plan, Inc.) that would be closely controlled by the parent agency. Because of its limited resource base and close working relationships with some large providers, however, SCAN decided to involve existing community providers much more closely in the SHMO than MJGC did. SCAN will use the Harriman Jones Clinics with a staff of 47 physicians for medical services, and St. Mary's Medical Center for hospital services. Both of these partners will be paid primarily on a capitation basis with relatively strong risk incentive provisions, especially in the case of the hospital. An interesting question to ask during the Demonstration will be whether these internal controls will be more or less effective than the total system performance rewards used at the other long-term care sites.

Integration of Service Delivery

By consolidating the provider system on the organizational level, the SHMO model lays the basis for integrated service delivery. The advantages are threefold. First, service integration gives rise to better care, including opportunities to achieve innovation and improvement in coordination, continuity of care, access, quality, and comprehensive assessment. Second, an integrated system of professionals should improve efficiency in service provision, which in turn will be the source of savings for increased benefits. Third, the development of a case-management system that allows prediction and control of the costs of long-term care for the membership is a basic requirement for developing an insurance mechanism for community-based chronic care.

In order to create a service delivery system that achieves these advantages, two types of issues must be addressed: (1) practical issues related to the integration of acute and chronic care and (2) issues concerning the allocation of resources (in the form of services) to members. The SHMO needs both to integrate services operationally and to allocate the services to members in a cost-effective and equitable manner. The practical issues that arise in attempting to integrate acute and chronic care services involve finding ways to harness the full power of the model. The SHMO expands both the "span" and "scope" (Austin 1983) of professionals' authority. Span of authority—that is, the number of services over which the professional has impact—is enhanced by consolidating a full range of acute and chronic care services and personnel. Scope of authority—that is, the breadth of a professional's impact on service use, is maximized because most services are prepaid. Accordingly, resources can be allocated on the basis of clinical assessment of need, not on the basis of whether or not the service is available or reimbursable, as in fee-for-service practice. Since many services are substitutes for one another at the margins, the SHMO offers opportunities for new divisions of labor and authority.

To achieve the full potential of consolidated professional practice one must address issues that parallel the ones involved in consolidating the organizations in which professionals work. That is, one must devise mechanisms to structure authority and incentives, and one must strike a balance between interdependence and autonomy. Once again, it is one thing to specify new divisions of labor and authority and another thing to gain acceptance of change by those involved. If nurse practitioners are to assume additional medical responsibilities, physicians will need to grant those responsibilities. If nursing homes are to develop beds at higher skill levels to reduce hospital costs, physicians and hospital discharge planners must use them. If physicians are to become more involved in chronic care, case managers must be ready to accept this powerful potential competitor in decision making.

Sites' choices concerning the practical issues of system integration are discussed in chapter 3. Their general approach to structuring practice has been to plan for work around the interfaces of services and professionals. Multidisciplinary planning teams were formed at each site to avoid reproducing fragmented systems. Key mechanisms to promote integration will be (1) protocols for communications and transfer of responsibility and (2) linkage staff, usually in the form of nurse practitioners or physicians' assistants.

Resource allocation is one of the most difficult issues confronted in planning SHMOs, and perhaps the most important. SHMOs will enroll a membership and offer the members "comprehensive care," including both acute and chronic care services. But comprehensiveness is limited by funding constraints, especially for private-pay members whose care must be financed out of current Medicare spending levels and additional private premiums. This means that choices must be made concerning which services to provide, which members to serve, and how much to provide them. These areas of choice can be labeled more precisely as benefit structure, targeting and eligibility, and prescription norms.

Decisions on these issues shape the nature of the SHMO and the types of philosophies, policies, and professional practices that will be reflected in it. They also have important implications for marketing and finance. In theory, the model is flexible on such issues. It allows a test of different philosophies and policies concerning the mix and distribution of health care resources—for example, the relative mix of acute versus chronic care, prevention and maintenance versus cure, and formal versus informal care. Different SHMOs could conceivably experiment with different philosophies, so long as providers find a market for their priorities, and public funders approve.

In the reality of the Demonstration, SHMO planners have been limited by both policy and knowledge constraints from making dramatic changes in current resource allocation practices. Most important, marketing considerations and HCFA requirements to provide all Medicare services have compelled all sites to offer a very rich acute care package along the lines of competing plans and medical practice. Thus, in benefit structure, targeting, and prescription practices, flexibility has largely been limited to the chronic care area. Making decisions on these issues has not been easy. Prior programs offer some examples on how to address them individually, but there is little basis for predicting the impact of choices made simultaneously in a comprehensive, prepaid model.

First, *benefit structure* refers to what benefits will be available on what terms. Dimensions of the issue include whether or not a service will be covered at all, whether it will be covered fully or only in part, how coinsurance is structured, and renewability. Such choices mean the allocation of chronic care resources to members differentially, according to their levels and types of impairment, income levels, place of residence, and other characteristics. Choices also have impacts on finance and marketing. For example, not covering emergency electronic alarm systems may hurt members who have special needs for these services. The policy may or may not decrease costs, depending on whether monitoring can serve as a substitute for more expensive services rather than simply be an add-on. Covering services fully rather than requiring coinsurance may be a good marketing attraction, and it also reduces the importance of ability to pay as a determinant of receipt of services. However, so long as funding is held constant, it also reduces the depth of coverage. Charging a large deductible before chronic care coverage takes effect may not be an easy provision to market, but it does stretch funds to improve depth of coverage. It will also be more favorable to the most severely impaired than the moderately impaired, since the latter group may not use enough services to become the fully covered. Finally, making chronic care benefits in one setting (such as the home) more easily renewable than in another (such as the nursing home) is one way to control costs, but it obviously favors those who are able to maintain a community residence.

Choices made by Demonstration sites on these benefit structure issues were similar. All accepted Brandeis's recommended core benefit package which includes a relatively full range of chronic care services; and all chose rather moderate coinsurance levels (on the order of 10 to 20 percent of costs) rather than a deductible structure. Two of the sites, however, chose to limit the renewability of institutional long-term care benefits, while home care benefits will be renewable at all sites. The levels of chronic care benefits for Medicare-only members range between $6,250 and $12,000 per member per year (before coinsurance), with differences due in part to available financing and targeting considerations. While these benefits will cover home and community services quite well, they will cover only a fraction of the costs of members who must enter nursing homes. These benefit structure decisions are described more fully in chapter 4, while marketing and finance influences on benefits are discussed in chapters 5 and 6 respectively.

Second, issues concerning the development of *eligibility* or *targeting* criteria for chronic care services are also crucial to both program finances and patient care. In terms of finance, an obvious point is that a broad definition of eligibility will mean more users of chronic care services, and probably higher costs, than will a narrow definition. But this is probably less important than the need for definitions to be as clear and precise as possible, since the program is selling insurance for chronic care on a contractual basis. Meaningful insurance for community-based chronic care does not now exist, largely because the fear of "moral hazard" has made community treatment of chronic illness virtually uninsurable. That is, since many home- and community-based chronic care services are clearly attractive to a broad spectrum of elderly people (who wouldn't like a homemaker or a hot meal?), some people might misrepresent their needs or circumstances to try to qualify for the services. The SHMO's work on eligibility criteria needs to address these problems.

The impact of eligibility definitions on patient care is clear. Such definitions determine who will receive long-term care benefits and who will not. The balanced membership gives the SHMO the full spectrum of the population to care for, but the Demonstration sponsors have had to choose who will qualify for chronic care. Various alternatives are defensible, such as limiting eligibility to the most "severely impaired" or those at "immediate risk" of entering nursing homes, or also including "moderately impaired" members in order to maintain functioning and prevent deterioration. Each targeting alternative involves tradeoffs, both financially and in the nature of care in the program. In chapter 4 it will be seen that the various sites each chose a somewhat different targeting option.

The implementation of a targeting system requires a system for assessing need in the membership. The SHMO's assessment system must have both a broad and a detailed information-gathering capacity—the former to identify possible need across the entire membership and the latter to confirm eligibility among those who appear to qualify. Brandeis and the sites devised the following process to determine who in the broad-based SHMO membership may be in need of services and who will be eligible to receive them (see chapter 4 for details). All sites will mail new members a forty-four-item Health Status Form (HSF). Certain responses and patterns of responses will trigger further assessment—either a medical one or one to test chronic care need. For the latter, a Comprehensive Assessment Form (CAF) will be used. Information from the CAF will not only form the basis for care planning, but will also be used to determine whether the impaired member meets state nursing home certification (NHC) standards. NHC status is being used by sites as a major eligibility criterion for receiving SHMO chronic care benefits.

The third issue in service delivery—the development of *prescription norms* for practice in consolidated geriatric care—is the most difficult. Practitioners need to devise norms about issues such as vertical and horizontal equity, the relative importance of acute versus chronic care services, the role of resource constraints and financial incentives in norms of practice, how to incorporate informal care in formal service provision, and what standards to set for quality and quantity of care. Precedent exists regarding some of these issues, but they are faced more starkly in the SHMO with its full range of services, its resource constraints, and its balanced membership which has contracted for benefits.

The influence of resource constraints on prescription norms in the SHMO must be closely examined. The practice of prepayment to consolidated systems of medical care (that is, HMOs) came about only after many years of fee-for-service experience with separate parts. Prepayment comes early in the life of consolidated chronic care, at a time when the potential for substituting community-based care for institutional care has been explored in only a preliminary way in the various long-term care demonstration projects (Zadwadski 1983). By fixing the long-term care budget in advance under the assumption that cost-saving substitutions will occur, the SHMO establishes cost consciousness as a much more prominent foundation of chronic care practice than in previous long-term care demonstrations, and certainly more so than in prepaid acute care. The limited long-term care benefit will put tremendous pressure on case managers at the same time that they are trying to implement new procedures for screening, assessment, eligibility determination, and care planning and giving. Lest they succumb to the burnout phenomenon, they will need help in carrying this load, from fellow practitioners, administrators, public policymakers, researchers, and the members and their families.

Because of the lack of relevant precedent, most sites did not attempt to devise detailed norms of chronic care practice during the planning phase. Rather, most will begin by developing criteria heuristically—allowing experienced case managers to use their judgment in allocating chronic care services to eligible members. However, Ebenezer did set up a "client pathway" system that lays out a general approach to caring for particular client types. To control costs, professional judgment will be aided by dollar-limited chronic care benefits and specific eligibility guidelines. Brandeis and the sites have made the development of norms of chronic care practice a priority area for developmental research during operations. Included in the developmental effort will be work on quality assurance standards, measures, and procedures.

One significant external limit was placed on service delivery development during the demonstration phase: HCFA prohibited sites from deleting or diluting current Medicare coverage. This restriction kept programs from merging acute and chronic care resources in radically new ways. The consequences are (1) to limit the scope of resource allocation guidelines (perhaps not a bad idea to start) and (2) to force SHMOs to continue to make internal distinctions between Medicare-type and chronic-type home health and nursing home care. It is important to point out that these are accounting rather than medical care distinctions, since HCFA requires that Medicare-type care be covered at least as well as under Medicare, while chronic-type care can be subject to limits on long-term care coverage. The sites will be developing explicit technical criteria to manage the distinction.

In summary, SHMOs will develop benefit structures, targeting guidelines, and prescription norms for professional practice, all of which will be sensitive not only to medical knowledge but also to social and political standards, cost constraints, and equity issues. The SHMO concept is thus in the mainstream of current public policy initiatives that try to use external cost constraints to force providers to address these issues. The SHMO could be a laboratory for the creation of standards for benefits, targeting according to long-term care need, assessment criteria, resource allocation mechanisms, equity in treatment, and so on. It is also a good setting for testing who should take part in making the decisions, and how. Providers, professionals, different levels of government, members, and families can all be involved. During the Demonstration phase, care has been taken to select providers that are sensitive to these concerns about equity, quality, and the needs of vulnerable elders. Until policy and professional practice are well established in this area, it is advisable for the government to continue to select provider sponsors and their partners very carefully.

Attracting and Maintaining a Balanced Membership

The third essential feature of the SHMO model is that a balanced membership is enrolled. That is, the health status of the membership roughly reflects that of the local community's population, especially in regard to chronic impairment. The Demonstration places some additional membership requirements in order to test the model's potential in the competitive open market. Sites will be enrolling members voluntarily through conventional marketing techniques, and both Medicare-only and Medicare-Medicaid elderly will be enrolled. Initial target membership is in the range of 4,000 at each site within a year of the start of marketing.

The general rationale for the balanced membership has been mentioned already: the need to create an insurance mechanism through the premium, and to demonstrate how the care of the entire population can be managed. The overriding obstacle in trying to obtain a balanced population is the danger of selection bias, that is, the possibility of attracting and enrolling a population that is either "sicker" or "healthier" than the desired population. Obviously, the potential for selection bias is enhanced by the open-market model. (Hypothetically, if the programs were set up to serve the entire elderly population in a community, or if members were randomly assigned to the program and compelled to join, the potential for selection bias would not arise, except in a statistical sense.)

Developing a marketing strategy that helps produce a balanced membership is a major task for sponsors, and it encompasses three sequential activities. First, the position of the sponsors in their internal and external environments must be clearly defined. Second, clear objectives must be specified. Third, a market strategy for meeting the objectives must be developed and implemented. Since the situation of each site will be different, this analysis must be carefully tailored to conform with local conditions. A background discussion on these three stages of market analysis is found in chapter 5, which also discusses the market analyses and strategies of each site in turn.

The starting point of the situation analysis is that the SHMO will be a new product in every community in which it is being offered, and the organizations offering it are in most cases new combinations of agencies. Sponsors have some flexibility in defining both themselves and the product in order to best respond to the opportunities and potential obstacles they face. For example, Demonstration sponsors facing an external environment with significant HMO penetration of the elderly market (such as Medicare Partners) have had to plan their market positions differently than sponsors in environments with no significant HMO competition (such as Elderplan), and both differ from Kaiser, which already has a major share of the elderly market with little HMO competition. The sponsors' images in the community are also important. Are they well known to the local elderly, and are they known for serving a particular type of clientele, for example, in the case of a long-term care sponsor, the impaired?

Internal situations are also a consideration. The organizational section above indicated that the sponsors have different long-term plans for the SHMO. It makes a difference whether they see it as an experiment in a new line of business in addition to their major line (a regular HMO line at Kaiser), or as their main business in the future (Elderplan and SCAN). What are the internal financial situations of the sponsors? Can they afford to be bold and aggressively market the SHMO, or do they need to be cautious for fear of depleting their limited venture capital? These issues and choices are primarily analyzed below as organizational questions (chapter 2), but they have also had to be addressed from a marketing perspective.

An assessment of the local elderly health care market is a second key task in a situation analysis. Conventional market analysis often divides the potential market into distinct segments based on such factors as geography, age, income, and health care coverage, and then targets marketing efforts to those segments that promise to yield the desired membership in terms of numbers, composition, and willingness to join. While the market for conventional health care coverage is well established, little if anything is known about the market for long-term care in conjunction with health care coverage. Again, the questions outnumber the answers. Will the well elderly pay substantial new premiums for long-term care insurance, or will their primary interest be in comprehensive acute care coverage? Will the low- and moderate-income elderly be willing to pay to join the SHMO, or will a substantial premium mean that the program is primarily for those who are relatively well-off? Can the program effectively attract both the Medicaid and non-Medicaid markets, and what will be the program's relative points of appeal to each? It is clear that the model cannot be all things to all people and that choices must be made on these and other issues.

To learn more about their local target populations, all the Demonstration sites gathered and analyzed local information on potential segments of the market. This included an analysis of available geographic, demographic, and health status information. All of the sites, except Kaiser, also conducted formal market surveys of the local elderly population to obtain information specific to the elderly's response to the SHMO concept and the sponsoring providers. Results of these surveys are reported in the site section of chapter 5.

The information from the situation analysis forms the basis for setting marketing and membership objectives, and these in turn form the basis for marketing strategy. The key decisions in this stage concern product and pricing, because such decisions will have significant effects on the general marketability of the program as well as its appeal to various segments. Product and pricing decisions must also be made in the context of the local competition. For example, a SHMO facing significant HMO competition may decide that it can attract a membership by putting more of its benefit dollars into long-term care coverage at the expense of covering "extras" such as prescription drugs, eyeglasses, and dental care. Or will this turn out to be exactly the wrong strategy in that it will lead to adverse selection? Similarly, given limited funds for long-term care benefits, should long-term care coverage be "deep" or "shallow"? That is, should there be a large deductible or very high initial coinsurance for chronic care benefits, in order to offer catastrophic coverage for those with the greatest needs, or should the program offer first-dollar coverage with a consequent lower limit on the maximum benefit? Should there be optional or multiple benefit packages for applicants to choose from (such as a higher chronic care package for additional premiums or a supplemental medical plan for drugs, dental, and the like), or should there be only one basic option for all? Again, the issue of selection bias must be considered in such decisions. Pricing decisions must be considered in a similar light. How much more than the local competition in the Medicare supplement market can the SHMO charge for premiums without bringing on adverse selection? If the answer is that it can charge substantially more, the long-term care benefit can be richer.

The most significant finding of the sites' market analyses was that the SHMO would have to compete with Medicare supplementation insurance on the private side of the market. Price became the key factor (supplementation policy costs could not be exceeded by more than $10 or $15 if a balanced membership was to be achieved) and product had to follow suit (long-term care insurance could not drive the premium too high). This led to a limit on the level of chronic care benefits to be offered to private pay members. Experience, it is hoped, will allow most sites to increase the depth of their coverage.

It should also be noted that price and product considerations are radically different for the Medicaid segment of the market. The Medicaid elderly already have comprehensive long-term care coverage at little or no cost in most communities (at least for nursing home care). Therefore, competitive prices and new benefits are not important inducements for Medicaid beneficiaries to join. Sites are stressing high quality and assured access to comprehensive services as inducements, but it is unclear whether these advantages will overcome the loss of freedom to "shop around" with Medicare and Medicaid cards. Sites and states did have the option of restricting freedom of choice (through section 2175 of the Omnibus Budget Reconciliation Act of 1981) and requiring Medicaid beneficiaries to join the SHMO. No site or state took this option, but Medicare Partners and Elderplan chose to restrict disenrollment of Medicaid members to six-month intervals.

Once decisions are made about pricing, product, the segments to be targeted, and the position of the SHMO in the market, methods for promoting the program must be devised that are consistent with these decisions. Here the sponsor must choose from the various promotional techniques used by HMOs, including mailings, the print and electronic media, open houses, endorsements, and community presentations, among others. The overriding issue in making choices among the options is the SHMO's unique and potentially confusing combination of acute and chronic care benefits in a prepaid, membership (HMO) model. On the one hand, in order to avoid dissatisfaction and disenrollment, the prospective applicant needs to understand the limitations of the program. These include the lock-in feature characteristic of all HMOs, the limited duration of the waivered experiment, and the need to give up current physicians and insurance arrangements. On the other hand, the SHMO's positive features must also be clearly communicated to prospective members, in order to attract the several thousand members required.

Deciding how to describe and how much to emphasize the program's new chronic care coverage is especially important in all promotional efforts. Should chronic care benefits be featured prominently by highlighting how much more than current Medicare coverage is being offered, or should they be downplayed in the context of a strategy that emphasizes features like comprehensiveness, coordinated care, and quality. The latter strategy was the choice at the Demonstration sites, and once again the issue of selection bias was a primary consideration.

There is a very real possibility of obtaining a membership that is biased toward those needing chronic care, and thus the option of supplementing open marketing and enrollment strategies with more direct controls on the balance of the membership has also had to be considered. Health insurance plans commonly employ health screens to exclude from eligibility those with certain prior health conditions, and such screens have also been used by some HMOs serving the Medicare population (Galblum and Trieger 1982). An alternative to the "pure" health screen (which only excludes) is a quota or queuing system, whereby "fair shares" of the population with particular health characteristics are defined in advance. Queuing at the point of application can then be used to enroll the quota in each category on a first-come, first-served basis.

The screening and queuing strategies must be considered in light of their immediate effects on promotional efforts. Will they confuse people or discourage them from enrolling? These strategies must also be considered in light of the long-term balance in the risk pool. For example, while a pure screen may seem attractive in obtaining a healthy population to which extensive long-term care benefits can be offered, the membership will age over time and become more impaired. Of course, this problem could be addressed by building up substantial reserves against such future liabilities. The quota method offers a more stable approach to membership balance, since the case-mix of the program can be monitored over time and new members enrolled to fill openings in each category. Both SCAN and Elderplan decided to use queuing from the start of marketing, while Kaiser and Medicare Partners will use it only if membership becomes significantly imbalanced. All sites that queue will use a standard procedure developed by Brandeis that seeks to enroll a representative sample (in terms of impairment levels) of the local elderly population. Applicants will be grouped into queues according to their answers to questions about physical impairment on application forms and on an initial Health Status Form. They will then be accepted into the program on a first-come, first-served basis by queue. Once again, it must be emphasized that these issues are new and that the techniques for dealing with them are untested.

Consolidated Financing

SHMO financing is based on simple but powerful concepts: "prospective, capitated reimbursement" and "funds pooling." Payment on a prospective, capitation basis is the same principle used in HMOs. The program is paid in advance, *before* it provides service, and payments are made on a per person or premium basis—not a per-service basis. Prospective capitated reimbursement with a balanced membership is also the mechanism through which the SHMO creates a "risk pool" of long-term care insurance. Part of the premium from each member goes into the risk pool, even though only a small minority will receive chronic care services.

Funds pooling means that premiums from payers are merged into a single account at the level of the SHMO entity. Pooling is not a new idea either—it occurs in HMOs—but pooling has never before included so many payers in a program that provides a full range of acute and chronic care services to a full spectrum of the elderly population. Medicare will pay premiums into the program to cover Medicare-type service costs for all members; Medicaid will pay premiums to cover Medicaid-type service costs for members who are Medicaid beneficiaries; and private-pay members will pay premiums and coinsurance to cover their benefit costs beyond what Medicare covers.

Because the SHMO promises to deliver each payer's existing package of services more efficiently than does the current fee-for-service system, "savings" should be achieved, especially in the area of institutional costs. The extent to which the SHMO actually achieves such savings and the ways savings are allocated are very important in determining how far the model can expand long-term care benefits.

While the model has the potential to achieve substantial savings through downward substitutions and other economies, it is important to avoid the fantasy of seeing the SHMO as a means to finance the long-term care out of "fat" from the Medicare system. The total bill for chronic care is much larger than such savings, and that bill must be paid more directly. The central financing issues for the SHMO are therefore (1) how much long-term care will cost and (2) how to pay for it.

In fact, the SHMO needs to answer each of these two questions twice: once for Medicaid members and again for members covered by Medicare only. On the one hand, since Medicaid is already responsible for full long-term care costs for its beneficiaries, Medicaid decision makers should be willing to set the programs's reimbursement rate high enough to cover a full chronic care benefit in the SHMO. The practical problems here are estimating how much full coverage will cost for this population and deciding how, and how much, Medicaid should pay. On the other hand, additional funds to pay for chronic care for Medicare-only members must come from the members themselves—either indirectly through the insurance mechanism and/or through coinsurance from those who use the services. It is doubtful whether a high enough premium can be charged to finance full long-term care without also bringing on adverse selection, and thus the private long-term care benefit will not cover full costs for the most costly members. In other words, it will be less than the Medicaid benefit. The practical questions here are how much can be raised through the premium, and how much of a benefit these funds can support. Secondarily, this becomes a question of how to structure the funds into a limited long-term care benefit, using coinsurance as a part of this structuring.

Thus, the Demonstration should yield important program and policy experience on two different types of long-term care financing models: one for full prepaid coverage by the public sector and another for limited coverage through private insurance. The Demonstration faces substantial barriers initially in devising the pieces of these models, both in terms of devising third-party reimbursement and private pay arrangements and on the question of estimating the two sets of costs. An overview of these will be presented next in order to suggest the magnitude of the tasks, the ways in which SHMOs can address them, and the difficult policy issues faced by Medicare and Medicaid.

The task of devising reimbursement systems for the SHMO requires some groundbreaking in terms of information development, technique, and policy. Each payer presents a different set of issues. Medicare policy and methodology are the most well-established of the three payers. Early in the planning stage, Medicare agreed to pay SHMOs the equivalent of what the members would have cost the program under the fee-for-service system, as estimated through Medicare's prospective reimbursement mechanism—the adjusted average per capita costs (AAPCC). Medicare also agreed to allow savings on the AAPCC to be allocated to currently uncovered services, including, most importantly, chronic care costs. However, the existing AAPCC formula posed SHMOs with a perverse incentive. The AAPCC formula approximately doubles Medicare reimbursement when a member living in the community becomes a long-term nursing home resident. Since the SHMO needs to spend considerable sums on community-based services designed to keep people *out* of nursing homes, the AAPCC formula rewards the program for failure and penalizes success. A major issue with Medicare, therefore, involved finding a way to alter the formula to remove this bias toward institutionalization. The solution adopted for the Demonstration is to pay SHMOs at the current formula's institutional rate for SHMO members found to meet state nursing home preadmission standards (see chapter 6). This important new policy will be closely researched and refined during operations.

Prepaid, capitated reimbursement systems for Medicaid beneficiaries are in a much earlier stage of development than Medicare's AAPCC. Few states have experimented with capitation for *any* of their services for *any* populations served. Capitating payments for acute *and* chronic care for the elderly in conjunction with Medicare prepayment is an order of magnitude beyond the current state of development of Medicaid reimbursement policy. Limitations of data, staff time, technical expertise, and policy precedent were all more significant than anticipated at the Medicaid agencies participating in the Demonstration. Furthermore, policies and methods for Medicaid reimbursement had to be developed separately in *each* agency. Every state and locality posed a different set of opportunities and obstacles on a whole variety of variables.

Probably the most important policy question that the SHMO poses to both Medicare and Medicaid is what to do with the savings that the model hopes to achieve. As was pointed out above, Medicare has made its decision on this issue (at least for the course of the Demonstration): Savings will remain in the program and can be used to reduce premiums and expand benefits. Medicaid faces a similar decision: Should it follow Medicare and base its reimbursement rate on a fee-for-service equivalent model, or should it try to reduce its current costs by realizing some of the model's savings immediately?

There are several ways Medicaid could realize both direct and indirect savings through the SHMO. Direct savings could be achieved by paying the program on the basis of actual SHMO costs for services usually covered by

Medicaid. Since the model should reduce hospital backup and unnecessary nursing home admissions, significant reductions from current spending levels should be achieved, and it may be difficult for many Medicaid agencies to pass up these types of savings.

In fact, this is what happened to some extent in the process of establishing initial Medicaid rates at the sites (see chapter 6). While Minnesota and California followed a fee-for-service equivalent methodology to calculate rates, these states will pay only 95 percent of fee-for-service costs, as opposed to Medicare's 100 percent of AAPCC. Residual approaches were proposed by the sites in New York and Oregon. The New York rate is calculated to approximate estimated member costs minus Medicare reimbursement. Kaiser's rate proposal to Oregon was based on an overall adjusted community rate less Medicare reimbursement. By using these approaches, the state will reap some of the benefits of savings on Medicare reimbursement.

The most significant source of indirect savings to Medicaid comes through the SHMO's expanded benefits for private-pay members, especially in the long-term care area. These benefits should reduce the incidence of spend-downs that would have been expected among the membership without the SHMO, and to the extent that spend-downs are avoided Medicaid will save money indirectly. The policy issue for Medicaid is whether it should share these savings by somehow compensating the SHMO for reducing spend-down costs. During the initial period of the Demonstration, no rate element for spend-down prevention was included in Medicaid reimbursement. Since there are real problems in estimating the magnitude of potential savings, the issue will receive close study during operations.

It becomes clear that policy decisions by both Medicare and Medicaid relating to reimbursement levels and the legitimate components of reimbursement rates have important effects on the private premium and private member benefits. The more public payers (especially Medicaid) capture the model's savings for themselves, the less savings are left over for private members' benefits, which in turn puts more of the financing burden for these benefits on the nascent insurance mechanism. The alternative of taking little or no savings should not be rejected out of hand, at least to start. Some or all of both the direct and indirect subsidies could be allowed to flow into private-pay benefits. Such a strategy would not only increase these benefits directly, it would also increase the attractiveness of the program to private-pay elderly, probably allow a higher premium to be charged, and thus allow a further increase in benefit levels. Such insurance could provide some relief to the spend-down problem.

Turning now to the task of estimating service costs, it is clear that this is an inexact science at best. While there are relatively good data available from the Medicare HMO demonstrations on acute care costs for the elderly in a prepaid system, these data vary considerably across the HMO sites.

They also represent only initial experience, and they may reflect a healthier population than the SHMOs. The SHMO sponsor must determine which of the programs most closely reflect what its own experience will be—no mean feat for a sponsor that is not teamed up with an established HMO, as two of the Demonstration sites are not. Additionally, SHMO cost estimates must attempt to predict what effect the availability of good chronic care services will have on the utilization of acute care services. Since the chronically impaired use a disproportionate share of acute care resources, integrated and coordinated care in the home and in the nursing home could easily prevent many hospital admissions and shorten others.

Estimating long-term care utilization and costs is much more difficult than estimating costs for acute care. Data on long-term care are more limited and variable than acute care data. Furthermore, interpretation of the available program data is severely hampered by differences among the programs in terms of population served, eligibility guidelines, services offered, and financial incentives in the programs toward saving and economy. Most importantly, the key estimate that the SHMO must make (that is, the porportion of the membership that will use chronic care services) can be made only very indirectly from prior long-term care demonstrations. Also, most of the long-term care demonstration programs were not integrated with the acute care system or even with the institutional long-term care system. Thus, there is only limited precedent for the SHMO's integration of home- and community-based chronic care benefits with institutional long-term care benefits.

Each site developed methodologies and data for estimating capitation costs, but no one is terribly confident about the accuracy of the estimates. Expecially in the long-term care area, a whole series of assumptions had to be made about population, eligibility, and assistance from informal caregivers. Because of these unknowns it was very difficult to estimate in advance the costs of offering a particular package for chronic care services—even assuming that SHMO experience would be the same as that of prior demonstrations. Sites were conservative about making additional assumptions that would account for the new types of substitutions that are expected to occur in a fully consolidated model.

Across the sites, total cost estimates for 1984 ranged between $225 and $283 per member per month (PMPM) for Medicare-only members and $348 and $882 PMPM for Medicaid members. These costs were within the range of current fee-for-service spending by Medicare, Medicaid, and individuals at all sites. The large range of the Medicaid per-member costs reflects differences in coverage levels and case-mix. The low Medicaid estimate is from Kaiser, which was not able to reach agreement with its state Medicaid agency on a long-term care rate, and thus this estimate includes only medical and related services (see chapter 6).

Distributing Financial Risk

A required element of the SHMO model is that providers face financial risk. That is, the SHMO is paid in advance for the services it is to deliver to the membership, and it is expected to serve them within the constraints of the prepaid budget. Incorrect estimates of service requirements can have many effects, which are in part dependent on the organization of the SHMO. In a contracted system such as Elderplan, the effects can be significant losses or surpluses in plan budgets. In fully owned and controlled systems such as Kaiser, incorrect estimates of revenues or utilization can result in a budget imbalance, but internal control over other parameters (such as queues, occupancy, waiting times) may make this a less likely outcome than in more decentralized systems. In either case, significant miscalculations are unpleasant.

Thus, prepaid, at-risk reimbursement encourages cost consciousness in resource use, and it should lead to efficiency in operations. Risk enforces the SHMO's responsibility for managing the service system, and indeed it is difficult to see how a policy of prospective reimbursement could work without risk. If providers were paid in advance for expected costs, were then allowed to deliver an expanded package of services without outside review as to appropriateness, and then could ask for the balance of costs over prospective payments, there would be no control over system costs for third parties—not even the current provisions to review billing for appropriateness of costs and services.

Thus risk is a necessary feature of the model, and the practical and policy questions are (1) how much risk there should be for the SHMO entity, (2) what service costs should be protected through reinsurance or risk sharing, and (3) how third parties might share in the risk of cost overruns. On each of these questions the SHMO pushes back the boundaries of current policy and practice and demands thinking about new models.

In considering how much risk to incorporate into the SHMO entity, it is important to examine the kinds of risks faced by SHMO providers. A half century ago Knight (1921) made the distinction between the concepts of *risk* and *uncertainty* in business ventures. The term risk can be applied to possible future events that can be predicted statistically, that is, the possible outcomes are known, and one can assign probabilities to each. In contrast, uncertainty implies that there is not enough information to assign probabilities to various outcomes, and indeed the range of outcomes may not even be known. It is safe to say that at this point the SHMO is full of uncertainties, including effectiveness in integrating the service system, appeal in the market, structure of new benefits, accuracy of cost estimates, aging of the membership, and adequacy of reimbursement arrangements with third parties (see chapter 7).

Because of the magnitude of these risks and uncertainties in the

Demonstration, sponsors cannot be expected to have a great degree of control over these various systems or the overall financial outcomes, at least at the start. Following the policy that financial responsibility should flow from control (Leighton 1979; Zelten 1981), it may be bad policy to put the SHMO at full risk for service costs because the SHMO cannot expect to have a predictable level of control. Too much risk for providers would likely lead to extremely conservative, protective, and possibly dysfunctional behavior—certainly in the areas of cost estimates and benefit levels, and possibly in caregiving decisions. Even with conservative strategies, the possibility of bankruptcy for sponsors could not be ruled out.

Recognizing the potential adverse effects of full risk—and because conventional private reinsurance for this type of experimental program is unavailable—Medicare and most Medicaid agencies agreed to share risk with the Demonstration sites—at least in the initial years of the project. That is, SHMOs will still stand to earn or lose money for their efforts, but third parties will step in to limit losses (or gains) under conditions agreed on in advance. Such risk sharing should maintain efficiency incentives but at the same time protect against the dysfunctional effects of excessive risk. Prior to examining the potential and actual risk-sharing roles of the third parties, it is necessary to briefly review existing models for reinsurance and risk sharing.

Many HMOs obtain reinsurance against potentially catastrophic cost overruns. Two common models are "individual stop-loss," through which the third party takes over responsibility for costs after an individual member's costs exceed a set dollar threshold; and "aggregate stop-loss," through which the third party takes responsibility for the costs of the entire membership after a set threshold is passed. Both individual and aggregate kinds of stop-loss coverage are usually obtained on an individual service, particularly hospitals (Miller 1981). In HMOs these are typically reinsurance arrangements; that is, a premium is paid for the coverage. This is distinguished from risk sharing, where no premium is paid but where gains as well as losses can be shared. One important approach to risk sharing, at least in the literature (Leighton 1979), is a risk-sharing "corridor." Through this mechanism, the provider and the third party can share set proportions of a particular risk over set ranges of loss (or gain), rather than simply handing the full risk from one to the other at the threshold.

All of these models and features are important precedents, but there are problems with using some of the predominant models in the SHMO. Most important, the practice of insuring against costs only in a particular service area is problematic because of the ability to substitute services within the consolidated system. If, for example, a SHMO followed the common practice of insuring only against hospital costs, in the context of hospital cost overruns, it might be cheaper for the program to keep a patient in the hospital than it would to pay for more appropriate nursing home care (which was not protected by risk sharing). The same might be said for chronic nursing home care and home care. Thus, the SHMO calls for risk-sharing models that not only protect against major costs such as hospital care but also are sensitive to the full range of service costs for which the program is responsible.

But there is a second problem with insuring against particular areas of service costs—a problem that applies even if a range of cost areas are covered. Aggregate stop-loss (and to a lesser extent individual stop-loss) arrangements rely on setting a threshold or performance goal as a trigger for coverage. This makes sense in an HMO (especially an experienced one) where performance standards have been established. The performance potential of the SHMO has not been established, and setting a priori standards could easily distort outcomes. Performance targets for various service areas could acquire a life of their own, whether or not they represented the most efficient and effective mix of services for the membership. Thus, risk-sharing arrangements that treat internal decisions neutrally are the most desirable. The arrangement that does this most effectively is aggregate stop-loss coverage on total plan losses and gains. This "bottom-line" risk sharing gives generalized incentives toward efficiency without specifying what "efficiency" means in each particular service area.

Bottom-line risk sharing arrangements were recommended for the Demonstration by Brandeis, and they form the basic structure of risk sharing at most sites (see chapter 7). Medicare Partners and Elderplan will begin operations sharing bottom-line risk in preset proportions with Medicare and Medicaid, with total loss (and gain) limits for the providers set at $250,000 and $150,000 respectively in the first year. Medicare Partners also has a variety of risk-sharing corridors with Medicaid on long-term care services. Kaiser and SCAN will begin risk sharing under selective approaches only. Kaiser will give risk on long-term care gains and losses to Medicare, but will take full risk for acute care. SCAN has asked both Medicare and Medicaid for individual stop-loss coverage on hospital costs as its primary risk protection. It has also, however, asked for a bottom-line arrangement, but at a much higher level than the other sites (up to $800,000) (see chapter 7).

Brandeis's original proposal for risk sharing was that initial experience in the Demonstration would shape the types and levels of risk sharing in the future. The goal was always to increase provider risk substantially in year 2 and hopefully to go to full risk in year 3. The SHMO legislation (see the foreword) makes full risk in year 3 a requirement. While full risk is an appropriate ultimate goal for the SHMO, it is a goal that should be approached with caution. Until providers have proven their ability to control the service costs of the membership at a level consistent with both reimbursement levels and high quality care, and until standards for quality and benefits are established, the strength of risk incentives should probably be limited to levels that providers can absorb without disaster. One of the most important tasks of the Demonstration will be to develop these controls and standards in the short time available.

Notes

1. Similar issues must also be addressed at the service delivery and professional levels. Integration issues at these levels are discussed in chapter 3.

2. A list of foundation and corporate sponsors is included in the acknowledgments.

2
Organizational Development

The fragmented systems of acute and long-term care outlined in chapter 1 have their organizational analogue. In the current system the many types of professionals and organizations that provide health care services—such as physicians, hospitals, home health agencies, and nursing homes—have neither the means nor the motivation to cooperate effectively. Each is responsible for only a portion of the service universe, and each faces different incentives and tests of success—both financial and professional. Each is relatively autonomous, and their autonomy contributes to the maintenance of the fragmented system.

While these organizations work separately from day to day, there is in fact a high degree of interdependence among them. In the current fee-for-service system, this interdependence is often handled poorly. From the point of view of services to clients, the problem shows up in quality and continuity of care issues. From the point of view of organizational behavior, it shows up in protective behavior and inefficient use of resources. For example, with DRG reimbursement, hospitals will want to discharge patients much sooner than before to postacute care in nursing homes and home health care. However, these providers will not want to take a sicker grade of patients unless they receive corresponding increases in payments. But such increases have not been included as part of the DRG system.

Such interdependence gives health care organizations reason to establish relationships with one another. By associating, they can control "contingencies," that is, aspects of their environments that have important impacts on their work, success, and profitability. Various interorganizational ties expand the scope of one's own organization so that the important parts of the environment are included within one's own boundaries. The goal is a greater appreciation of the impact of decisions made in one place on other parts of the system. This is what providers do in the HMO model, and this is what providers find attractive about the SHMO.

There is a limit, however, to interdependencies and consolidation. In the instance of health care in general and the SHMO in particular, the need for integration must be tempered by the need of the constituent parts to maintain professional and organizational autonomy. In part this is true because it is obviously unreasonable to expect that agencies and professionals with a history of independence will be willing to cede a great deal of that control. But perhaps more important, consolidation must be limited because caring for the elderly requires highly skilled professionals with the autonomy to exercise their trained judgment. Strict centralized control is not possible because the information needed to make sound health care decisions cannot easily be transmitted in standardized ways. Nor can a small group have the range of skills necessary to evaluate all the facts about patients' needs and define solutions to them. Concern for quality of care, therefore, sparks the need both to integrate the system (to have continuity and case management) and to limit the extent of that integration.

Thus, the overriding task of organizational design for the SHMO is to find a workable balance between integration and autonomy of the parts. Also, in varying circumstances different balances will prove appropriate, and obviously various organizational structures may prove equally acceptable. The challenge for planners is to define the reasonable choices and approaches and to recognize the advantages and disadvantages of each, given the particular circumstances of the site.

The analysis that follows approaches these questions of integration and autonomy at two levels: first at the level of structure and then at the level of control of the system.[1] The discussion is meant to help potential SHMO sponsors answer such structural questions as:

Who should (and should not) sponsor a SHMO and why?

What kinds of other providers should be brought in as partners in the SHMO?

How should the sponsor and partners formally associate to offer the SHMO?

Control issues for sponsors to consider include:

Defining desired behavior for the various partners and components;

Motivating the participants to perform according to expectations;

Monitoring the performance of the participants.

The format of the presentation in each section will be a discussion of the general issues followed by a site-by-site description of the choices made in the Demonstration.

Designing the SHMO: How Can the Sponsor and Partners Structure Their Relationships?

The design of the SHMO system has three components: the provider agency that sponsors the project, the partner agencies that are likely to be needed to complete the system, and the structuring of relationships among the various participants. Before turning to detailed descriptions of these three components at each of the SHMO Demonstration sites, the generic issues related to the three aspects of design need to be more fully developed.

First, in examining the sponsorship question, a brief history of the actual process of site selection may be useful. In 1980 Brandeis and two sites applied for HCFA support for a demonstration of SHMOs. HCFA funded Brandeis to develop demonstration protocols and procedures and to locate additional sponsors, but site development funding was not granted. During its first grant year Brandeis solicited support from foundations for site development and contacted scores of additional health care providers across the country. The providers included HMOs, hospitals, medical groups, long-term care agencies, and nursing homes. While nearly all were interested and supportive, most did not feel prepared to sponsor the Demonstration. Fewer than a dozen submitted formal applications, and most of these (including one of the original applicants) voluntarily withdrew after examining their internal and external situations and the prospect of a long, uncertain development and testing period. In the end, five competent sponsors were selected. While it was clear that there were several others that could have done the job, Brandeis and HCFA decided that limitations on staff and outside funding required that no further sponsors be designated.

Factors considered in the selection process (both by Brandeis and during self-selection by providers) included financial resources and stability; reputation of the sponsor among the elderly; the amount of community competition; experience of the sponsor in mounting new programs requiring planning, applications, negotiations, and so on; attitudes toward risk and uncertainty; and experience with government bureaucracies in negotiating such permissions as licensure, and certificate of need. SHMO development extends into each of these areas and more, and sponsors must feel comfortable conducting a multifaceted planning and development effort.

It became clear early on that most SHMO sponsors (except perhaps large HMOs) would need partners to complete the system of care required in the model. It was also clear that partners would be chosen on the basis of such factors as their ability to provide the rest of the services, their resources (e.g., financial, experiential, political), and their willingness to adapt their operating procedures and systems to the SHMO effort.

One particular question that arises in the selection of partner providers is relative size. While picking a large partner (such as an HMO) may appear attractive to a small sponsor in terms of acquiring access to funds, market, experience, and other benefits, it may be more difficult to influence a large partner to conform to SHMO system goals than a small partner. A large agency may be less willing to adapt to the needs of a small one; or, more simply, if the SHMO is a small part of an agency's business, it may not make sense to make significant modifications in its predominant operations to accommodate an experimental program. Size also affects the number of partners needed to generate a complete delivery system. Small partners, especially if their participation is on a contract basis or if there is competition among them, may be more easily influenced by the sponsor. However, a large number of providers increases coordination problems—at least proportionately.

The third aspect of organizational structure is the formal relationships among the sponsor and the partners. The structuring of these relationships must take into account the need to (1) see the system through the planning and development phase; (2) integrate the providers toward mutually accepted goals related to the SHMO; and (3) retain sufficient autonomy for provider agencies and professionals to allow them to maintain high-quality care and take care of their other corporate interests.

It should be obvious that there is no "best" way to structure such relationships. The relationships at each site must fit the nature of the sponsors and other participants. Solutions must also be sensitive to the legal, financial, and policy constraints of critical outside actors, most notably the government and the local market. While there is probably a limited range of distinct legal relationships (such as partnerships, independent corporations, subsidiary corporations, contractual service agreements) these basic forms can be modified and shaped to fit particular needs and circumstances. Site-by-site analyses of the Demonstration sponsors' solutions to these problems follow.

Mercy Hospital, Springfield, Massachusetts

Mercy Hospital was one of the two sites that applied with Brandeis for the original SHMO grant in 1980.[2] When HCFA funded Brandeis but not the sites, Mercy sought and obtained outside foundation support for planning and development. After a year of planning and analysis, Mercy decided that it was not a feasible SHMO site, and the hospital dropped out of the Demonstration. Mercy staff members involved in the effort have related their experiences in some detail (Popko and Lasky 1982), but it is useful to provide here a summary from Brandeis's perspective. The Mercy experience offers useful insight into the process of deciding whether or not to become a SHMO sponsor.

Mercy is a 311-bed general hospital serving the city of Springfield and eight surrounding communities. Mercy was attracted to the SHMO concept because of a large and increasing elderly census in the hospital and a growing AND[3] problem. The hospital had plans for converting a building on its grounds into an extended care facility and also for setting up a comprehensive referral network with existing local community service agencies. The SHMO was seen as a mechanism that could integrate this whole system of planning and service delivery.

As planning began, the most important element of the SHMO system that was lacking at Mercy was a physicians' component. While the hospital's affiliated physicians had relatively elderly patient panels, these doctors were largely individual private practitioners. The hospital administration had two options for organizing the prepaid group practice required for a SHMO. First, the start of SHMO planning coincided with the formation in the Springfield area of an IPA-model HMO[4] by a large insurance company. Mercy physicians could simply join the new HMO, and the SHMO could form a relationship as well. The other option was to turn a recently formed physicians' group at Mercy into an HMO—following either an IPA or a group model.

While both these options seemed reasonable from an organizational point of view, it turned out that the hospital's most powerful and established physicians supported neither of them. First, there was already resentment among these physicians against the hospital's new medical group. The young physicians who staffed it were not about to embark on a prepaid group of their own, if the area's most powerful doctors had the potential of shutting them out of the referral network. Second, toward the end of the initial planning year, it became clear that the new IPA was failing, an event that appeared to confirm the older physicians' faith in individual private practice.

In itself, the lack of a viable medical services component was sufficient to make the SHMO infeasible at Mercy. However, there were other factors. One was a change in state reimbursement practices and levels for hospitals and nursing homes. When the state rate-setting agency cut rates (and there were rumors of more severe cuts in the future), the idea of expanding into extended care no longer seemed as prudent as a policy of contraction. Another factor was a more informed market analysis for a SHMO in the Springfield area. Since there were only 40,000 elderly persons in the Mercy service area, the program would have needed a relatively high penetration rate to reach the desired goal of 4,000 members.

In retrospect, it is clear that some of these barriers to SHMO development at Mercy could have been foreseen, but some could not. Also, at the time of the original application to HCFA and foundations, there simply was not enough knowledge on the part of either Mercy or Brandeis to recognize the importance of various factors in feasibility. The loss of the Mercy site led to a much closer examination of potential sponsors, as well as to additional work in detailing the specifications of SHMO Demonstration requirements.

Metropolitan Jewish Geriatric Center, Brooklyn, New York

The Metropolitan Jewish Geriatric Center was designated as a sponsor in August 1981. The core services of MJGC are provided by two long-term care facilities totaling 915 beds. In recent years MJGC has expanded its institutional base to include a day hospital, respite care, and other community services. MJGC's leaders found the SHMO consistent with their long-range plan, which is to become a major multilevel gerontological health care provider in the community (Kodner 1981, 1984). MJGC had demonstrated its capacity to mount new and innovative efforts in community-based care by its sponsorship of a Nursing Home Without Walls demonstration in New York's Long-Term Home Health Care Program (Kodner, Mossey, and Dapello 1983). This program attempts to keep impaired Medicaid recipients out of nursing homes through the provision of home and community-based services. The agency's history of innovative programs, its experience in negotiating with local government, its commitment from executive and board leadership, and its fiscally sound and substantial resource base all combined to make MJGC a strong sponsor for the Demonstration.

The major developmental efforts facing MJGC were to arrange for physicians and hospital services. Affiliating with the only major HMO in the New York City area was never seriously considered, in part because the HMO has a mixed reputation in the community but, probably more important, also because of power considerations. Working with a large existing HMO would have made it difficult for MJGC to create the type of geriatric practice that was consistent with its treatment philosophy. However, rejecting this option meant that MJGC had to create its own HMO and its own medical group. Both meant major developmental efforts for MJGC but did not create a barrier, since having these two components was consistent with the agency's long-range plans.

Starting an HMO is not an easy task in any state, but few can match the bureaucratic complexity of the process in New York. The major actors include the State Health Department, the State Insurance Department, and the Department of State. The major steps of the process are incorporation (very easy), Certificate of Need, and licensure (the latter two being very difficult and time consuming). The incorporation of Elderplan, Inc., took place in the spring of 1982, but licensure is still pending as of this writing (November 1984). MJGC's efforts to obtain licensure illustrate problems encountered at all the sites in establishing relationships with state and local agencies. As a rule, government agencies are not equipped to handle demonstration programs, especially demonstrations that cut across so many bureaucratic domains and break so much new policy ground. Negotiating this political thicket has been a major task for all sites, but especially for MJGC.

MJGC will maintain very close control of the new HMO–two-thirds of the board members of the new corporation are MJGC trustees, and the executive director of MJGC holds the same position at Elderplan. He will function as a chief executive officer, responsible for integrating Elderplan with the rest of MJGC. Day-to-day operations will be handled by a general director, whose position will be analogous to chief operating officer. The general director also serves as the project's principal investigator.

Forming the required prepaid group practice was somewhat easier. The most promising opportunity lay in an existing relationship with the Cornell University Medical College's Division of Geriatrics and Gerontology. One of the first graduates of the division's fellowship program, an assistant professor of medicine at Cornell, was interested in heading a medical group that would become the medical component of the SHMO. Under the leadership of the division director at Cornell, the Geriatric Medicine Associates (GMA) was incorporated in the fall of 1982 as a professional corporation (PC). Because the GMA and SHMO planning staffs worked closely together during the developmental phases of both programs, there is a strong likelihood that the medical component will be consistent with the goals and procedures of the SHMO.

MJGC also had some clear choices in the development of its hospital component. An obvious choice was the 619-bed Maimonides Medical Center—to which MJGC's skilled nursing facility is physically connected, and which enjoys a good reputation in the community. But once again MJGC did not make the obvious choice. Again, the choice was probably made in part for reasons of control: MJGC, though large, could easily have been overshadowed by Maimonides. But perhaps the more important and practical reasons were related to cost and bed availability. Since it is a teaching hospital, beds at Maimonides cost more than average for its community. Furthermore, Maimonides was operating close to capacity. Since a major part of the SHMO's financial underpinning is based on saving on hospital costs, starting out with a high-cost institutional provider would put the new venture in the hole from the start. Given these considerations, MJGC very early decided they could strike a better deal with a community hospital with available beds and a lower per diem charge. The choice was the nearby Brooklyn Hospital–Caledonian Hospital. It will be the primary SHMO facility, with Maimonides available for back-up specialty care.

One other piece of the SHMO delivery system missing at MJGC was home health services. While MJGC delivered home health services in the Nursing Home Without Walls project, it had state authorization to deliver such services only to Medicaid eligibles enrolled in that project. To serve the broader Elderplan population, Elderplan would need to start its own home health agency or contract with an existing agency. The problem with contracting was that state regulations required that services be purchased in minimum blocks of four hours. This could raise costs unnecessarily in Elderplan, since in most cases a shorter visit is appropriate. When negotiations with local home health agencies and public officials failed to produce an alternative to the purchase of unwanted hours, MJGC decided to develop its own home health agency and began the required applications. While this decision entailed another significant developmental and political effort, the sponsor saw the effort as worthwhile, since home health represents another component in the long-range plans for a comprehensive gerontological health delivery system.

In summary, the SHMO sponsored by MJGC looks very much like an

HMO in terms of participants and formal relationships, except of course for the long-term care sponsor and services. A satellite corporation—Elderplan— is formed by a sponsor, and that corporation becomes an HMO. The HMO contracts with a physicians group for medical services, a hospital for acute care services, and its parent corporation for home health, nursing home, and other home- and community-based services. Relative to the other sites, the planning and development efforts were very significant at MJGC—requiring more than two years and $1.1 million in foundation support and contributions from the sponsor. However, because some of the key service components were created explicitly for the SHMO this is a powerful model for marshaling the necessary organizational control to manage the SHMO system success-fully.

Kaiser Permanente Medical Care Program, Portland, Oregon

Kaiser-Portland was designated as a SHMO site in December 1981. The Portland region of the KPMCP is in many ways the flagship unit for the 4.2-million member Kaiser system. Kaiser-Portland houses the Center for Health Research (formerly the Kaiser Health Services Research Center), which has sponsored many research and demonstration projects, including most recently the Medicare Plus Program, KPMCP's entry in the Medicare HMO prospective payment demonstration (Greenlick et al. 1983; Galblum and Trieger 1982). In launching Medicare Plus, Kaiser made a decision to expand its share of the elderly market. It now has nearly 10 percent of its 268,000 members over age 65, and the SHMO promises to increase the proportion of elderly. Medicare's prospective payment system is attractive to Kaiser, since it both simplifies reimbursement procedures and raises the level of revenue. That is, under its cost contract for Medicare eligibles (the only arrangement available prior to the HMO demonstration), Kaiser is paid only for the Medicare-covered services its members actually use. Even more important, the basis for calculating the costs of these services excludes key cost areas such as capital formation. Because of these exclusions and Kaiser's lower utilization patterns, reimbursement to Kaiser under the cost contract averages out to about 80 percent of Medicare's fee-for-service spending. Under the risk reimbursement in the HMO demonstration Kaiser is paid 95 percent of fee-for-service costs, and in the SHMO it receives 100 percent. The additional funds can be used to enrich benefits and/or reduce premiums for members.

While these are clearly strong incentives for Kaiser to participate in such systems, key sectors of the Kaiser system had reservations about the project. First, officials at corporate headquarters were concerned about taking risk for long-term care services, since Kaiser had no experience with these services. Second, the medical group was not enthusiastic about the increased time and complexity of serving additional elderly members, especially members who might be more impaired than the Medicare Plus Members. Kaiser adjusts its community rate to account for time and complexity in figuring costs for Medicare reimbursement, but physicians are paid on the basis of a single community rate. While the higher costs of SHMO members will be factored in to increase the community rate, there is at least a year's lag in the adjustment. Finally, the two Kaiser hospitals serving the region were running close to capacity. In later chapters it will be seen that these concerns were met by allowing Kaiser to recruit half of its SHMO members internally (chapter 5) and to give third parties full initial risk for long-term care (chapter 7).

In terms of its need to expand system capacity to encompass the full range of SHMO services, Kaiser was in the opposite situation from MJGC. Kaiser-Portland owns two hospitals and includes a multispecialty physicians' group. While the SHMO required potential sites to examine the capacity of the participating hospitals and doctors to take on more patients, there was never any question at Kaiser of looking for alternative providers. There was a need, however, to find a vehicle to provide the SHMO's additional long-term care services which were not in the Kaiser system. Kaiser staff decided not to affiliate with an existing provider of these services, in part because there were few obvious candidates. But, probably more important, Kaiser has a tradition of controlling its entire system. Kaiser chose to develop the additional home care services by expanding its existing home health unit. At the start it will contract with existing institutional long-term care providers, holding out the possibility of acquiring its own nursing home at a future date. The SHMO will be called Medicare Plus II, a name that builds on the established reputation of Medicare Plus.

Thus, the entire SHMO service system has been developed internally at Kaiser without partners. The planning effort was not nearly as extensive and expensive as efforts were at the other sites. Kaiser's total external foundation funding was less than $250,000. This is certainly an underestimate of actual costs, however, since donated time by the sponsor was more considerable at Kaiser than at the other sites.

Ebenezer Society, Minneapolis, Minnesota

Ebenezer Society was designated as a Demonstration site in December 1981. Ebenezer has been serving the elderly in Minneapolis since 1917, under the sponsorship of a consortium of Lutheran churches. Its services are wide-ranging and now include the management of 1,382 congregate housing units (400 of them owned by Ebenezer) and 670 nursing home beds in six facilities. Ebenezer also operates a Medicare-certified home health agency, a homemaker–home health aide program, an adult day care program, respite care, and other advocacy and support services for the elderly (Carter and Kennedy 1983).

Ebenezer's motivation for becoming a SHMO was in part its desire for more stable, sound, and rational financing for its community-based services. But there was also a large measure of altruism in the effort: Ebenezer's leaders wanted the SHMO simply because they saw it as a better system of care for local elders.[5] In other words, somewhat in contrast to MJGC there seemed to be no desire on Ebenezer's part to transform itself into something new. If anything, there was some internal hesitancy about change and expansion, and there was certainly concern about financial risk, given some recent financial difficulties in connection with some of the new Ebenezer housing.

These concerns were important, not only in Ebenezer's deliberations about whether or not to sponsor the SHMO, but also in the agency's choice of a medical partner. In fact, the decision to seek designation as a Demonstration site and proceed with planning and development was premised on the choice of a particular partner—Group Health, Inc. (formerly Group Health Plan, Inc.), the oldest and largest HMO in the very competitive Minneapolis HMO market. An agreement from Group Health to participate was obtained prior to the designation of Ebenezer as a sponsor. Group Health was seen as bringing not only the full range of medical services with a good array of clinics near the Ebenezer campus; it also brought experience, financial resources, a good reputation with local elderly, and a community service ethic similar to Ebenezer's. This is reflected in Group Health's status as a cooperative, with a board of directors composed entirely of plan members.

The most difficult issue at the Ebenezer–Group Health site was finding a way to structure the integration of the two partners while still preserving the autonomy that each desired in particular areas. The difficulties were not the result of philosophical disagreements or any lack of goodwill. For example, there was an early understanding that the two agencies would approach the Demonstration as an "equal" or "shared" venture. However, there was some difficulty working out the division of responsibility for services. Between them the two sponsors controlled all SHMO services, but there was one point of service overlap—home health care. Staff at Group Health wanted to maintain their control over discharge planning and postacute home health, while Ebenezer planners wanted to centralize all delivery of home care at one agency (Ebenezer) to avoid confusion and discontinuity. As will be detailed in chapter 3, a compromise was reached.

The most problematic issue, however, was how to structure formal relationships. The basic options were clear from the beginning. The first option was forming a jointly sponsored satellite corporation. Similar to MJGC's Elderplan, it would be licensed as an HMO that would contract with the two partners for services. This was the best model for sharing control and for insulating the sponsors from risk, but it had the disadvantage of having to go through the state licensure process. It posed another potential disadvantage for Group Health: How could GHI be sure that the SHMO might not eventually end up competing with it in the already crowded Twin Cities HMO market? This could not be discounted, when by law, 40 percent of the new HMO board of directors would be required to be composed of plan members.

The second option was forming the SHMO as a legal partnership between the two sponsors. The problems here were twofold. first, a little legal research showed that partnerships could not be licensed as HMOs in Minnesota. Second, partnerships do not protect the individual partners from the legal liabilities of the other partner.

The third option was to turn the tables and make Group Health the formal sponsor of the Demonstration, with Ebenezer a contracted provider. This arrangement had the advantage of being the cleanest legally and organizationally. Group Health's HMO license would be used; no new corporations would need to be formed; and the vagaries of partnership liabilities would be avoided. However, such an arrangement would clearly make Ebenezer the junior partner—if a partner at all—and that would be contrary to Ebenezer's original mission to infuse its long-term care philosophy and expertise into the SHMO system.

The negotiation of these conflicting demands took nearly two years. The resolution was a hybrid between options two and three—that is, a legal partnership that uses the Group Health HMO license. In other words, the elderly who join the SHMO in Minneapolis (aptly called Medicare Partners) will legally be members of Group Health, Inc. Similarly, the third-party service contracts will be made with Group Health. However, the joint business of Medicare Partners will be shared between the two partners in a very explicit and, it is hoped, equal manner. Details of the agreements will be outlined in the section to follow on management control systems.

In summary, the Ebenezer site was relatively simple to plan and develop from the point of view of choosing partners and developing the service system capacity: Ebenezer's partner, Group Health, provided all that was needed in a single package. Not surprisingly, the $598,000 in planning and development support was significantly less than the amount required at MJGC. The real challenge during planning was to find a way to integrate the two agencies around the SHMO, and the long-run workability of their method of formal integration will be one of the ongoing issues at this site.

Senior Care Action Network, Long Beach, California

The Senior Care Action Network (SCAN) was designated as a site sponsor in February 1982. SCAN is the smallest and youngest of the sponsors, but its record of innovation and mobilization of the Long Beach provider community makes it a strong choice. As a brokerage-model case-management agency, SCAN is a small operation that controls no services of its own except case management. Founded in 1978, SCAN has been a site in the Multipurpose Senior Services Program (MSSP) for several years. MSSP is a state-sponsored home- and community-based services project similar to MJGC's Nursing Home Without Walls. MSSP achieved status as a permanent state program in July 1983. SCAN staff's entrepreneurial skills were also demonstrated in its formation of a physicians' service program for the poor and near-poor elderly, in conjunction with a network of local providers.

The leadership at SCAN saw the SHMO in much the same way as MJGC did. The SHMO could be a vehicle to establish a broader reach for the agency, as well as a more sound and stable long-term financial footing. Establishing a basis for long-term survival was an especially strong motivation for SCAN, since much of its budget was dependent on state demonstration programs, fund raising, and support from major providers—most prominently the St. Mary's Medical Center.

In deciding how to structure a SHMO, SCAN faced options similar to both MJGC and Ebenezer. Should they use an established HMO or form a new one? Should they use an existing medical group or create a new one? Which hospital should they choose from among several in the community? Once again the history of the agency, local conditions, and the sponsor's long-term plan for the SHMO all influenced the choices that were made.

First, the idea of selecting an existing HMO as medical partner was never seriously considered. None of the three leading HMOs in the Long Beach area was involved in the elderly market (although one of them has since entered the elderly market under the expanded HMO Medicare Demonstration Program). SCAN saw that there was clearly room for another HMO in the market, and sponsoring one was consistent with SCAN's need for a broader and more secure base. Thus, SCAN formed the SCAN Health Plan, Inc., a not-for-profit corporation that applied in late 1983 for licensure as an HMO in California. The application is pending as of this writing. SHP is a satellite of SCAN, with the majority of its board composed of current SCAN directors. The details of the licensure procedures (which were less complex than in New York but still demanding) need not be repeated here, except for one important provision to be further addressed below. The government required a $1 million performance bond—a sum that was clearly well beyond SCAN's small reserves.

SCAN differed from MJGC in its choice for a medical component for the SHMO. Rather than forming its own affiliated medical group, it chose as a partner the Harriman Jones Clinic, a forty-seven-doctor group practice with a fifty-year history in the Long Beach area. Harriman Jones has three clinics in the area, and one-third of its patients are over age 65. SCAN viewed its connection with Harriman Jones as a strong advantage in terms of both quality of care and marketability.

The choice of a hospital was the most difficult decision facing SCAN. Three hospitals in Long Beach were very interested in participating, since there is excess hospital capacity in the community (occupancy rates are 70 to 75 percent). St. Mary's was an obvious choice because of its long working relationship with SCAN and its substantial material support over the years. However, because it was a medical center, it was feared that St. Mary's might not be able to offer competitive prices. The two other hospitals also offered high-quality care, but their standard per diem rates were somewhat lower. Also, one of these two was the primary hospital used by Harriman Jones physicians. SCAN decided to use another criterion on its choice of a hospital, in addition to a hospital's past relationship with SCAN, its reputation, and the competitiveness of its per diem rate. The hospital had to agree to make a subordinated loan to SHP to cover the $1 million HMO performance bond.

When SCAN reviewed the proposals from the three hospitals and further negotiations took place, it turned out that the St. Mary's proposal was best. The St. Mary's per diem rate was ultimately competitive with those of the other proposals, and SHP had its loan. The St. Mary's proposal went even further. The hospital agreed to provide not only acute care services but also pharmacy and institutional long-term care services. The offer served to round out SCAN's SHMO delivery system, since SHP had planned all along to use SCAN's case managers and existing network of home care and day health service providers.

In summary, SCAN followed a path similar to MJGC's but with some important differences in detail. Both agencies formed new closely controlled HMOs that would sponsor the SHMO, and both made sure that the SHMO would contract with the parent agency for long-term care services currently offered by the parent. But they followed different courses of action in terms of physicians and hospital services. By contracting with a large established group, SHP obtains the benefit of the group's reputation but may have more difficulty shaping the practice of the group to fit the practice that best serves the SHMO. But the biggest difference between SCAN and MJGC lies in the hospital area: By placing the hospitals into competition with each other, SCAN was able to strike a very favorable bargain for SHP. The terms of the hospital agreement also bring St. Mary's into a much more integrated position in the SHMO system than is the case with Brooklyn-Caledonian at Elderplan. This point will become clearer in the next section as the mechanisms for achieving internal control in the SHMO system are analyzed.

Planning and development costs covered by foundation grants to SCAN were comparable to such costs at Ebenezer. A total of $407,500 has been raised as of this writing.

Managing the System: How Can Internal Control of Operations Be Achieved?

The second level of organizational integration to be addressed in this chapter is the establishment of internal systems of control. Once again, decisions about integrating the system must balance the tension between the interdependence of the participants and their needs for some autonomy. From the standpoint of patient care, one needs somehow to obtain cross-specialization interactions and modifications of practice without compromising the quality of care. From the standpoint of system efficiency, one needs somehow to make the components work toward efficient resource allocation *across* the system, rather than simply toward the narrower efficiency of the individual agencies or groups.

There are three aspects to internal system control:

1. Defining what the SHMO expects from each component;
2. Developing methods of encouraging and enforcing compliance; and
3. Devising methods to monitor compliance.

In the SHMO all three aspects of control are played out primarily around systems for internal reimbursement and risk sharing. Issues and options concerning internal financial arrangements will be detailed presently, but first the three aspects require some elaboration.

In defining the behavior that is expected of someone it is necessary both to have an idea of the kinds of outcomes that actor can influence and to be able to define the specific outcome or range of outcomes that are desirable or acceptable. It makes sense only to hold people responsible for outcomes they can control and for outcomes that can be defined. However, in a system such as the SHMO, where responsibility is often shared or sequential, expecting to define individual responsibility for outcomes is often unrealistic. And in a radically new system whose goals are to change significantly the current pattern of outcomes, there is no relevant experience for setting standards. Of course, some responsibilities and standards need to be set even in the beginning, but these first measures need to be general ones.

Assuming that responsibilities and standards have been set (either specifically or generally), the next task is to develop methods of encouraging and enforcing compliance. For changes in behavior to occur, individuals and organizations must not only know what is expected, they must also be motivated toward compliance and cooperation. Internal control systems can offer incentives to comply. These can be positive or negative, financial or nonfinancial, but whatever their form, the incentives must be perceived by the actors as both relevant and valid.

For organizations, financial incentives are the most important and the easiest and clearest to implement. Financial incentives may also be important for individuals, but it may not be possible or even desirable to tie individual or team behavior to pay. It should not be forgotten—especially with professionals—that other incentives can also play a role. Wanting to see a "job well done," or to maintain "professional standards," or even simply wanting to do what is expected are all important motivators and should be utilized.

Expectations for changes in behavior should not be unrealistic. Among well-entrenched professionals and organizations, it is difficult to change "standard operating procedures." Also, the scale of incentives is important obviously in the financial sense, but also in terms of the importance of the SHMO in the actor's existence. If the project is only a tiny part of the individual's or the organization's work, it is not reasonable to expect direct incentives to have much effect. Direct convincing is the only measure that is likely to work in such an instance.

Effective monitoring of internal control relies on access to information. Since the information must relate to the definitions of desired behavior and outcomes, outcomes that cannot be measured and monitored should be avoided as standards. The organizational structure and the capacity and resources of the providers also play roles in designing monitoring systems. A large organization with a sophisticated management information system (MIS) that can monitor individual behavior can take one approach, while a contract system with a number of small providers will generate different information. Of course, the information needs will differ in various structures. For example, if the SHMO has a performance contract with a provider, monitoring direct providers is probably neither important nor even possible. However, monitoring contract compliance may be critical, and this will require a particular system and kind of expertise.

It is the responsibility of managers to implement and operate internal control systems. Managers monitor, deliver the incentives, and set and revise the performance expectations. Once again, the structure, style, and power of management will reflect the structure of the particular SHMO system. And the variables are the same: scale, amount of consolidation versus contracting, the extent to which the components have traditionally maintained their autonomy.

Communication is an important management tool in dealing with professionals in highly differentiated organizations. It is often necessary to gain some degree of agreement from professionals as to the goals and tests of compliance. Methods such as task forces and committees do elicit such participation, and that is part of their appeal—but these methods swallow up personnel time. An organization can invest too heavily in communications, and how much communication is enough will depend on the likelihood of noncompliance. This, in turn depends on whether everyone understands what is called for and on whether they think the new arrangements are a good idea. This reflects back to the initial selection of partners who are experienced in the sort of work being done and who are committed to the SHMO concept.

Overview of Internal Risk-Sharing Issues

One of the most fundamental questions related to internal control systems in the SHMO is the manner in which financial responsibilities and incentives are allocated among the parties involved. One-provider sites are likely to be rare, and future sponsors and their partners must work out plans for such "internal risk sharing." Before the sites' internal risk sharing and other internal control aspects are discussed in detail, three questions will be explored here:

1. What types of risks are there?
2. Who should be responsible for what types of risks?
3. What models are there for sharing risks?

Types of Risk to Be Shared. Before looking at the types of risk in the SHMO, it is useful to say a few words about the concept of risk. Zelten (1981) makes a useful distinction between "pure risk" and "speculative risk": "the former refers to situations that tend to produce negative financial consequences only, while the latter's consequences can be either positive or negative." Fires and thefts are examples of the former, and most risks assumed by both HMO and SHMO providers are in the latter category. Thus, when one says that SHMO providers are "at risk," one means that these providers stand either to lose or to gain, as is true in most other business ventures. It is also important to point out that the positive and negative consequences of miscalculations in an at-risk venture can show up in places other than the "bottom line." For example, when a fully integrated HMO such as Kaiser makes mistakes in estimating revenues or service demand, it can often stay within its budget by altering other system parameters (such as the length of queues).

The magnitude of risk in the initial period of the SHMO Demonstration is so great that providers are not being asked to take full risk. While the magnitude of these risks is better addressed in chapter 7, it is relevant here to list the types of risk. Again, Zelten provides a useful classification using five major areas:

Unit cost risk: will cost per service be higher or lower than predicted?

Utilization risk: will members use more or less of each service than predicted?

Contract mix risk: if there is a subsidy across contract types, will the target balance be achieved (families and individuals, or in the SHMO, Medicaid versus private members)?

Age–sex risk (in the SHMO, also impairment-level risk): will the membership be more or less costly according to these factors than predicted?

Enrollment risk: will enrollment of new members be faster or slower than predicted?

All of these risks are present in the SHMO, with the possible exception of contract mix risk. At least in theory, most SHMO Demonstration sites are not planning cross-subsidies. However, it is in fact likely that there *will* be cross-subsidies, although it is difficult to predict whether Medicaid will subsidize private individuals or vice versa.

Allocating Risk among Providers. Which provider should take responsibility for which risks? A very basic principle to apply here is that those who have control should take responsibility. A corollary is that where control is shared, responsibility should also be shared. A major recurring task in designing internal risk-sharing arrangements in the SHMO is defining where control ends and begins and, in turn, where a provider's risk should end and begin. A second principle that applies here is that the risk-sharing arrangements should provide incentives that are in the "right" direction; that is, they should encourage cost-effective outcomes *for the system overall,* and the financial incentives of each individual provider should not conflict with these system incentives. Realizing this principle in the SHMO is more difficult than in an HMO because of the wider range of services and providers in the SHMO.

Potential Arrangements in a SHMO System. This is not the proper context in which to detail every specific model or mechanism for internal risk sharing. The references cited earlier already do that well. A simple example from the most common type of HMO—a plan, a medical group, and a hospital—will illustrate how the principles of control and incentive can be applied to allocating the various types of risk described above, using the most common risk-sharing models. If the HMO allocated internal risk according to the principle of control, the "plan"—which organized the HMO—would take risk for contract mix, age–sex, and enrollment risks. The medical group would take risk for unit costs and utilization in acute medical care on a capitation basis and, perhaps, take some risk for hospital utilization. The hospital would be paid on a per diem basis, thus taking unit cost risk for the major expenditure of the HMO.

The most difficult challenge in SHMO internal risk sharing is deciding how to allocate risk for acute and long-term care. In the HMO model, physicians have control over the utilization of both ambulatory and in-patient services. Thus, it is easy to capitate physicians for the former and put them at some kind of joint risk for the latter, giving the decision makers incentives to economize across the entire system. There is a broader system to span in the SHMO, but systemwide incentives still make sense. For example, physicians will obviously have some control over the utilization of long-term care services in the SHMO. It can be argued that they should therefore share some risk for these services. Conversely, the long-term care providers should probably share some risk for hospital costs. If they don't, and physicians don't share risk for long-term care, why should the long-term care providers make their best effort to get patients out of the hospital? These issues would be much easier to work out if there were known, acceptable standards of performance available for each of the various providers. Since there are no such standards, and since a major aim of the Demonstration is that significant changes in current patterns will occur in the model, it may be dangerous to have a great deal of risk tied to a target performance level for any of the particular, individual providers. To get around this problem, a "bottom-line" approach to internal risk sharing was recommended by Brandeis to the sites. All sites considered the approach, and some accepted it, as outlined below.

Choices at the Sites on Internal Control Systems

Medicare Partners. Ebenezer and Group Health attempted to follow their "equal partners" approach in designing their internal control systems. Their arrangements for reimbursement, risk-sharing incentives, and management all rely on shared responsibility. For the services each partner delivers in the SHMO that partner will receive a monthly payment equal to estimated costs. The payment will be adjusted periodically if costs depart significantly from predictions, and at year-end, payments to each will be adjusted to reflect actual aggregate costs. Any overall profits or losses remaining after these calculations will be shared fifty-fifty by the partners. Thus, the policy of giving systemwide economizing incentives (as opposed to setting performance incentives for each individual agency or service area) is fully incorporated in the Medicare Partners arrangements.

The major source of information to monitor these agreements is a new MIS that is concurrently being introduced at Group Health. It includes modules for financial and membership accounting, utilization reporting, case management, and evaluation. The basic Group Health system is being modified and expanded to include the Ebenezer component and other requirements of the SHMO.

The Medicare Partners management design also aims for joint control. The SHMO's executive director is supervised jointly by the chief executive officers of Ebenezer and Group Health. Day-to-day organizational liaison will be carried out by designated senior staff members from each partner. Reporting to the executive director will be an assistant director, an administrative assistant, a part-time medical director, a case-management director, and a member services director. The case-management teams will report to the case-management director. The SHMO will take advantage of some key administrative services that already exist at Group Health, including member registration, billing, accounting, claims processing, and MIS. Purchasing these services, together with marketing services, at cost from

Group Health, makes it possible for Medicare Partners to keep its staff to a minimum.

While the Medicare Partners highly value the equal partners concept, and while they have also tried to implement the concept in their internal control systems, they face some challenges in practice. First, there are issues of scale. SHMO business will be only a small portion of Group Health business, while it will be a major share for Ebenezer (20 to 25 percent). Will the Medicare Partners management arrangements and the financial incentives in the risk-sharing agreement be strong enough to affect the far-flung Group Health management and provider systems? It seems likely that the cooperation of Group Health providers will be gained not so much by compulsion as by convincing the providers of the efficacy of integrating their practice with the new elements in the SHMO system. The next chapter will show that planning has taken this route, through joint task forces, but it remains to be seen how well this process will work.

In contrast, Ebenezer providers are likely to be much more aware of the importance of the SHMO to their agency, and more in tune with its potential for elderly clients. Furthermore, the services to be provided by Ebenezer will be directly prescribed by SHMO staff (that is, the case managers). SHMO managers will clearly need to work hard to bring GHI staff "in line" with the program. One direct acknowledgment of this need was the appointment of an Ebenezer staff member as the executive director of Medicare Partners.

A second challenge for the partners was to work out ways to manage the autonomy and interdependence of the partners within the context of the formal partnership agreement. Three issues were paramount. First, the bane of partnership arrangements—the liability of each partner for the other's business—was handled through a series of covenants in the partnership contract that limit financial obligations to the joint business and that declare each immune from the negligence of the other. Second, since the third-party and membership contracts will be signed with Group Health (not Ebenezer), the possibility exists that Group Health could offer the SHMO in the future without Ebenezer, while there is little possibility that Ebenezer could turn the tables and do without Group Health. The former possibility was guarded against in the partnership contract with language that prohibits either partner from marketing a product resembling a SHMO without the other, until a stated number of years have passed.

The third difficult autonomy issue was Group Health's desire to market a conventional HMO package to the Twin Cities elderly under the HMO Medicare Demonstration Project. Since both partners agreed that simultaneous marketing might lead to adverse selection in the SHMO, the partners negotiated a detailed system for monitoring the dual offering's impact on selection in each of the two programs. The agreement stipulates that GHI's risk share will increase to 70 percent if adverse selection occurs in the SHMO.

Elderplan. Elderplan's approach to internal control systems more closely resembles a conventional HMO model than does the approach at Medicare Partners, but it also integrates some financial incentives at the bottom line. Following HMO practice, Elderplan will pay the medical group a monthly capitation for medical services and will pay the hospital on a monthly capitation basis for a fixed number of inpatient beds.[6] Payments to MJGC for long-term care will be on a fee-for-service basis. Total system profits or losses will be shared between GMA and Elderplan in set proportions (40 and 60 percent respectively, in the initial period).

Along with this bottom-line arrangement there will be an incentive payment system for GMA physicians. Payments from a "medical service incentive pool" will be made by Elderplan if GMA's per member, per month costs for a set package of medical services are below budget. Similar payments from an "institutional services pool" will be made if hospital utilization is below budgeted costs. These incentive payments are designed to motivate physicians to continue to economize on medical costs even if they are losing money on the bottom line because of such factors as cost overruns in long-term care or marketing problems.

A way to monitor these internal control systems at Elderplan had to be developed from scratch, since MJGC had a very limited MIS capacity compared to that which is needed for a SHMO. The new system will be an automated MIS designed expressly for the SHMO. Elderplan issued MIS vendors a detailed request for proposal that outlined Elderplan's need for a full range of systems for enrollment, billing, finance, patient care, and so on. The winning bid came from COMTEC of Southfield, Michigan, which will install a modification of the system it has developed for Medicare HMOs.

The management structure of Elderplan is similar to that of Medicare Partners, but, not surprisingly, it is a little larger. MJGC's formal control at the board level is mirrored at the management level. MJGC's executive director holds the same formal title in Elderplan (on a part-time basis). Reporting to the executive director is a general director who is assisted by a plan administrator, a special projects director, and an administrative assistant. Reporting to the general director through the plan administrator are directors for marketing and research, finance, case management, and professional affairs; an MIS coordinator; and a health education coordinator. The various directors will each have sufficient staff to perform the full range of HMO-type functions required by Elderplan. Thus, management and administrative functions will be more centralized in Elderplan than in Medicare Partners, where many administrative functions will be performed by existing Group Health units.

The Elderplan model for internal controls and management comprises what could be a very well integrated SHMO system. The bottom-line risk-sharing arrangement should motivate staff in all service sectors to be conscious of system performance rather than thinking in terms of narrower performance objectives. In contrast to the Medicare Partners system, for example, the Elderplan incentives might be more meaningful to all participants. The SHMO will be GMA's only line of business, and the SHMO's functioning will have the attention of MJGC and GMA staff from the standpoint of both practice and material incentives. The only significant actor that lacks system incentives is the hospital, which has incentives only to control its per diem cost. However, as will be detailed in the next chapter, Elderplan staff will control both admission and discharge for Elderplan patients, and thus the hospital need not be incorporated any further initially.

One future problem may be the capacity of GMA to continue to bear such a large proportion of the system's bottom-line risk. The device being used initially to cover GMA's risk share (a capitation withhold) works well with limited total bottom-line risk levels. Still, one must question the capacity of a small group to handle open-ended risk exposure of the magnitude that will exist in the SHMO later. Obviously, modifications in risk shares are possible and are anticipated by both parties.

Finally, there is one other problem that Elderplan faces to a much lesser extent than does Medicare Partners—that is, managing the degree of integration and autonomy of the formal partners. As was outlined in the previous section, the goals of MJGC in forming a SHMO have remained clear from the outset. MJGC wants to be in charge, and they have implemented their authority both by closely controlling the governance and administration of Elderplan and by devising dependent relationships with the other actors. The medical group is small and closely affiliated with the purchaser of its services, and the hospital is kept at arm's length through a per diem arrangement of reimbursement. The provider agencies are allowed autonomy in their own areas of expertise, but their practice must be consistent with SHMO system objectives. Finally, there is some reciprocity in Elderplan's organization of its provider network through the provision of seats on the Elderplan board to GMA, Brooklyn-Caledonian, and Maimonides.

SCAN Health Plan *(SHP)*. SHP's approach to internal control systems departs significantly from that of the other sites in that it brings in the hospital as a major risk bearer from the start. The previous section showed that SCAN increased St. Mary's stake in the system by requiring its hospital partner to provide a $1 million loan. St. Mary's in turn raised the stake by offering to take on responsibility for pharmacy and institutional long-term care. Another provision stemming from the initial negotiation was that the hospital would be paid on a capitated, risk-sharing basis for acute inpatient care. In other words, the hospital will be paid for an expected number of days of acute care per year for each SHMO member. If total days are fewer than the preset number, the hospital will make money; if total days exceed the number, the hospital will lose. A separate "hospital incentive pool" will also be established that will reward Harriman Jones and SHP for holding utilization below target levels and will partially compensate St. Mary's for losses if utilization exceeds target levels. Similar arrangements will be made for pharmacy and inpatient long-term care. The actual figures for the performance targets, the levels of internal risk, and the incentive payments are confidential, but it can be said that the targets are ambitious and that the hospital's first-year risk exposure is several times higher than that of any single party at the Elderplan or Medicare Partners sites.

Financial arrangements with Harriman Jones also call for a capitated monthly rate for medical services, but Harriman Jones is not taking nearly as much risk as the hospital. SHP will also provide the medical group with $6,000 in individual stop-loss coverage on medical services (see chapter 7 for an explanation of individual stop-loss). As noted above, Harriman Jones will also receive incentive payments for meeting performance in service areas for which it is not being paid but in which it has a good deal of control over costs (such as hospital days).

SHP will be at risk for community-based long-term care services, and it will acquire these services through cost-based contracts with the SCAN parent agency. SHP will also be responsible for the costs in the physicians' and the hospital's capitations after the set risk-sharing and reinsurance corridors are exceeded. As will be seen in chapter 7, it will cover these exposures first through funded reserves, and then through third-party risk-sharing arrangements.

The SHP management structure is similar to that of Elderplan. A plan administrator is responsible for the day-to-day operations of the plan, assisted by a finance director, case management director, marketing director (half-time), and medical director (quarter-time). Other professional staff include an MIS director, a marketing specialist, a health educator, and three case managers. SHP also has a management service contract with SCAN, which secures the services of the executive director (half-time), public information coordinator (40 percent time), finance manager (40 percent time), and support staff. Thus, as in Elderplan's arrangements, the CEO of the parent organization maintains authority over the operations of the subsidiary, but at SHP this authority appears to be more active and direct than at Elderplan.

Information requirements at SHP will be met through an MIS system acquired from an established HMO vendor. The system will be able to meet HCFA and state reporting requirements as well as the demands for internal accounting. Harriman Jones already has an on-line patient records system, which will be used for SHMO members as well.

Since there will be no bottom-line internal risk-sharing arrangements at this site, the SHP model can be used to illustrate the importance of examining each kind of risk and who should bear it. The examination reveals several ways in which the partners may have different incentives and interests. First, the model shifts a great deal more risk onto the hospital than a per diem arrangement would. For example, consider a very "bad" enrollment mix in terms of age, sex, and impairment. Hospital costs would understandably be much higher than anticipated, but the hospital would be paid on the basis of a healthier population. SHP, in the meantime, might show a substantial surplus, since its reimbursement would be increased through the Medicare reimbursement formula (see chapter 6). The physicians' group would also be likely to suffer a loss in this hypothetical situation, but probably not as large a loss as the hospital's. The plan could find itself in the opposite position if the enrollment turned out to be much healthier than expected. In this case, the members' utilization of both hospital and physician services would be lower than the target capitation numbers, but the plan would still have to pay a good portion of the target capitation figures. In the meantime, the Medicare reimbursement formula would adjust for the healthier population, and the plan might easily suffer losses. These effects could be moderated by adjusting the internal capitation payments according to changes in third-party payments.

A second potential danger in the SHP internal incentive system is that there could be internal cost shifting. If a partner stands to gain more by attending to its own individual performance goals than by meeting system goals, it could pursue the former even at the expense of latter. For example, if the SHP case manager chooses to save SHP money by shifting an expensive home care client into an even more expensive nursing home (because nursing homes are the hospital's responsibility), the system will lose.

A third danger with setting up significant gains and losses around service-specific performance targets is that some individual provider partners could be rewarded (and others penalized) for meeting the wrong standards. And when it is time to renegotiate the internal reimbursement and risk arrangements, partners with "easy" standards can be expected to try to hold onto them, while partners who have lost will want their standards relaxed. Such negotiations would be necessary in any model of internal control, but the negotiations will be easier with more experience and with lower individual stakes. Partners could be forced into the position of having to protect their financial autonomy at the expense of integration. Patient care could also be adversely affected if provider partners worked to the wrong standard in terms of mix of services.

SCAN planners and their partner providers considered these potential disadvantages, but they concluded that the advantage of having strong individual agency savings incentives—especially for all parties on hospital costs—outweighed the potential dangers.

Medicare Plus II. The internal control issues at the Kaiser-Portland site are quite different from the other sites, except for some similarities to Group Health, the other large HMO. The key features accounting for Kaiser's differences from other sites are (1) size and (2) degree of existing consolidation of the medical system. On the acute care side Medicare Plus II's 4,000 members will be incorporated into a 268,000-member HMO that has well-developed ways of handling patient care, as well as established corporate management and financial structures. Obviously SHMO planners can and will set performance expectations in the utilization of acute care services, but this alone will not provide results, since there is no way to enforce these expectations on sectors of the system through financial penalties or rewards.

The physicians, for example, are paid at a community rate for all members across the system, so there is no mechanism available to materially motivate physicians to reach targets for SHMO members specifically. Even if the medical capitation could be adjusted to performance, such a device would probably not affect behavior when SHMO members comprise such a small proportion of physicians' practices. Nevertheless, there are clear (and apparently effective) savings incentives and mechanisms working across the entire medical system, and Plus II will be able to take advantage of these for its membership. Since Kaiser is taking full risk for medical costs (see chapter 7), Kaiser staff have some confidence that this system will work for Plus II members in terms of their medical services.

Integrating long-term care into existing internal control systems is obviously Kaiser's major challenge. The only available approach was to convince rather than coerce the rest of the system to comply, and this was accomplished through a number of means. First, from previous work, the Kaiser Research Center was able to draw on a good deal of experience and prestige in gaining the attention and cooperation of decision makers. Second, the method of obtaining compliance was the formation of four planning and implementation committees, including a large umbrella committee representing medical, hospital, corporate, and research staff (with more than two dozen members in all) and smaller ones for marketing, finances, and new services development. Third, the goal of the committees was to incorporate Medicare Plus II as much as possible into the existing Kaiser systems. With Medicare Plus II coming on the heels of Medicare Plus, this was easily accomplished in some areas. From the existing Kaiser systems, Plus II will obtain all information and management services in the areas of marketing, enrollment, finances, and acute care utilization and costs.

Only one new unit will be created, which will manage the new chronic care services. These services will be housed administratively in a special assessment unit managed by the director of the "expanded care benefit program." This unit will include the case managers and will have its own automated MIS to monitor costs and utilization of long-term care services as well as individual client characteristics and care plans.

It remains to be seen how these arrangements will compare to the other models in effectively creating an integrated system of health and long-term care services. Success will depend on a combination of professional development and administrative integration through internal control mechanisms. The large and established system of Kaiser physicians and hospitals will have the option of guarding their current autonomy from the changes that Medicare Plus II could bring them. It is hoped that the advantages of the new system can be sold and the potential for increased interdependence can be exploited, to the benefit of professionals and members alike.

Conclusion

In summary, it is very difficult to generalize from these five sites about what kind of models and what kind of sponsors are possible (let alone best) for starting and operating a SHMO. Each of the current sites designed a formal structure and a system of internal controls that were shaped by the site's goals for the project and the constraints it faced. The three long-term care sponsors illustrate the point. Two sponsors with very similar current services and histories (Ebenezer and MJGC) made very different choices, based on their goals and their local environments. The third long-term care sponsor (SCAN) seemed to have goals similar to MJGC's, but its more limited independent resource base required that it devise a structure that more fully integrated larger existing providers.

The one HMO sponsor faced a much more limited set of options because of its large existing system, which could not be overhauled to accommodate a small demonstration program. The important question to track at Kaiser—and also at Group Health—is whether the SHMO model's full potential to alter the pattern of service delivery can be realized in the context of an established HMO.

The failure of the one hospital sponsor (Mercy Hospital) does not mean that hospitals cannot successfully sponsor SHMOs. The Mercy experience does illustrate, however, the importance of being certain early in the feasibility stage that all key program components are "on board." While hospitals should be aware from the beginning that the goal of the SHMO is to reduce hospital use, this goal should not scare hospitals as long as they can identify an expanded market for themselves.

Finally, it is important to comment on the mix of sponsor types found in the initial Demonstration period. Brandeis staff had initially expected that HMOs would be most likely sponsors for SHMOs, followed by hospitals and then long-term care agencies. The reasoning was that HMOs and hospitals would be likely to have more of the required system already in place and would also have the resources and experience to pull together the rest of the system.

The providers that stepped forward in the Demonstration period proved Brandeis wrong, but a different pattern may prevail in the future. During the time that sponsors were being sought, few HMOs had experience with the elderly and most of those contacted clearly thought that their immediate futures would center on the under-65 market. This has all changed with the TEFRA legislation.[7] In general, hospitals also had no immediate reasons to try a program related to the elderly market, since Medicare took care of hospitals' needs quite well. Now that situation has changed as well, with DRGs and proposals to restructure Medicare.

While long-term care sponsors will most likely continue to find the SHMO attractive, the resource issue may in fact turn out to be decisive in the future. The Demonstration's long-term care sponsors were fortunate in obtaining substantial foundation support for their extensive planning and development efforts, but it is unlikely that such support will continue to be available once the SHMO is no longer an experimental program. Unless the government changes its policy and decides to underwrite planning and development, future SHMOs will probably need to rely on the existing delivery systems and the more extensive resources of larger medical care systems. It remains to be seen whether these types of partners or sponsors will be amenable to incorporating the knowledge and expertise of long-term care providers into truly integrated systems of acute and chronic care. The outcomes at the Demonstration sites should shed some light on the question.

Notes

1. Of course the concepts of integration and autonomy apply equally well to the service delivery level of the system. While it is often hard to draw the line between organizational and service delivery issues, this chapter deals largely with the former and chapter 3 addresses the latter.

2. The other was Contra Costa County, California.

3. Administratively necessary days; that is, backup of patients in hospitals for lack of nursing home beds.

4. IPA stands for independent practice association, an HMO model that conracts

with individual physicians rather than contract with a medical group or employ staff physicians.

5. Saying this is in no way meant to discount the importance of improving services to the elderly to the other site sponsors. None would have chosen the SHMO had they not seen it as a potential means of improving care.

6. The primary hospital agreement has some flexibility up and down, however, based on demand fluctuations, as well as provision for use of unfilled beds by MJGC's nursing homes.

7. The 1982 Tax Equity and Fiscal Responsibility Act (P.L. 97-248), section 114 of which allows HMOs to enter the elderly market under provisions similar to the Medicare HMO Demonstrations.

3
The Organization of Service Delivery

I t is difficult to exaggerate the importance of service delivery to the success of the SHMO. The creation of an effective, efficient, and equitable pattern of service delivery is at the heart of the project's rationale. The model's strategy of consolidation brings all the services and providers in the health and long-term care systems into a single system. Its flexibility allows these agents to structure new relationships and modes of practice that are oriented toward the goals of appropriate, cost-conscious, and high-quality care for the elderly. To a large extent, all the other features of the SHMO—organizational systems, finance, marketing and enrollment, and risk management—are designed to create and encourage a service delivery system that meets these goals. In turn, an efficient and effective service delivery system is what makes the SHMO attractive to the elderly and financially feasible to the government and providers.

The major areas of concern here are threefold: first, how to structure and control the service system itself; second, how to allocate resources to members, including most important the creation of norms of professional practice and paths to downward substitution in a consolidated system of care; and third, how to assure high-quality and appropriate care. These areas are obviously interrelated, and planning approaches must be coordinated and internally consistent. However, the issues are sufficiently distinct and are so complex and detailed that two separate chapters are required to do them justice. Therefore, this chapter addresses the organizational issues related to structure and control, while chapter 4 takes up the issues of resource allocation and quality assurance.

In each chapter, the exposition follows the format of chapter 2: a discussion of the generic issues and options, followed by descriptions of the choices made by each site in turn. Thus, the reader can trace site descriptions across chapters, and thereby derive a coherent and complete picture of each SHMO model being tested.

Introduction to the Organization
Of Service Delivery

The issues concerning the organization of the service system were outlined in the previous chapter and can be quickly summarized. In the fragmented fee-for-service system, individual service providers have neither the means nor the motivation to effectively cooperate and coordinate their efforts. Each group of professionals—whether physicians in private practice, hospital discharge nurses, home health nurses, or nursing home administrators and service staff—exists and functions in relative autonomy and responds to its own motivations and tests of success. Concurrently, however, there is a great deal of interdependence among these groups (Scott 1982), with the "output" of one becoming the "input" of the next. The interfaces are at present handled poorly—both at the level of the clients, who often experience discontinuities and poor quality care, and at the level of the larger system, where common outcomes are protective behavior and inefficiencies.

The challenge in organizing the SHMO's service delivery system is to find a workable balance between the need for autonomy on the part of the various professionals and service providers, and the need for better defining and managing the areas where services and professionals are interdependent. It is not difficult for professionals to acknowledge interdependence and the need to work more closely with others to manage their "contingencies," but actually drawing the lines in professional and agency battles over turf is another matter. While everyone gains from improved patient care and overall system efficiency, and from extended control over resources afforded by the multidisciplinary team approach, each must also face the possibility of losing some responsibility, autonomy, and authority.

Each site has the same general objective of structuring and managing a comprehensive service system, but each faces unique challenges arising from its own unique organizational environment. Once decisions were made at the corporate level to bring organizations together in the SHMO system, decisions became necessary at the service level concerning how to integrate the services of the organization. Three questions had to be addressed:

What elements of a continuum of care should be included in the SHMO?

What staff members will be needed in the SHMO, and how should responsibilities and authority be divided among them?

What systems of management can be used to control service provision across the continuum?

Creating a Continuum of Care

When a minimum benefit package was formed early in the planning period, the national Demonstration largely defined the range of services to be included in the SHMO's continuum of care. The minimum package included a full range of acute and chronic care services in a core package to be offered by all sites and a set of optional benefits to be offered at the discretion of the site.

As shown in table 3–1 each site will provide all Medicare part A and part B services without the copayments and deductibles associated with these services. In addition, acute care benefits include among others dentures, prescription drugs, optometry, audiometry, eyeglasses, hearing aids, and preventive visits. Some of these will have copays as shown in table 3–1. All sites offer unlimited hospital days, and two sites have significantly extended "Medicare type" SNF benefits.

The core chronic care benefit package at each site includes case management, home nursing and therapies, personal care and homemaker services, adult day care, medical transportation, hospice care, home-delivered meals, as well as chronic care in an SNF or ICF. At their discretion, most sites also will include or arrange for electronic response systems, chore and escort services, and other necessary transportation.

The details of benefit structure (such as copay requirements and chronic care benefit limits) will be addressed in the next chapter. The concern here is the impact of the benefit requirement on the service system. It is clear that these benefit requirements go a long way in defining the basic service delivery components that need to be included in the SHMO system. These components are illustrated in the abstract in figure 3–1. Actual sites, of course, can combine the components in different manners. For example, home care or the day care center may be attached to the medical center, the hospital, the nursing home, or another community agency.

As sponsors and partners look at the services currently delivered by each of them, the initial question is whether there are gaps in the required basic delivery system and how to fill them. Next they must decide whether there are additional services that should be provided along the continuum. The options are many and include

1. Subacute units in nursing homes could be used to reduce the length of hospital stays and even prevent hospital admissions;
2. Primary care delivered in nursing homes and at home could reduce nursing home use (Master et al. 1980);
3. Electronic alarm or "lifeline" systems could be more appropriate and economical than human attendants for some patients;
4. Volunteers could perform many social support services; and
5. Well-targeted respite care could enhance the strength and reliability of family supports.

While many of these services are attractive in theory, each site must develop them in the context of the organizational units and staff that currently exist.

Table 3–1
SHMO Benefits Package Compared with Medicare Part A and Part B Coverage

Service	Medicare Benefit	SHMO Benefit
Institutional services		
Acute hospital	90 days each benefit period plus 60-day lifetime reserve. $356 deductible per spell of illness on part A benefits required. Copays noted below are 1984 figures and assume deductible has been paid. For each day between 61st and 90th day the beneficiary pays $89. For each reserve day, the payment is $178.	Unlimited number of days for prescribed hospitalization at hospital approved by SHMO. Complete hospital services (inpatient and outpatient) including all physicians' and surgeons' services. No deductibles, no charges.
Psychiatric hospital	190 days lifetime. Copayments same as inpatient hospital.	190 days lifetime. No copays, no charges.
Skilled nursing facility care meeting Medicare criteria	After 3 consecutive days in hospital and then transferred to SNF: first 20 days no charge; 21st thru 100th day: $44.50 per day.	No prior hospitalization requirement. No deductibles, no charges. Kaiser and SCAN: 100 days. Elderplan: 365 days. Medicare Partners: unlimited days.
Skilled and intermediate nursing facility care of a custodial nature	Not covered.	Covered up to limits of chronic care benefit. Kaiser: 100 days. Elderplan: $6,500. Medicare Partners: $6,250. SCAN: $7,500. Coinsurance and benefit periods vary (see table 4–1).
Medical and related services		
Physician's services	Medicare pays 80 percent of allowable charges after $75 annual deductible on part B benefits is paid. Includes ambulatory (outpatient) surgery. Physicals and preventive care not covered.	Covers Medicare deductible and coinsurance. Ambulatory surgery, routine physician exams, preventive care included. Kaiser: $2 per visit. Elderplan includes authorized house calls by physician or physician extender.
Nurse practitioner and physician assistant services	80 percent of allowable charges when provided incident to physician services.	Covered in full. Kaiser $2 per visit.
Mental health OP visits	80 percent of doctor charges up to $250 maximum (after $75 deductible). 80 percent of other professional charges.	Kaiser: 6 visits per year to psychiatrist; no limit to other professionals. Other sites: 20 visits per year. Copay per visit: Kaiser $2; Elderplan $5; Medicare Partners $10; SCAN no charges.

Service		
Foot care	Routine foot care services not covered except when performed as necessary part of a covered medical service. Medicare pays 80 percent of allowable charges.	Medically necessary podiatry. Kaiser $2 copay, other sites no charges. Elderplan in addition provides routine foot care at $2 per visit.
Blood	First 3 pints not covered; then 80 percent of allowable.	Covered in full.
Medical equipment and supplies	80 percent of allowable charges on durable medical equipment, prosthetic devices, and supplies.	Durable medical equipment, prosthetic devices and supplies covered in full when ordered and provided by plan.
Lab and X-ray	Part B services: 80 percent of allowable charges.	Covered in full.
Dentistry	80 percent of allowable charges *only* if it involves *surgery of the jaw*, setting fractures of the jaw and facial bones, treatment of oral infection, dental procedures that are integral part of medical procedures. Routine dental services not covered.	Medicare benefits covered in full—no charges. In addition, all sites cover dentures under the chronic care benefit limits, with copays (Kaiser 10 percent; Medicare Parnters 20 percent; Elderplan and SCAN $50). SCAN also covers routine care; Medicare Partners covers diagnostic and preventive care; Elderplan covers erupted tooth extractions and denture repair ($15 copay).
Outpatient physical therapy and speech pathology services	Part B services: 80 percent of allowable charges.	Medicare outpatient physical therapy speech pathology services covered in full by sites. No charges except Kaiser $2 regular fee.
Out of plan services	Emergency and nonemergency services covered anywhere in the United States.	Approved emergency services covered anywhere in the world. Kaiser and SCAN: no charges. Elderplan and Medicare Partners: 80 percent coverage of first $500, then same coverage as hospital and medical services described above.
Pharmacy	Not covered.	Prescription drugs covered at all sites. Copay range $1 to $3.50.
Optometry	Only covered if related to treatment of aphakia or if part of a covered medical service.	Covered in full. Kaiser $2 copay. Elderplan specifies one exam per year.
Audiometry	Not covered.	Covered in full. Elderplan and Medicare Partners specify one exam per year. Kaiser $2 copay.

Table 3–1 (*continued*)
SHMO Benefits Package Compared with Medicare Part A and Part B Coverage

Service	Medicare Benefit	SHMO Benefit
Institutional services		
Eyeglasses	Not covered (contact lenses for postcataract surgery patients: approximately 80/20 per part B).	Covers one pair glasses in each 24-month period. Kaiser and SCAN: no charge. Elderplan $10 copay; Medicare Partners 50 percent copay.
Hearing aids	Not covered.	Covers one hearing aid in each 24-month period. Kaiser no charge. Copays: Elderplan $40; SCAN $50; Medicare Partners 50 percent.
Home health and other community based services		
Medicare home health services (includes visiting nurse, home health aide; occupational, speech and physical therapies; and social work services)	100 percent of allowable costs, skilled care criteria and homebound.	Medicare home health covered in full. Coverage expanded beyond skilled care and homebound criteria when approved for long-term care plan.
In-home support services (includes homemaker, personal health aide, medical transportation, medical day treatment, respite care; and arranging and coordination of other services such as home-delivered meals, chore services, additional transportation, electronic monitoring)	Not covered.	Covered with limits, copays and renewability conditions as specified in text and table 4–1 (varies by site).
Hospice (includes home health care, inpatient treatment for acute and chronic symptom control, family respite, outpatient drugs, counseling and volunteer services for terminal cancer patients)	5 percent copay or $5 per prescription for outpatient drugs, whichever is less. 5 percent copay for in-patient respite costs, up to a maximum of $304. All other hospice services are fully covered.	Covered in full (no copays).

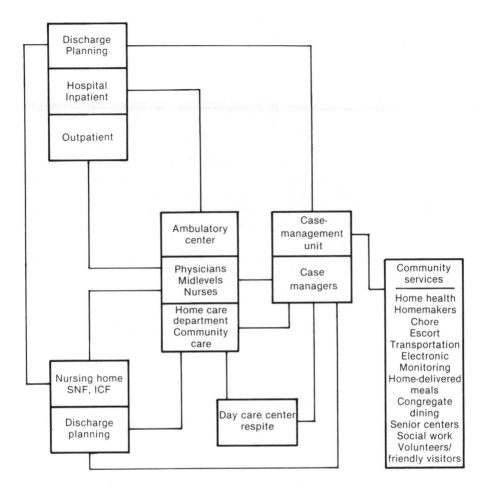

Figure 3–1. SHMO Service Delivery Components

Staffing and Division of Labor

The second type of question raised in creating the continuum of care concerns the divisions of labor and responsibility among the staff and service units of the participating organizations. These questions may be most difficult for partners trying to integrate existing service systems rather than creating some new ones. There are likely to be overlaps among the participating units and professionals, and the possibility of creating new steps in a continuum of care raises the prospect of further duplication of services and functions.

There are no pat answers to questions such as these, but there are some general guidelines for action and orientation. To work effectively in this setting, all staff members involved need to be flexible, challenged by innovation, accepting of interdisciplinary teamwork, and interested in developing integrated approaches to geriatric care. However, even among committed staff it should be anticipated that turf conflicts will develop (for example, when SHMO case managers take over functions of existing units such as hospital discharge departments). It is hoped that participating professionals will be willing to make trade-offs between loss of control and achievement of the multidisciplinary coordination required by an integrated system. For providers experienced in geriatric care, there are high costs and many frustrations involved in attempting to coordinate the current fragmented system, and the SHMO offers a solution to these problems. The need for such trade-offs also has implications for staff selection, recruitment, and key leadership in the SHMO.

The actual selection of certain staff members is a crucial step. The key provider leaders in the SHMO care delivery system are (1) the medical director and primary physicians and (2) the case-management director and the case managers. These individuals can set the tone for a smooth working out of innovative approaches and provider interdependence across the whole system.

The following are some of the issues to be considered by physicians as they weigh their willingness to participate or take a leading role in the SHMO program:

There will be a change in case mix resulting from expanded Medicare clientele. How many and which physicians are ready for this change?

A new focus of services may be appropriate for an elderly clientele, such as increased emphasis on health education, self-care techniques, and preventive interventions.

There is increased time and complexity in treating elderly clients, which will affect productivity, staff planning, and recruitment schedules.

There may be a change in the level of specialization needed to serve the enrolled SHMO population. For primary care needs, mainly internists and some family practitioners may be involved, but certain specialties (such as orthopedics and urology) may be affected by expanded Medicare enrollment. Should the group hire more specialists, or increase referrals, and what are the cost implications of each alternative? Should a geriatrician be hired to assist with care of the frail enrollees?

Multidisciplinary team work requires that physicians allow time for additional consultation, conferencing, and medical supervision of other team members. Physician input is required for care plans; community nurses, nurse practitioners, and physician assistants working in the home or nursing home require available and timely physician consultation when client health status changes or emergencies occur in those settings.[1]

Staffing issues of concern to case management in long-term care include the following:

What professional disciplines, or mix of disciplines, result in the most effective case management teams? Nurses (with community experience) and social workers (with some medical experience) were most frequently selected in past case-management demonstrations. The mix of these professions may vary.

What level of professional qualification (master's, bachelor's, associate degree) should case-management directors and case managers have? Is professional qualification necessary, and if so, for what positions? Could experienced case aides function as case managers?

Management and Control Issues

Turning now from the structure and staffing of the service system to its control, the key task is to find the means to make the continuum work as an integrated system of care. Onto the continuum of care an overlay of management must be constructed that includes definitions of responsibilities, authority structures, work groups, and the like. The discussion that follows first takes up the key concept of the locus of authority for patient care management and then reviews some of the more specific mechanisms for management of the system, including staff linkage roles and case management in chronic care. While the details of the SHMO model differ at each site, the following general elements are included at all sites.

Locus of Authority. As elderly clients move through the continuum of care, they require different levels and intensities of care at different times. As the client's needs change, so does the team of professionals; and the locus of major responsibility may shift from the physician to the case manager, from the acute medical care team to the long-term care providers, and vice versa. Some elderly clients find themselves in a fluid, constantly changing situation.

This changing locus of authority has been one of the key issues in working out the interdependence of the SHMO service delivery system. Protocols and job descriptions have been developed that clearly specify the respective responsibilities of each team professional. While models differ in detail, across the sites there are two constants. First, the primary physician is always responsible for medical decisions and will supervise and act as backup for physician extenders, nurses, and other medical providers who may need to change medical prescriptions while serving clients in their homes. Second, the case manager is responsible for authorizing all chronic care services prescribed (beyond medical and Medicare home health services). Even though several providers may have developed the care plan as a team or in consultation, the case manager is always accountable for the chronic care budget and has the final say over long-term care resource allocation. Other providers such as physical and speech therapists, social workers, and community nurses have authority to perform within their specific disciplines, but chronic care plans cannot be changed by any provider without the authorization of the case manager.

The ultimate locus of authority, therefore, moves between the primary physician and the case manager, depending on the type of services prescribed, and these two professionals must work together closely. Within that structure, and within their own disciplines, other professionals have limited authority but are ultimately accountable to either the primary physician or the case manager.

Staff Linkage and Communication Flow. Two further ingredients in an interdependent system are the staff who link the components of the system together, and the appropriate flow of communication among the system's various units. Both bind together the components of the system and keep it running smoothly. Linkage roles and functions may include such activities as physicians consultation with case managers, mid-level assistants, and nurses working in the community; the case manager's function in discharge planning; staff interface between the case management unit and home care–continuing care units of large medical groups; and the case manager's role and functions in linking together all community services. The definitions of these roles and divisions of labor need to be clearly specified in protocols and job descriptions.

The need for a sophisticated scheme of communication is one of the costs of a highly integrated system, as compared with a system of relatively autonomous hierarchical units, where communication is mainly vertical. The sites have used various mechanisms to maintain communication, including:

Specific interdisciplinary provider task forces (essential in the planning phase);

Case-centered team conferences;

Issue-specific staff conferences;

Protocols for required consultation and supervision functions;

Defined critieria for referring clients to the medical and case-management components, due to change in health or social status (all providers, at all levels of the system should be oriented to these criteria);

A client record system (including medical and care plan records) that is accessible to all appropriate providers;

Staff orientation and in-service training programs on an ongoing basis.

Case management. The long-term care component of the SHMO will be controlled through the case-management function. As the term *case management* implies, there are both clinical and control aspects to this function, and it is the latter aspect that this section addresses. The clinical aspect of case management (that is, the prescription of services to clients based on assessed needs) will be addressed in chapter 4.

In their management function, case managers are responsible both for coordinating the individual client's long-term care services and for controlling the allocation of long-term care resources in general. It is in this latter function that SHMO case-management systems build on and consolidate some of the trends that have been developing in the field. Austin's (1983) analysis of long-term care projects shows that case manager discretion over resource allocation has depended on both their "span of authority" (range of services controlled) and their "scope of authority" (breadth of impact in control of specific services). Similarly, Callahan (1981) argues that one measure of the power of case management is the extent of control over entry into the system, especially through eligibility determination mechanisms. Financial incentives for case managers—such as projected budgets and budget ceilings—have also been tested as methods for resource allocation control (HCFA 1982).

All of these trends are being consolidated in the SHMO case-management systems. In fact, all of the Demonstration sites have chosen to define their case-management system as the client's single entry point into long-term care. All the sites have also assigned major client assessment responsibility to the case manager and have given the case manager full responsibiliity for authorizing all chronic care services. Sites have varied in the scope of authority given to case managers in such areas as discharge planning, monitoring of clients in different settings, and resource allocation of postacute services. These are areas for negotiation among the respective SHMO components, the agencies to which those components are attached, and the case-management units.

Generically, there are three basic models for how case managers relate to service providers (Abrahams and Leutz 1983; Wecksler, Durmaskin, and Kodner 1983):

Model 1. Case managers are entirely separate from direct service provision but perform all of the traditional case-management tasks related to intake, assessment, eligibility determination, care planning, service coordination, and follow-up. When all service provision is contracted, this is known as the brokerage model of case management.

Model 2. Case managers perform some of the traditional case-management tasks (e.g., intake, assessment, reassessment) but other case-management tasks (e.g., care plans, coordination, monitoring) are performed by direct service providers involved with the client. Some form of communication among these various actors must take place through team consultations or conferences.

Model 3. All case-management tasks are undertaken by various qualified direct service providers. This is often called a fully consolidated model of case management and requires close working team relationships among all those concerned with a specific client.

Channeling and MSSP (California) are examples of model 1. OnLok and Urban Medical Group are examples of model 3. The latter are both relatively small organizations that focus on frail clients and operate with close teamwork. An advantage claimed for this model is that under a tight budget, it eliminates an administrative layer between the direct service provider and the client. Model 2, a hybrid, is used in many long-term care agencies that have a case-management unit. The SHMO may use any of these models. Choices are likely to be made in relation to existing provider responsibility and turf compromises between system components.

Whatever the model of case management, the case manager in the SHMO is likely to feel considerable strain as a function of both the "middle management position" and the expanded case manager role (Austin 1981, 1983). Middle management staff are often caught in the gap between agency administration and direct service workers. On the one hand they must translate, interpret, and implement administrative directions to workers, and on the other they must absorb workers' concerns and communicate them to management.

In addition to shouldering this "middle position" strain, case managers in a fixed-budget system may find themselves in a position of both advocating for and possibly having to deny services for clients. They will also be in the middle of situations in which clients receiving home care services either run out of their benefits or become unable to meet their copayments. Responses to these situations are likely to take two directions: (1) development by case managers and their supervisors of various intrastaff support mechanisms; (2) increasing pressure to develop standardized protocols and criteria for resource allocation that will buffer the strain of decision making. Issues concerning the development of such criteria and norms of practice are analyzed in chapter 4.

Site Descriptions of Service Delivery Organization

There is no need to repeat in detail the previous chapter's description of the issues and options faced by each site in organizing the components of its SHMO service system. The issue here is how the sites have each chosen to structure and manage the services and staff in the components as an integrated system of care. The site descriptions therefore begin with a review of the key elements of each site's continuum of care (with more detail on innovative features). The descriptions continue with discussions of staffing and divisions of labor in the system, and conclude with an analysis of the elements of control and communication that bind the system into a working whole.

Elderplan (Brooklyn, New York)

Elderplan's challenge in forming a SHMO was to create key elements of the service delivery system from the ground up. The challenge was softened by the fact that there would be fewer chances for conflict and fewer requirements for compromise than there would be with existing systems and personnel. The most important opportunities for Elderplan were in the creation of a new medical group and a new HMO, both of which would have team-oriented staff and a specific focus on geriatric practice.

Key Elements in the Continuum of Care at Elderplan
Chronic Care. MJGC entered the demonstration with experience in managing and delivering the full range of chronic care services. The center is a site in the New York State Long-Term Home Health Care Program (Nursing Home Without Walls). Elderplan will build on this experience and the provider and service delivery relationships established within it. These include a centralized case-management unit located in the Elderplan HMO entity, a medical day care unit at MJGC, and contracted arrangements for home-delivered meals, medical transportation, and social day care (Kodner 1984).

Home support and home health services will be obtained from MJGC's newly formed home health agency, which received determination-of-need approval in relation to the Elderplan initiative. Sponsor ownership of this home health agency will avoid the restrictions in both staffing and service prescription that are imposed through the major local home health agencies. These restrictions are the four-hour visit minimum, which is not necessary for all clients, and the customary use of different levels of staff for personal care, homemaker, and home attendant functions. Through its own home health agency, each of Elderplan's personal care workers will perform any or all of these functions at the same hourly rate. Also, Elderplan will be billed only for the number of hours actually required by each client.

In addition to offering all the core chronic care benefits listed above, Elderplan will offer electronic monitoring or "lifeline" services, and respite care (both in-home and institutional). All of these services enhance the possibility that frail elderly will be able to remain in the home and concurrently that the need for institutional care will be delayed or prevented. These services are all supportive of family caregivers and can help to sustain the informal support networks.

In the area of institutional chronic care, MJGC owns and operates two long-term care facilities in Brooklyn: an ICF and an SNF, with a combined total of 915 beds. Elderplan will contract with MJGC for assured access to a certain number of beds on both a postacute and chronic basis. Furthermore, Elderplan plans to use a special maximum care unit (MCU) located in the MJGC SNF. It is equipped for intensive nursing care and restorative services. Arrangements for preferential admission of SHMO enrollees, as required, have been negotiated with MJGC. Inclusion of the MCU in the continuum of care allows for flexibility and downward substitution, both in shortening hospital stays and in preventing hospital admissions for some clients who may be admitted from the community.

Medical Services. MJGC's key challenge in constructing the SHMO system was in the medical services area. Working with Cornell University Medical College, MJGC helped to incorporate Geriatric Medicine Associates, find a director for the group—the first fellow to complete Cornell's Geriatric Fellowship program—and assure that the structure and philosophy of the practice would be consistent with the goals and operations of MJGC and Elderplan. GMA will serve Elderplan members exclusively and be housed in a newly renovated 2,500-square-foot primary ambulatory care center, located in MJGC's SNF. The center is at street level and has its own entrance. The practice will therefore be convenient to the MCU and the majority of MJGC's nursing home beds. GMA will be responsible for all medical services through a capitation arrangement with Elderplan and will make referrals to specialty care, as described below.

Health Education. Both Elderplan and GMA have given particular attention to the role of health education in geriatric care, and they obtained a private foundation grant during the planning phase to develop a health education–self-care program for SHMO enrollees. This program will be implemented by both GMA staff and long-term care workers and will be directed by a health education coordinator. The program will address the needs and concerns of both well and impaired elderly (Glazer, Snyder, and Kodner 1985).

Volunteers. Elderplan intends to establish a volunteer system in conjunction with the SHMO, perhaps along Sager's (1983) model of informal care "credits." Under the system Sager suggested, individuals obtain and "bank" credits for informal care they provide while they are healthy. If they later become impaired, they can draw on their credits—even in the form of formal services. Elderplan staff are interested in testing if this system can reduce the costs of service provision.

Hospital Services. Elderplan's primary hosptial is Brooklyn Hospital–Caledonian Hospital, a nearby community hospital that offers available capacity and reasonable costs. The hospital is seriously committed to integration with the SHMO, and a special geriatric unit is being formed in the hospital, with major planning input from the GMA medical director and hospital management and medical staff. Beds will be made available on a modified per diem arrangement, with guaranteed access. The back-up hospital is the Maimonides Medical Center—located across the street from the SNF and actually linked to it through an enclosed passage. Tertiary care will also be available at Cornell Medical Center in Manhattan.

The HMO. The system of care will be linked financially and organizationally by Elderplan, Inc., an incorporated HMO. Elderplan's key link to the service system is its case-management unit.

In summary, Elderplan has an almost fully consolidated model of service delivery, with contractual arrangements only for the hospital and a few community services, such as home-delivered meals, medical transportation, and social day care. All other services are available through MJGC or GMA under the umbrella of the Elderplan HMO.

Staffing and Division of Labor. In contrast to the other sites—especially Kaiser and Ebenezer–Group Health—where the challenges have been to redefine staff responsibilities and the division of labor, Elderplan's designers had to develop *initial definitions* in these areas. Whereas other sites had to find and select interested and suitable practitioners from existing staff, Elderplan could externally recruit professionals interested in a team approach to geriatric care.

Staffing Geriatric Medicine Associates. In concept this new medical group is unique among the sites, since it is established specifically for serving SHMO enrollees. In other words, GMA is the medical program of Elderplan. Its medical director is a geriatrician who brings considerable clinical experience as a geriatric consultant in private practice and as the medical director of a nursing home. He has worked extensively with the team approach to geriatric care and is strongly committed to redefining roles and relationships between physicians and physician extenders.

Other GMA physicians will include internists and family practitioners, the latter expanding the spectrum of skills (such as family practitioners for minor in-office surgery). Physician's assistants (PAs) and nurse practitioners (NPs) will be utilized for direct care in the home and nursing home, as well as in the ambulatory center. A psychiatric nurse clinician will take care of most psychiatric needs, with occasional referral to a psychiatrist. When Elderplan enrollment reaches 4,000, the GMA medical group will include:

1. 4.5 FTE physicians (including medical director);
2. 3.0 FTE physician's assistants;
3. 3.0 FTE nurse practitioners;
4. 1.0 FTE psychiatric nurse clinician;
5. 1.0 FTE medical assistant.

Specialty Referrals. Since GMA is a small medical group, it will have to rely heavily on specialty referrals. Two options considered for obtaining these services were contracting with outside fee-for-service specialists and hiring part-time subspecialists for a given number of hours or sessions per week. Advantages of the contract approach include: guaranteed specialist availability during specified hours; increased control over referrals; potential for higher productivity with efficient patient scheduling; expansion of group size and collegial relationships; and improved negotiating power for expanding admitting privileges to other hospitals. The major drawbacks are the potential for excessive availability of specialists and incentives for GMA physicians to fill session time with unnecessary referrals. Advantages of the fee-for-service option include: paying only for services actually used, the chance to test various specialists for their compatibility with GMA, and the possibility of negotiating discounted volume rates. Disadvantages of this approach are a lower degree of control over utilization, potentially greater costs, and dilution of collegial relationships.

Decisions are not yet final, but GMA will most likely rely on a combination of arrangements. It will use hourly service contracts for heavily utilized specialties or for specialists with whom there is a strong reason to associate (such as a specialist with a compatible practice or with desired admitting privileges) and will rely on fee-for-service arrangements at negotiated rates for less-utilized subspecialties. The short-term goal is to identify a network of "preferred providers" and to confine referrals to them. Ultimately, GMA may evolve into a multispeciality group.

The Division of Labor between Physicians and Physician Extenders. Each enrollee will be assigned to a regular physician and physician extender (PE). Both PAs and NPs will practice in the ambulatory center, and it is expected that these PEs will provide 50 percent of all primary ambulatory care. In addition, PAs will provide primary care in the nursing home, while NPs will provide such care in the client's home. It is estimated that 90 percent of direct care in the home and nursing home will be provided by PEs.

The greatest proportion of physician and PA time will be scheduled for office visits. Physicians will participate in twice as many office visits as will PAs, with each physician visit averaging twenty minutes, each PA visit thirty minutes. PAs will collect most baseline data, while physicians will review diagnostic–assessment information, interview patients, and perform further examinations as needed. Medical protocols will guide patient scheduling with the physician or PE.

The experience of GMA's medical director indicates that geriatric clients form attachments to their PEs as well as to their physicians, and the assignment of a regular MD–PE team to each enrollee will foster such patient–provider relationships. PEs are trained to spend time listening to patients, and the extra scheduled PE time allows for this function. Physician consultation and backup will always be available to all PEs, whether working at the ambulatory center or in the home or nursing home.

Elderplan has faced some potential turf problems in relationships between MJGC's current nursing home medical staff and GMA's PAs. Protocols are still being developed as of this writing. Negotiations have been facilitated by the appointment of the nursing home medical director as director of professional services for the SHMO. This individual will have an overseer's role in the SHMO medical service system and will participate in quality assurance committees.

Chronic Care Staffing Pattern. Elderplan's case-management staffing follows a highly professional model. The case-management director is an M.S.W. experienced in long-term care and administration. Position responsibilities include training and supervision of case-management team members; development of policies, procedures, and protocols; coordination of discharge planning (hospital and nursing home); a lead role in chronic care quality assurance activities; and involvement in setting service-substitution and cost-containment targets.

Case-management teams will consist of a community health nurse and a social worker. Job descriptions for the nurses call for bachelor's degree training, strong health–functional assessment skills, and the ability to work effectively with physicians and other health care providers. Requirements for social workers include M.S.W. degrees and advocacy skills, and ability to work well with the community services network. Either the nurse or the social worker will lead the team for a case depending on the needs of the individual member.

A ratio of one case manager to seventy impaired members has been set as a target. Thus, for the expected enrollment of 700 impaired members (17 percent of 4,000 total members), it is projected that five case-management teams (ten case managers) will be required. Of the ten case managers, the functions of one may be largely supervisory, and another will have primarily a liaison function with the hospital.

Within an almost fully consolidated service delivery system, Elderplan's case-management model retains all of the traditional case-management functions within the case-management unit, including assessment, eligibility determination, development and authorization of care plans, monitoring, and reassessment. Case managers will consult with physicians, PEs, and other providers in development of care plans. Negotiations with hospital discharge planners are currently underway to define discharge planning responsibilities of Elderplan's case managers. Plans are to locate one case manager primarily at the hospital, to take major responsibility for discharge of SHMO enrollees.

The model most closely resembles case-management model 1 outlined above, although it is part of a consolidated, not a brokerage, system. Case managers will not provide direct services, nor will direct service providers assume responsibility for case-management tasks. At a total case-management staffing cost of $272,400 (per 4,000 enrollees), it is relatively expensive in the context of the Demonstration site case-management models. The Demonstration hopes to shed light on whether this most costly and most centralized system may be the best resource allocation model.

Communications, Linkages, and Control. With the formation of the new medical group, and with joint, cooperative planning involving the medical and case-management directors from the beginning, Elderplan's medical and long-term care systems have been designed with integration as a major focus. GMA physicians will provide daily supervision both at the ambulatory center and to PAs working in the nursing home and NPs working in the home. PEs who provide care to impaired enrollees will work closely with case managers, by attending case conferences and consulting with case managers in development of care plans, with physician backup as necessary. These defined staff linkage roles and functions facilitate system integration.

Figure 3–2 (from the Elderplan protocol) indicates the lines of direct and indirect control from system components to the continuum of services. The resource allocation decisions box represents the area of communication and information exchange among providers in the system, including case conferences, consultation, supervision, and patient record exchange. The physicians are always responsible for medical decisions; the case managers

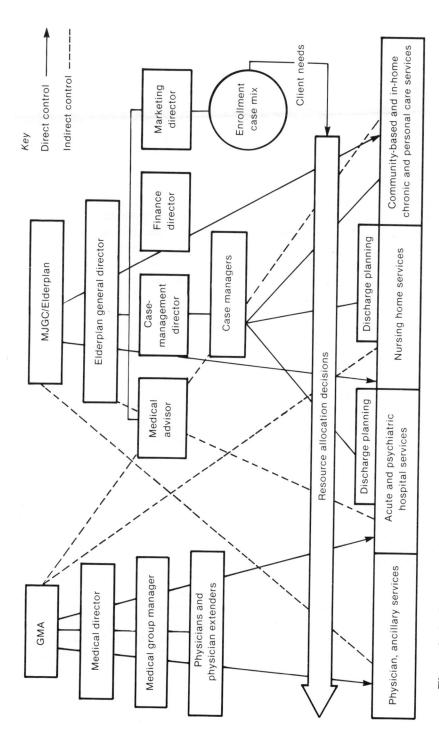

Figure 3–2. Authority and Resource Allocation at Elderplan

authorize all chronic care plans; and the ongoing interaction of PEs and case managers at the level of assessment, care plan development, service coordination, monitoring, discharge planning, and client record exchange will maintain the communication flow and link the care given in the home, the nursing home, the hospital, and the ambulatory center. Figure 3–3 indicates referral patterns and decision-making processes as the client moves through the continuum of care at Elderplan. It should be noted that each site has developed a similar flow chart.

Medicare Partners

Between them, Ebenezer Society and Group Health, Inc. (GHI) provide all the basic acute and long-term care services required in a SHMO. However, they still face two major challenges in creating a system of integrated geriatric care through their partnership arrangement. One challenge is to integrate two systems of service provision, one from each of these well-established agencies. This challenge applies especially to GHI, a large twenty-five-year-old group-model HMO that does not have a substantial number of elderly persons (less than 2 percent) among its 208,000 members. The second challenge is to redefine responsibilities and authority where the functions of the two agencies overlap, especially in relation to discharge planning and postacute home care–continuing care.

Another aspect of this site that differs somewhat from the other three sites is an agreement with the Hennepin County Medicaid agency to enroll 150 nursing home residents in the SHMO. This places a requirement on SHMO providers to establish appropriate mechanisms to care for this number of very frail institutionalized elders. As will be noted below, this has provided an impetus and justification for a group of GHI providers to begin to shape a geriatric care system within GHI that is different from the usual medical model. This system is the spearhead for development of interdependent, integrated SHMO practice.

Key Elements of the Continuum of Care in Medicare Partners

Medical Services. Through fourteen ambulatory centers (seven in Hennepin County), 190 physicians (staff model), and six dental clinics throughout the Twin Cities area, GHI offers all of the medical and related services in the core benefits package. GHI also has a continuing care department, with nurses involved in discharge planning and postacute care. In addition, GHI has a health education program run by a distinct health education department. GHI's clinics have the capacity to serve the SHMO enrollment, but some will require modification in terms of access ramps and other equipment. Two new medical centers have been opened in 1981 in the city of Minneapolis proper. This is where the Hennepin County elderly population is concentrated and where Ebenezer has its facilities.

Chronic Care Services. To this comprehensive range of medical services, Ebenezer adds six nursing homes (798 licensed beds), including a 185-bed facility providing specialized skilled care as an alternative to continued hospitalization for stabilized patients; as well as a comprehensive range of home health services, including visiting nurses, home health aides, homemakers, adult day care, respite, and a senior companion program. Finally, Ebenezer currently manages six congregate housing facilities with a total of 1,841 units, which provide a supportive system for continued independent living of elders. They have plans for five additional facilities to come on line during 1985–86. In addition to the core chronic care benefits listed above, Medicare Partners will offer an emergency response communication system and respite care.

Volunteers. Because of its sponsorship by Lutheran churches, Ebenezer has a history of involving volunteers in its programs. The SHMO planners decided to formalize this approach and obtain a grant to establish a volunteer services unit. The plan is to recruit volunteers among healthy and independent SHMO members to perform functions such as new-member orientation at the clinics, short-term respite care, peer counseling, as well as occasional light housekeeping, shopping, and personal care duties that do not require homemaker–home health aides. The goal is to create a reciprocal community of caring, in which volunteers gain satisfaction from helping others, and assurance that they will in turn be helped, should they have future need. The volunteers will be trained and supervised by staff according to specific job descriptions. No one yet knows the full potential of the volunteer approach, but the site plans to test that potential. If successful, the unit could be a significant and cost-effective addition to program resources and the continuum of care.

Staffing and Divisions of Labor and Control
Physicians. The sponsors realized that to change patterns of care in a large, long-established HMO would not be easy, especially since SHMO enrollment of 4,000 would represent only a small fraction of each physician's case load. GHI began the planning process by identifying a GHI internist who had a strong interest in and commitment to geriatric care and who could potentially become the Medicare Partners medical director. Under his leadership, a series of meetings were held with GHI internists, family practitioners, nurses, clinic managers, area coordinators, and program administrators to test both interest and commitment to the SHMO concept. Part of the discussion centered on the many implications of enrolling many more (and

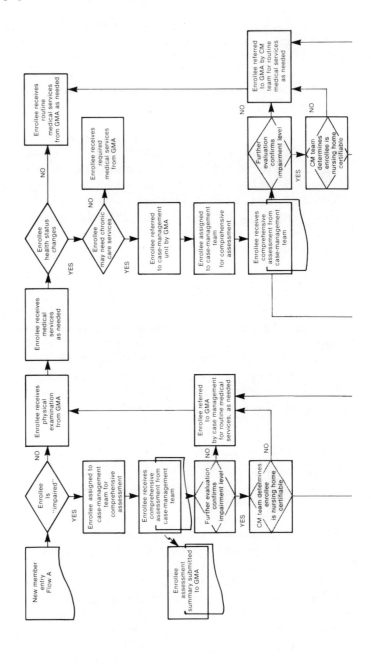

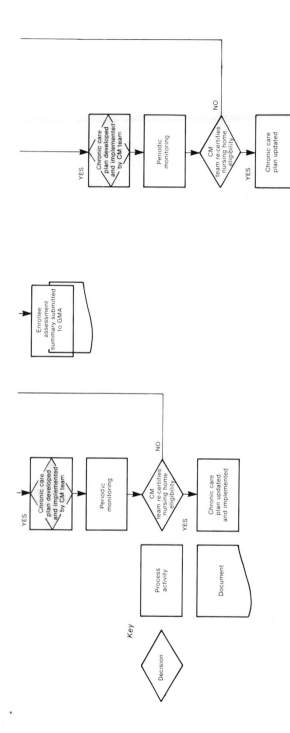

Figure 3–3. Elderplan's Referral System Flow Chart

frailer) Medicare elderly. Most of the physicians and administrators attending these meetings were in favor of the proposal. Some thought that since GHI already cared for Medicare enrollees, the influx of more elderly patients would not require significant changes. Some of the subspecialists (such as urologists) were enthusiastic to enroll more elderly, since these patients present challenges in terms of disease complexity. However, some reservations were expressed concerning (1) the potential financial risk involved; (2) whether funds would be made available for new staff; (3) the implications of the complexity of treating the elderly patient for staff planning and recruitment; and (4) some uncertainty about the federal government's commitment to Medicare.

The key issue that developed in these planning sessions was whether to integrate the Medicare Partners enrollees into the existing system of providers or to establish a special geriatric department. A majority of physicians seemed to favor integration, but as the planning process developed, a core group of internists and family practitioners emerged that had special interest in geriatric care and a commitment to developing new modes of practice. This group of physicians, known as the "geriatric resource team," now consists of about two-thirds internists and one-third family practitioners.

GHI's choice on the integration-versus-special-unit issue was to follow a hybrid approach. The well elderly will be integrated into the general clinic population, each having a choice of a primary physician from the available clinic staff. The frail elderly will be encouraged to choose a member of the geriatric resource team. Each of the seven Hennepin County ambulatory centers has at least one, and in most cases two, of these physicians on its staff. Case managers will consult directly with these physicians, as required, and develop care plans with the input of these physicians. All of the physicians who volunteered to participate in the team have agreed to allocate time to consult with NPs, nurses, and case managers.

The planning team concluded that with the addition of a consultant geriatrician, the current level of physician staffing both primary and specialty is adequate for geriatric medical care. When full SHMO enrollment is achieved, three new primary physicians will be required.

Physician Extenders. GHI currently has about sixteen NPs and six PAs on staff who practice in teams with physicians at the ambulatory centers. These teams will also provide direct care to their panels of Medicare Partners patients. A geriatric NP has already been hired and, as the SHMO nursing home enrollment grows, another geriatric NP will be recruited. These NPs are expected to spend 50 percent of their time providing direct care to nursing home residents, about 30 percent to 40 percent providing direct care to impaired enrollees at the ambulatory centers, and the remainder of their time in consultation and in-service education to other provider staff.

Long-Term Care. Based on their experience at Ebenezer, the SHMO planners chose case-management model 2. That is, some of the case-management functions can be delegated to other staff, and some services will be delivered by case managers. The most difficult problems encountered in making these divisions of labor and responsibility related to the GHI continuing care department. These difficulties will be detailed below, but first this section will describe basic case-management staffing and responsibilities.

The case-management director is a former Ebenezer staff member who is qualified at Master's-degree level and has strong experience in both long-term care and administration. Planners reasoned that the chronically impaired SHMO enrollees would primarily require social support services, and they therefore decided to recruit the core case-management staff in a social-worker-to-nurse ratio of two to one. At the start of operations, staffing of the case-management unit will include the case-management director, one public health nurse, and one social worker. Case managers will be added in the two to one ratio as enrollment increases, until such time as operational experience implies the need for modified ratios. Nurses will be required to have public health experience and social workers preferably to have geriatric and medical experience. A staff-to-chronic-care-client ratio of one to seventy is estimated, and at full enrollment six FTE case managers are projected, plus 1.5 FTE of nursing and social work consultation from existing Ebenezer staff.

In choosing model 2, planners decided that some traditional case-management functions (such as monitoring and input to care plan development) could be performed by direct service providers. Case managers and relevant GHI and Ebenezer staff will collaborate in performing quality assurance functions and utilization review. Case managers might provide some direct services. As planning proceeds, however, and the implications of case managers' accountability for a tight budget become clearer, the model may shift toward a model 1 structure that ensures tighter control within the case-management unit.

Communications, Linkages, and Control. The configuration of two established organizations, each with its own long-standing modes of operation, presented difficult issues to be negotiated concerning responsibility and authority for management of the new chronic care services. The issues revolve around divisions of labor, but their resolution raises the issue of control. The disagreements resembled a straightforward dispute over shared turf, but the ultimate resolution had to be sensitive to the unique roles and responsibilities of the case-management unit in the SHMO.

In the SHMO model, the case manager has responsibility for allocation of the chronic care benefit, which means that this manager controls eligibility determination for that benefit, and the authorization of care plans, all within a tight budget. The case manager is accountable for that budget, and the pressure is on the manager for downward substitution of services wherever possible and as soon as appropriate. It is also essential that case managers always know how fast their clients are using up their long-term care benefit, and how close they are to reaching the maximum copayment level. Especially for heavy users of chronic care, case managers must make utilization projections and plan ahead in order to avoid loss of benefit or spend-down. Given these requirements, close relationships between case managers and provider staff are important, and provider staff must be well-oriented to SHMO goals if case managers are going to delegate some of their functions to others.

Working out a procedure for delegation was not a major problem with Ebenezer staff, in part because of prior staff relationships, but probably more important because of the kinds of clients Ebenezer will serve. It was decided that the case-management director may delegate to some provider staff the functions of monitoring and making recommendations for care plans, for those clients in long-term, stable situations. For example, these functions may be delegated to adult day care staff or home care nurses.

In contrast, more significant problems of control emerged between case management and the continuing care department of GHI. This department has been responsible for hospital discharge planning and short-term, postacute home care, and GHI wanted to retain authority over these functions for SHMO enrollees. Initial negotiations attempted to define the boundaries of this responsibility in terms of "Medicare certifiable," postacute, skilled services, with a time duration of up to two months. However, the line between treatment that is "Medicare certifiable" and treatment that is not, even within a two-month period, is not always clear. If the postacute care is not Medicare certifiable, then it uses the client's chronic care benefit, for which the case manager is accountable. Some clients could start in a skilled, "Medicare-certifiable" treatment plan (controlled by the GHI nurse), then move into their chronic care benefit. Transferring the client to the case management unit also raises questions about continuity of provider-client relationships.

The resolution of these differences came through a decision that the GHI continuing care department will have the responsibility for discharge planning for all Medicare Partners enrollees, but will coordinate with the case manager in discharge planning for all Medicare Partners enrollees who require home care or nursing home services. The case managers will have responsibility for authorizing all home care plans and nursing home placements and for management of all home- and community-based services. This compromise allows a clear definition of responsibility and authority, and it greatly simplifies administration. Each agency will use its own data and management system to document costs and track utilization, and most important there will be only one system tracking home care costs and client copay billings. Only the case management unit will make the distinction between Medicare-type and chronic home care, and this unit will also be responsible for assessment and reassessment of nursing home certifiable (NHC) status.

Another positive force in establishing the legitimacy of case management has been the geriatric resource team. The SHMO medical director has pushed for increased geriatric expertise through the hiring of a consultant geriatrician and two geriatric NPs. One of the latter, already hired, devotes considerable time to in-service training and orienting other GHI staff to geriatric issues. The physicians of the geriatric resource team will link directly with case managers and nurses working in the community or nursing home and provide the medical back-up required by these staff in working with chronic care plans. They perceive themselves as both advisers and advocates for case managers.

Medicare Plus II

As described in chapter 2, Kaiser differs organizationally from the other three sponsors in that it has the capacity to develop the entire SHMO services system internally, without partnership arrangements. Furthermore, Kaiser has extensive experience in delivering medical services to the elderly. Its clients include not only a large number of members who have "aged into" the plan (more than 16,000), but also 8,000 members of Medicare Plus, the Kaiser program in the HMO Medicare Demonstration (now called Medicare Plus I). The creation of Medicare Plus II can thus be viewed as the next step in the development of care for the elderly at Kaiser, and indeed Kaiser's long-range plan is to incorporate a SHMO-like extended care benefit as its standard benefit for the elderly if the Demonstration is successful. The major challenge for Kaiser is to learn to deliver and manage chronic care and to incorporate it into Kaiser's existing medical system.

Key Elements in the Continuum of Care in Medicare Plus II

Medical Care. Kaiser-Portland is a large, long-established group-model HMO. Medical care is provided by nearly 300 physicians, including most kinds of specialists, assisted by a large number of PEs (both NPs and PAs). In the Medicare Plus I demonstration, about 70 percent of outpatient visits were attended by physicians, 9 percent by PEs, and 21 percent by optometrists, audiologists, or therpists, among others. Kaiser also has its own Medicare-certified home health agency, staffed by public health nurses and home health aides. In the Oregon Region, Kaiser owns two hospitals (one 200-bed and one 155-bed) and provides care at ten ambulatory facilities and four dental clinics.

Health Education. Kaiser-Portland does not have a separate health education department. Health education concepts are built into the HMO philosophy and are intended to be practiced by all providers. Often health education is particularly emphasized by PEs. Each of the Kaiser hospitals has a health education unit that implements programs related to specific diseases and other health issues. Within the Kaiser system, many departments run their own health education programs.

Chronic Care. In order to develop a SHMO, Kaiser only had to add to its current facilities a case-management unit, expand its home care services, and make arrangements for use of some nursing home beds and adult day care. In the initial SHMO operations phase, these last two services will be contracted from outside agencies; but as Medicare Plus II enrollment grows, Kaiser plans to develop its own geriatric center to provide and internally control all of these services. In addition to the core benefits Kaiser is offering respite care.

Volunteers. Kaiser has obtained a foundation grant to plan and develop an areawide network of 100 to 200 volunteers from among its current elderly members. This volunteer network will be availlble as an added option in providing care and support for SHMO enrollees who receive chronic care. Detailed job descriptions for these volunteers are being developed. A team of three professionals will train and supervise the volunteers, with each supervisor responsible for about fifty volunteers within a specific area.

Staffing and Division of Labor

Medical Staffing. Kaiser's large system of medical providers was assessed to be adequate to take care of SHMO enrollees without any specific dedicated hiring. One major challenge has been to gain support for the program from the physicians and other providers. Another has been orienting them to the benefits the program has to offer from the providers' perspective, and to the methods and mechanisms for taking advantage of these benefits. The Plus II program follows close upon the influx of nearly 6,000 new senior citizen members through Medicare Plus I,[2] and Kaiser providers have only recently absorbed the impact of that influx. Some physician resistance to the SHMO program had to be overcome (see chapter 2).

Fortunately, the SHMO planning staff were long-time Kaiser Research Center staff members with already established relationships of trust with service staff members. Following the Medicare Plus I development model, they set up several task forces early in the planning phase, two of which were especially relevant to service planning. First, a multidisciplinary provider task force was headed by an internist who had a special interest in geriatric care, who was on the executive board of the physicians' organization, and who later became the SHMO medical director. Given the politics of this large medical system, it was important that the SHMO's medical director be acceptable to the majority of physicians and that the person have some clout within the organization. Another internist, well known for his work in an earlier Kaiser experiment with extended geriatric care, participated in the task force and acted as consultant in further geriatric care planning. During the planning phase, the SHMO medical director made presentations to groups of physicians and other providers. His role was that of educator, public relations person, and SHMO advocate.

The second group established was the new services task force, which includes all providers likely to be involved with SHMO enrollees eligible for chronic care. Its function was to address issues of integration, authority, and responsibility. Specific demands that the SHMO would place upon the provider system were discussed from the perspectives of various providers. Subjects of discussion included orientation to the expanded chronic care benefits, triggers for referral to case management, contact persons, methods of communication and information exchange, patient records, data, and documentation.

Long-Term Care. The planners of Medicare Plus II recognized the important function of case managers in controlling the allocation of chronic care services. Two hurdles faced by the planners, however, were gaining acceptance for this function, and implementing it effectively within a large medical system that already had well-defined staff roles and responsibilities for medical care of the elderly. One measure of the sensitivity that was required in defining roles and responsibilities is the fact that from the beginning of planning, Kaiser has used the term *resource coordination* rather than *case management*. The case manager is seen at this site (as at Medicare Partners) as a coordinator of existing resources. This perception is even more pronounced at Kaiser than at Medicare Partners because of the total consolidation of the Kaiser system, and the attitude has implications for the type of team approach used in care planning.

Kaiser's choice for a director of the expanded care benefit (that is, the case-management director) is a staff member qualified at master's-degree level, with extensive experience in speech pathology and administration. Kaiser projects that about 5 percent of Plus II enrollees will qualify for the expanded chronic care benefit and that five FTE staff members will be required for the resource coordination unit. This is a ratio of one coordinator to every forty members served. At start of operations, it is likely that one nurse and one social worker will be recruited as resource coordinators. The remaining resource coordinators may be case aides or paraprofessionals. In hiring for these positions, Kaiser is focusing less on professional credentials than are the other three sites. The applicant's abilities, sensitivity, responsiveness, and capacity for training are considered by Kaiser to be more important than professional levels.

Kaiser has chosen case-management model 2, in which the case-management functions are divided among resource coordinators and direct service providers. The responsibilities of resource coordinators are more narrowly defined than they are at the other sites. This may be due in part to the experience base of the direct service providers with geriatric patients. Kaiser's home health agency staff are experienced in working with Medicare home care criteria and may have provided home care somewhat beyond these criteria in prescribing homemaker services under a capitated system for Medicare Plus I clients. They will continue to provide home care services for Plus II enrollees. They will also continue to develop care plans, in cooperation with hospital discharge planners, for Plus II enrollees requiring postacute Medicare-type home health care. However, for enrollees who are eligible for the chronic care benefit, postacute care plans will be developed in consultation with the resource coordinator, who must authorize these care plans.

The main functions of the resource cordinators are (1) to determine eligibility for the expanded chronic care benefit; (2) to manage the chronic care budget for eligible clients; (3) to coordinate the resources available within the system for provision of care to eligible clients; (4) to monitor care provision for eligible clients in terms of continuity, quality, downward substitution, and budget; and (5) to document client utilization and care plans. This division of labor may be easier to implement than at other sites because of eligibility criteria for the expanded chronic care benefit are relatively clear and more narrowly focused than at other sites. (The Oregon state criteria will be described in the next chapter.)

No data are available on the projected costs of the resource coordination unit, since this comes under administrative costs in the capitation estimates. However, given the staffing pattern, this case-management model is likely to be relatively inexpensive in the context of the four Demonstration sites.

Communications, Linkage, and Control. Integrated relationships at Kaiser are intrastaff, rather than interagency, and care plan decisions result from team consultations. In this system, the resource coordinators have the major linkage roles and functions. They consult with other professionals (including discharge planners, home care nurses, dietitians, therapists, pharmacists, and others as appropriate); they coordinate case conferences; they work closely with the primary physicians; they monitor all of the chronic-care–eligible clients; and they must keep ongoing documentation of changes in the client's situation. The paraprofessional resource coordinators are more likely to be involved in monitoring and follow-up activities, which may be extensive. The professional case managers will have responsibility for assessment, eligibility determination, and resource allocation for the chronic care benefit.

These limitations in the span and scope of case-management authority have made it relatively easy for Kaiser to integrate the case-management unit into the existing system, with a minimum of conflict with other providers. At another level of analysis, the integration of the case-management unit also illustrates the advantages of a fully controlled system. Once the Research Center had convinced top management and the physicians group to go ahead with the SHMO, the rest of the system had no option but to cooperate. Management has the power to make the decision; staff knows the change will take place; and it happens. There may be grumbling and some interpersonal issues at the level of individual staff, but those running a new program such as the SHMO simply have the authority to implement it.

It should be noted that Kaiser's plans for the resource coordination unit are the least structured of the four sites and are left somewhat open and fluid for development through the operations phase. A computerized data base has been developed to help the resource coordinators keep track of and continually update care plans, utilization, and the chronic care budget. This process will facilitate ongoing evaluation of this unit's structure and effectiveness.

SCAN Health Plan

SCAN's issues in developing a SHMO service delivery system were somewhat different from those faced at the other three sites. If Kaiser is at one end of the consolidation-of-services spectrum, SCAN is at the other end, using a contractual model with no direct control of service provision beyond that of case management. Whereas Elderplan and Medicare Partners developed respectively from MJGC's and Ebenezer's consolidated long-term care delivery systems, SCAN has operated as a brokerage case-management model, contracting for all direct services from a variety of providers in the community.

At first glance it therefore seems that, structurally, SCAN must overcome the toughest obstacles in developing an integrated service delivery system. The key challenges were in developing a medical component, including physicians and hospital services and obtaining a license for its new HMO entity—the SCAN Health Plan, Inc. (SHP). Like MJGC, SCAN viewed these challenges as opportunities—in this case, the opportunity to integrate its brokerage approach to long-term care provision, with a larger comprehensive system.

Key Elements in the Continuum of Care at SCAN Health Plan
Chronic Care. SCAN entered the Demonstration with five years of experience

in establishing and operating a number of geriatric health and social service programs in the Long Beach community. These programs include the Case Management Model Project, which added a case-management component to the city's Information, Assistance, and Referral Program; the SCAN Medical Program, which provided for all Medicare parts A and B benefits through referral and working agreements with the major hospitals and many physicians in the community; and the Multipurpose Senior Services Program (MSSP), which administered a complex case-management program for the frail elderly and included service contracts for both health and social support services, with defined fiscal controls. In addition to having ties with community health care providers, SCAN is also closely linked, through interlocking board memberships, with the major senior citizen groups and councils in the area.

In short, SCAN's relatively short history is characterized by extensive community participation; innovative, areawide planning and program development; ongoing involvement of the medical community; and testing of several case-management models using professionals, paraprofessionals, and volunteers. SCAN viewed the SHMO as a logical extension of the service delivery models it had already established. Based on SCAN's prior experience in contracting for community services, SHP has been working with several community vendors, for such services as home health and chore services, respite, adult day care, electronic monitoring, home-delivered meals, medical transportation, hearing aids, and durable medical equipment. SHP has also contracted with a state-licensed, prepaid dental and optical provider for comprehensive coverage on a capitated basis.

Structuring the Medical Component.. In view of the large geriatric market in the Long Beach area, and the competition among providers to increase their market shares, SCAN's successful track record with seniors made it a desirable partner from the viewpoint of other Long Beach providers wishing to penetrate this market. SCAN, therefore, was in a somewhat different position than the other sites were. Rather than seeking out partners, it could select from among very interested and competitive provider bids, especially among the hospitals.

The Medical Group. In structuring the medical component, SCAN considered various options, such as approaching a local HMO, but the attractiveness of the Harriman Jones Clinics outweighed other options. Founded in 1930, HJC is well-established in the community, and one-third of its patients are over age 65. HJC brings to the Demonstration forty-seven physicians representing primary care and many subspecialties, three clinics (a fourth opening shortly), and a successful, growing group practice with a strong interest in expanding into the geriatric market.

HJC currently has several HMO contracts and serves about 7,500 clients under prepayment. It has an effective internal utilization review process and has developed norms of practice for cost-conscious, as well as high-quality, medical care.

The Hospital. Three Long Beach hospitals were particularly interested in working with SCAN, and each put in a competitive bid for the contract. SCAN chose St. Mary's Medical Center, mainly because it had worked extensively with this hospital in the past and St. Mary's had funded some of SCAN's earlier programs. St. Mary's is a 540-bed general acute hospital owned by the Sisters of Charity of the Incarnate Word. Its inpatient census is about 60 percent Medicare, and it has a special geriatric out-patient clinic. The hospital also has a strong social services department that is knowledgeable about home assistance and community services, and with which SCAN case managers already had working relationships.

Unique among the SHMO sites, SCAN negotiated a risk agreement with this hospital (see chapter 2). The hospital will provide (and be at risk for) not only all acute inpatient services, but also pharmacy services and SNF care. In order to ensure SNF bed availability, the hospital has contracted with a local nursing home, as well as certifying some of its own beds as SNF.

The HMO. As described in chapter 2, the SCAN Health Plan was formed as a nonprofit subsidiary of SCAN. SHP has applied for HMO licensure and will be responsible for plan administration (management, finance, and marketing, for example) and the case-management function.

Staffing and Division of Labor

Medical Services. Planning for the integration of HJC medical services into the SHMO has been aided by the early leadership of HJC's administrator and medical director. A planning task force was established whose discussions and presentations were well received by the physicians and other providers in the group. One example of the strong interest was the expressed desire of the medical director and other physicians to attend case-management conferences during early operations—partly as a learning experience, but also to give time to such conferences as required, on an ongoing basis. The group also utilizes physician extenders significantly, and these professionals were early on identified as having linkage roles with case managers, as well as a role in providing direct service to SHP enrollees. In general, providers have been most enthusiastic about working with SCAN's case managers.

In deciding to work with a relatively large, established medical group, SHP might have expected to face many of the same obstacles as Medicare

Partners, in terms of its trying to change established divisions of labor and responsibility. Site staff report, however, that such has not been the case. Perhaps this is because HJC does not have a home health unit and generally leaves the responsibility for primary discharge planning to hospitals. SHP's control over these functions and over the chronic care benefit was acknowledged by the other parties from the outset.

Chronic Care Services. The case-management team will act as the glue that bonds chronic care and medical services. As with the other sites, the SHP case-management system serves as the client's single entry point into the chronic care benefit and will be operated by a special unit located close to the plan administration. The case-management director is responsible to the SHP administrator and consults with the SHP medical director. This case-management unit has the MSSP program's extensive experience on which to build and can use many of the protocols and procedures developed in that program, which also had to operate within defined fiscal constraints.

SHP's case-management staffing model is similar to the Elderplan model. Case-management teams will consist of a community health nurse and a social worker. Both team members are required to have assessment skills, experience in the gerontological health field, and ability to identify, enlist, coordinate, and monitor a diverse set of professional, community, and familial resources. Nurses are expected to have the ability to work effectively with physicians, PEs, and other health providers, while social workers must be skilled in dealing with emotional needs, advocacy, and working with the extensive network of human service agencies. Based on the MSSP experience, SHP is projecting an optimal staff-to-impaired-client ratio of one to fifty-five. SHP projects a somewhat healthier enrollment than most of the other sites do, and although they are targeting chronic care services to some of the "moderately" as well as "severely" impaired, when full enrollment is achieved, targeted clients will most likely amount to 10 to 12 percent of total enrollment (400 to 480 persons). To maintain their staff-to-client ratio, therefore, SHP would need approximately eight case managers, or four teams.

SHP chose a veteran of MSSP as its first case-management director. She holds an M.S.W. degree and has extensive experience in the areas of gerontological care and administration. Her responsibilities include training and supervision of case-management team members; development of policies, procedures, and protocols; coordination of discharge planning and long-term care quality assurance programs; and involvement in setting service-substitution and cost-containment targets.

Like Elderplan, SHP retains all of the traditional case-management functions within the case management unit—assessment, eligibility determination, care plan development and authorization, monitoring, and reassessment.

Communications, Linkages, and Control. In relation to care plan development, SHP places strong emphasis on team consultation. As described in their protocol, the SHP case manager develops an initial care plan after exploring the options with the client and informal caregivers. Providers appropriate to the care plan are then consulted and a case conference is arranged, with the primary physician and other providers participating. Following presentations of all pertinent information from team members, a final care plan is developed, which must be authorized by the case manager and case-management supervisor or case-management director. This care plan is then reviewed with the client and primary informal caregiver(s), and the client is asked to sign the care plan to indicate compliance and cooperation.

The case manager is then responsible for arranging, coordinating, and monitoring implementation of services prescribed. Procedures for further review of care plans by the medical or case-management director are defined for cases where there is unresolved disagreement among providers or with the client in relation to the care plan.

In this model there is a clear expectation, spelled out in protocols and procedures, for all providers (both medical and long-term care) to make themselves available for team consultation and case conferences. Consensus and sign-off procedures are detailed. The coordinated approach to encourage participation from all provider team members is structured and defined in protocols and procedures, to which all providers have been oriented through initial orientation and in-service training sessions.

Conclusion

It is difficult to summarize the experience of these four diverse sites, but it is clear that variables such as experience, staff commitment, power, and size made a difference in the planning processes and eventual choices at each site. Each of the long-term care sponsors worked hard to maintain the autonomy and authority of the case management function in its SHMO system, but each chose a somewhat different route toward integrating this authority with a medical provider. Both MJGC and SCAN entered the Demonstration with extensive case-management experience under state-sponsored programs that capped individual client service packages. Their staffing models are highly professional, and their medical partners were highly accepting of the expertise and authority of the case-management staff from the outset of planning. It appears that case-management authority will be strongest at these sites. At the two sites with large HMOs, case-management authority was a more thorny issue for medical providers. Even the term *case management* was controversial and was dropped in favor of the more neutral term *resource coordination*. Yet even with these disputes over turf and authority, site planners were able to establish and maintain ultimate power over the authorization of long-term care benefits in the case-management unit. Wecksler, Durmaskin, and Kodner (1983) contend that this is an appropriate division, since this allows physicians to focus on the medical decisions they are trained to make.

It is tempting to speculate that the service system will work better at the two sites where case-management authority is the most firmly established, but such an assumption may miss the point that the HMO providers seem to be making. The central requirement for successful service delivery in the SHMO is integration. At this early stage of the Demonstration, it is premature to say that there is only one appropriate model for integration. Perhaps the SHMO *does* need to drop the term *case management*, since it connotes responsibility only for the impaired and only for chronic care services. In the SHMO, the management of chronic care obviously needs to be more than that, and the management of medical care needs to encompass more than traditional medical treatments and considerations. Perhaps in the end the specific divisions of labor and authority will be less important to integration than the establishment of clear mechanisms for linkage, communication, transfer of responsibility, and delegation of authority. Underlying any successful arrangements will be a full understanding and appreciation on the part of all providers of what each has to offer and how to obtain one another's assistance.

Notes

1. Master et al. (1980) suggest that 40 to 50 percent of the primary physician's time needs be left flexible for such consultation. This was the experience of Boston's Urban Medical Group, a comprehensive geriatric care program for the mainly very frail urban elderly poor. It was also found that, with this level of consultation, only about 10 percent of the calls from the nurses working in the community required a subsequent physician visit to the home or emergency room.

2. About 2,000 of the original 8,000 members were conversions from aged-in members.

4
Resource Allocation and Quality

S HMOs must create not only an integrated system of services and providers, but a system whose mechanisms and norms efficiently and effectively allocate resources to the members. Resource allocation is a broad concept, and it is meant to encompass more than professional practice. While the professional's allocation of resources through prescription of services is the most important aspect of the concept, professionals in the SHMO (and especially in long-term care) will practice in the context of two prior if not separate decisions. First, resource allocation decisions are made in defining the benefit package. By deciding which benefits to cover, and how fully, one places limits on what professionals can prescribe. Second, resources are allocated through what might be called targeting or eligibility decisions. While eligibility for all benefits will ultimately be based on clinical decisions, the eligibility determination process for chronic care may well require more formal structuring—at least this is the choice of the Demonstration. Obviously, constraints on targeting and eligibility decision making will form another context for professionals' prescription of services to members.

A central goal of resource allocation in the SHMO is to deliver high-quality care in a cost-effective manner. Lest the term *cost-effectiveness* be confused with simple cost cutting, it must be emphasized that the SHMO's more appropriate use of acute and chronic care services should be consistent with reducing costs. That is, the general approach of making downward substitutions across the interfaces of the levels of care and professional practice not only saves resources, it also maintains or even improves quality of care. Furthermore, with long-term care services, less is often better, since excess care can create unnecessary dependencies.

The major challenge in devising cost-effective norms of practice and quality assurance protocols comes in the chronic care area. In part this is because there is less experience with prepaid practice in comprehensive chronic care systems than there is with acute care systems. But more importantly, there are stricter resource constraints. The SHMO will have limited funds for long-term care benefits, both for Medicaid members, whose benefit levels are limited by Medicaid budgets, and especially for private-pay members, whose benefits are limited by premiums and system savings levels. While the particular limits are not inherent in the model but rather lie in current financing, a limit on resources at some level is unavoidable. The challenge for policymakers and professionals in the SHMO is to devise norms of practice that lead to high-quality care delivered in an equitable manner, but that at the same time can hold chronic care costs of an enrolled population to budgeted levels.

The importance of predictable and cost-effective resource allocation decisions goes beyond the function of maintaining budgets, however. Such predictability and cost-effectiveness are also necessary if chronic care is to become insurable. Insurers have steered clear of chronic care (especially home care) largely because they do not know what chronic care benefits should be covered (and at what levels), who should be eligible to receive these services (and how many will qualify), or how to prescribe them (and how much eligibles will need). The Demonstration should thus make a valuable contribution to insurers outside the SHMO model.

The emphasis on chronic care is not meant to minimize the challenges that the SHMO presents to acute care. Physicians and other acute care providers will be working within a comprehensive geriatric system. The opportunities for improving the care of both independent and impaired elderly include preventive intervention, programs to support self-care and health education, and of course more effective integration of acute and chronic care. This chapter will emphasize questions directly related to caring for the SHMO member. That is, once the members enter this new system of care, how will the providers decide "who gets what"? This simple question requires a multidimensional answer, and the SHMO model once again creates a flexible space for fashioning a variety of responses. What the members receive will be determined in part by the services the program chooses to offer and emphasize and in part be a function of the level of resources available to support the services. Who receives care will primarily be determined by the targeting and prescription guidelines that define what conditions qualify an individual for a service and how much he or she should receive.

In the abstract, the SHMO model is rather wide open on these questions, which must consider the extent to which service will be oriented toward prevention as opposed to cure; toward life enhancement as opposed to maintenance; and toward costly high-technology approaches to prolonging life for the very few, as opposed to labor-intensive social support services that maintain independence for the chronically impaired. What level of services will be available is also an open question, which will depend on the level of government support and the level of premiums that the elderly are ultimately willing to pay, as well as the level of informal supports that are available to the members—either through their own networks or through networks created by the program.

These issues concern both resource allocation and quality and must be addressed at many levels of the SHMO. At the broadest level, the issues are philosophical. To what extent and in what ways is the SHMO a medical program, a social support program, a community-based life care program? At another level, the issues are political, expressed in the form of public policy toward the SHMO. What service will the government require the model to provide? How much financial support is it willing to give? How closely will it regulate care within the SHMO? At the level of the program, the issues become legal and contractual. That is, when an individual becomes a member and agrees to pay premiums, to what benefits does he or she become entitled, and under what circumstances? Finally, all of the decisions about issues made at other levels must be interpreted and applied at the level of professional practice. Here individual staff must assess the needs of the members and respond with appropriate strategies and services. Practice must integrate, coordinate, and be responsible for the patient's care across the full range of health and long-term care services, including the services of informal caregivers.

Creating and maintaining a high quality of care will be crucial in attracting both public payers and individual elderly to the program and in maintaining their participation. Since the model creates a fixed budget system with strong savings incentives, there is reason for concern that quality could be compromised in the interest of profits (or of avoiding losses). Somehow managers, practitioners, regulators, and members alike will need to learn to distinguish between well-managed efficiency and simple corner cutting, as they evaluate the quality of care in the SHMO.

SHMOs will need to follow the precedent of HMOs and create formal mechanisms with which to monitor, evaluate, and reinforce quality of care in all areas of the program. Sites face special challenges in the area of home- and community-based long-term care services, where quality standards and measures are underdeveloped compared to those of institutional and medical care, and where prescriptions will be constrained by the limited chronic care benefits being offered by the sites. Providers may occasionally find themselves walking a narrow line between maximizing informal resources and client independence, and providing an inadequate level of care to meet client needs.

The remainder of the chapter is divided into four sections:

A detailed analysis of the three components of resource allocation. Issues and options concerning benefit structure, targeting, and prescription norms are reviewed, and some of the key choices made in the Demonstration are described.

A description of the uniform assessment guidelines and instruments adopted by the participants in the Demonstration. These form an information base for decision making.

Detailed descriptions of the four sites' plans for allocating resources to their memberships. Discussions of benefits structure, targeting, and prescription procedures are included, with some detail on each state's nursing home prescreening criteria.

An analysis of quality assurance issues in the SHMO. Included are a discussion of possible approaches to quality assurance and descriptions of site systems.

Overview of Resource Allocation Issues and Options

Benefits Issues

The first resource allocation decisions are made when the program benefit package is devised. Decisions to make some benefits mandatory in a core package, others optional on an individual basis, and others not available at all have the effect of allocating resources. Decisions about the level of benefits available (such as covered in full, covered to a unit of service or cost limit, covered with coinsurance) have a similar effect. In short, given a limited level of resources, the decision to cover a particular benefit in a particular manner affects the capacity to cover others.

The national Demonstration placed some specific requirements on the sites in their decision making about benefits, but it also allowed flexibility. The core benefit package that Brandeis recommended to the sites contained stronger requirements for some benefits than for others. HCFA strictly required that all current Medicare benefits be covered at least at their current levels. Brandeis made strong recommendations to include a full "buy-out" of Medicare copays and deductibles, a series of supplemental medical benefits (such as drugs, hearing aids, eyeglasses, dentures), and a specific range of long-term care services. In fact, the sites were able to negotiate some discretion concerning these individual Brandeis recommendations, except for the need to include both institutional and noninstitutional long-term care. In the end, however, sites chose not to leave out very much of the core package (see figure 3–1). As will be seen in the next chapter, this decision stemmed largely from marketing considerations and the patterns of traditional HMO coverage: HMOs generally offer a range of fully covered medical benefits, and these benefits are attractive to the target population.

While the national Demonstration's core benefit recommendations were quite specific in terms of the type of benefits to be offered, sites had considerable latitude in terms of the structure and level of benefits in the long-term care area. The areas of latitude include:

1. Allocating funds into institutional versus community-based benefits;
2. Defining the benefit period and the renewability of the benefit; and
3. Deciding on cost-sharing levels and mechanisms.

Institutional versus Noninstitutional Coverage. The allocation of funds to community-based versus institutional benefits has been a matter of some internal debate in the Demonstration, since it goes to the heart of the model. That is, an important concept in the SHMO is the placing of providers at risk for a full range of long-term care services, including nursing home care. Providers then have incentives to maintain members in the community when that option is more appropriate and less costly than institutional care. Of course, this would work best if providers were responsible for *all* long-term care costs (as with Medicaid members), but the incentives are still important with the limited benefits of the Medicare-only members.

In order to maintain incentives for keeping members in the community, Brandeis recommended making the financial risk for institutional costs about equal to the risk for community-based costs. Given this concept, what models are available? The first approach tried was to make the dollar value of benefits in each area approximately equal. Members would have a certain dollar value in home care benefits, plus an equal value in nursing home care. However, since this split the funds for chronic care into two benefits, the maximum value of each had to be less than the value of the two combined. The problem with this model is that if a member needs (and wants) only home care, he or she cannot obtain the value of the chronic care benefit covering institutional care (and vice versa).

The solution to these problems was another model: the "intertwined" benefit. The intertwined chronic care benefit is defined in dollar terms, which can be applied to care in either or both settings up to the maximum per benefit period. This model maximizes the potential value of community-based services.

Benefit Periods and Renewability. There are several dimensions to the benefit period issue. First, should the benefit be defined in monthly or annual terms? The monthly benefit has the advantage of assuring that benefits will extend for a full year. However, they may fall short of meeting full needs for the most impaired. Under the annual benefit structure, all needs are met while benefits last, but the benefits may expire completely before the year is out. Under the annual approach, it may be easier to arrange a Medicaid "spend-down" internal to the SHMO for those whose benefits run out. A spend-down threshold would be harder to reach if new benefits were available each month.

Another dimension of the benefit period issue is renewability of the institutional benefits. As the membership ages, some proportion of the SHMO membership will consist of persons residing in nursing homes. If the program must pay the benefit for every year of a member's stay, costs will build up, and community-based benefit levels will thus have to be cut. This would reduce the program's capacity to *prevent* nursing home admissions— and such prevention is a major original goal of the SHMO model. So goes the argument for making the benefit nonrenewable. On the other side is the provider-incentive issue: With a nonrenewable benefit, it becomes much cheaper to have an impaired member in an institution. Clearly, sponsors offering nonrenewable institutional benefits should require strict utilization review, quality assurance, member education, and grievance protocols, to make sure the sponsor persists in trying to keep members out of nursing homes. Obviously, the whole renewability issue is fraught with multiple, conflicting objectives, and either solution involves trade-offs.

Coinsurance Structures. Sponsors have a great variety of approaches available to them in structuring cost sharing for long-term care services for private members. The approach used should reflect conscious choices on how cost sharing should be used to manage the demand for long-term care and to distribute long-term care benefits among members. These issues have implications not only for service delivery, but also for marketing and finance.

First, there has been a good deal of study of the effects of cost sharing on the demand for medical services (Rand 1981), but little is known about how cost sharing affects demand for long-term care services (Bishop 1981; Pollak 1973). Although little is known about the elasticity of demand for these services, it seems certain that price will affect demand. The question is how much to control costs through market mechanisms and how much to control them through case management. If, on one hand, planners worry about the inability to control moral hazard[1], a 50 percent copay would go a long way in addressing their concern. If, on the other hand, the plan wants case managers to be the major actors in resource allocation decisions, a lower copay level would be indicated. Hybrids are of course possible.

Second, the way copays are structured will distribute benefits to specific groups. The most important point in this regard is that for any given level of revenue to be raised by copays, the most impaired will be better off with a structure that puts costs on the "front end" (a deductible) than with a flat-rate-per-service or percentage charge. The worst option for the most impaired is free service up to a threshold, followed by cost sharing. Also, the more copays are used as a revenue source, the more the level (both gross and net) of the chronic care benefit can be raised. This is because higher copays will both dampen overall demand (more benefits left for those who do use) and also raise the proportions of costs paid by low and moderate users. The result should be that heavy users convert to full cost sharing later.

The site description section of this chapter will show that the Demonstration sites chose not to require substantial initial cost sharing to control long-term care service utilization because site planners are assuming that such utilization will be quite effectively controlled by case management. Any cost sharing is likely to have utilization effects on two types of enrollees—that is, those whose incomes are marginal and those who currently have a system of informal support. Regrettably, the SHMO does not have the resources to compensate for inequities in income distribution, and some enrollees will have difficulty with any cost-sharing requirement. This is one reason cost-sharing requirements were kept rather low. Finally, it could be argued that it is important for enrollees and their families to experience some price for SHMO support services, since free service might encourage many informal caregivers to withdraw some of their support.

Targeting Issues

The second level of decision making in resource allocation is targeting services to the membership. Two aspects of targeting should be distinguished: first, a preliminary and general identification of those who may need a service; and second, an in-depth determination of whether those people actually do need or qualify for the service. Since SHMOs are responsible for the full range of health care for their members, the first aspect of targeting is central to the model. SHMOs have the opportunity if not the obligation to actively seek those who may benefit from a service rather than operating in the usual mode of waiting for patient demand. For example, broad prevention and health education programs could be not only beneficial to the membership, but also cost-effective. As will be detailed presently, SHMO sites will survey the health status of all members on entry, and annually thereafter. This will provide a good data base for formulating and conducting a variety of proactive targeting efforts.

The second aspect of targeting brings in the restrictive sense of the term. It applies most clearly to the model's new long-term care benefits, which are offered under strict resource constraints and risks, and which are likely to be demanded at levels that are greater than the sites will be ready to satisfy. This is the eligibility screening dimension of targeting, and it has received detailed consideration in the planning phase of the project.

The formal eligibility screening issue does not arise in acute care the way it does in chronic care. At least in the medical ideal, the physician prescribes services solely on the basis of clinical need, and it is assumed that the resources will be provided. There is no such assumption in chronic care—at least in the current system, or in the SHMO Demonstration sites either. Rather, the practitioner's first role is as the "gatekeeper" who applies preset standards of eligibility to potential clients. These standards have varied considerably in previous programs, ranging from the very loose ones of Triage I ("need" for long-term care), to the stricter but still open-ended ones in Triage II ("at risk" of institutional placement) (Quinn 1982), to the very strict and closed-ended ones in Channeling (so many assessed deficits in activities of daily living (ADL) functioning, instrumental ADL functioning, and combinations thereof) (Baxter et al. 1983). Obviously, the stricter and more closed-ended the eligibility standards are, the less discretion is available to the professional to apply clinical standards; the more open-ended the standards, the more discretion for professionals (Greenberg and Pollak 1981).

The national Demonstration set no requirements concerning who among the broad-based membership should be eligible to receive the SHMO's expanded chronic care benefits. Rather, eligibility decisions were left to individual sites. There was a good deal of exchange across sites, and between Brandeis and the sites, in deciding on targeting, and prior demonstrations were also examined. It can be argued that early, lower-intensity, less costly interventions with the moderately impaired might delay functional decline and prevent or delay institutionalization for an increased number of people, and therefore result in greater cost saving (Willemain 1980). However, there is little information on how people's functional levels decline over time.

Given the current level of knowledge and the SHMO's limited budget for long-term care, a reasonable argument can be made for targeting benefits to the most frail. Those with the most severe impairment are presumably most likely to enter nursing homes without extensive support in the community, and the SHMO therefore, could prove to be more effective if it saved limited resources for these members. An even stricter rationing mechanism might dictate serving only the severely impaired who are at imminent risk of entering a nursing home.

Ultimately, a financial decision provided the central component of the sites' eligibility determination processes and criteria. This was the agreement by HCFA and some state Medicaid agencies to pay a higher rate for members who were assessed to meet state nursing home certification standards. Since the programs would be paid more for these nursing home certifiable (NHC) members, it made sense to tie eligibility for chronic care services (at least in part) to NHC status. While all sites adopted this approach, the site descriptions will show that there are significant differences among the state standards, including differences in the amount of clinical discretion in deciding classifications. Furthermore, within these constraints, each site still has room for incorporating organizational values and philosophies into eligibility and targeting criteria—for example, by being more or less strict than state standards, or by including prevention criteria. All in all, the flexibility means that sites may derive significantly different outcomes from the eligibility processes.

One reason for giving the sites latitude in defining eligibility for the chronic care benefit is to see how services can best be targeted to impaired elderly clients, within current budget constraints. Descriptive documentation of clients who do and do not qualify for the long-term care system will be a major evaluative task of this demonstration. This documentation will be facilitated by the availability of data gathered by uniform assessment instruments and procedures. With careful documentation of who gains access to services at each site, the SHMOs may be able to refine the screening process and develop some uniform criteria, based on documented optimum targeting related to outcomes.

Norms of Professional Practice

The final and most complex step in the resource allocation process involves professional practice itself. Prescription of care through professional practice starts where the benefit package and targeting rules leave off: It allocates the available benefits to appropriate members according to their assessed needs. Norms of practice for matching services to needs must be developed that meet the SHMO's goals of efficiency, effectiveness, and equity in delivering services.

Once again the primary focus for development in the Demonstration will be on norms of practice for chronic care. The overall goal is to develop norms that have some of the key characteristics of medical practice—that is, a base of knowledge and interventions, broad acceptance, replicability, and insurability. These norms must take a form that can be clearly articulated and communicated not only to clinical staff, but also third parties, clients, and family members. Members and third parties are buying insurance in the SHMO, and they have a right to know how insured benefits are distributed. This is especially important for members and families, since they will be a part of the decision-making process.

It may at first seem contradictory to say that chronic care practice must become more like medical practice, and also say that norms must be understandable to clients and families. But the contradiction merely reflects the fact that there are differences between the two areas of practice. After analyzing some of these differences here, potential models for developing chronic care practice will be explored. A survey of past efforts in this area shows that there is limited experience for developing new norms of practice and that the SHMO sites have a major developmental effort ahead of them.

Differences between Acute and Chronic Care Practice. There are three important differences between acute and chronic care practice that must be taken into account in the development of norms of practice. First, to obtain a true picture of need for services, assessment and care planning must take into account not only such clinical factors as mental and physical impairment levels, but also a set of environmental, economic, and social factors. Basing service provision only on clinical assessments is likely to produce an inefficient or inappropriate allocation of resources. Environmental and economic factors include whether or not the client lives alone and whether the home is handicapped-accessible and safe. Economic resources influence the client's opportunity to buy additional care or change the environment. A range of social factors is even more important, especially the level of informal support the impaired member receives. A goal adopted by all parties concerned with the Demonstration was to avoid substituting formal services for existing levels of informal support provided by family and friends. While it may make sense in many cases to augment, improve, or rearrange the informal support of impaired clients, the program is not likely to be financially feasible if it creates a significant "add-on" effect.

Assessment and care planning concerning the informal support system should take into account both the system's strength and its resiliency. Strength may be evaluated by whether or not the primary caretaker is working at a job outside the home, whether the person is responsible for the care of other family, and whether he or she is healthy. Resiliency is a measure of whether the care will be available for as long as it is needed and as much as it is needed (that is, could the caregiver possibly do more?). Resiliency can be measured by how strongly the caregiver feels a responsibility for the impaired person, whether there is a reciprocal relationship between the caregiver and receiver, and whether there is affection between them. Finally, an assessment of the informal system should take into account the character and attitudes of the impaired client. Preferences as to community versus institutional living are often strong factors in whether or not impaired individuals enter nursing homes.

A second key difference between chronic care practice and medical practice is that specific budget constraints will be placed on case managers' prescriptions for chronic care services. Whereas the service of physicians and hospitals are virtually unlimited for members at SHMO sites, the services of home care workers and nursing homes will be strictly limited. While the limits are lower than most of the sites would like, most practitioners accept that some sort of resource constraint on long-term care is essential. Compared to medical services, the demand for many chronic care services is more elastic, long-lasting, and patient-initiated. It may turn out that impaired SHMO members who pay premiums for services will feel entitled to press the project staff for more services. In this context, benefit limits (along with eligibility guidelines and coinsurance) will help case managers moderate the pressures. Also, there is a strong feeling among the long-term care workers at the sites that there are significant ill effects from prescribing too many long-term social support services. They feel that maximum client independence in functioning is the primary goal of care, and that in some cases a budget constraint can assist all concerned in maximizing client functioning and informal support.

Of course, there will be situations where the budget constraints prohibit practitioners from prescribing services that are essential for client well-being, especially when individual benefit levels are as limited as they are at some of the sites. Finding the resources to meet such needs and developing the flexibility in prescription norms to allow practitioners to use them are key questions for the future.

A third difference from medical practice is that chronic care practitioners have not defined what might be called a "necessary and sufficient" array of services for comprehensive chronic care. The Demonstration's core benefit package takes a rather inclusive approach, and the supplemental benefits round out a range that includes most if not all of what previous programs have offered. The Demonstration sites have incorporated pretty much the full package, with only minor modifications of detail in their listed benefits. While case managers at the various sites will therefore have rather similar arrays to choose from, it does not follow that they will make the same choices in using the services, or that services with the same names will have the same content across sites. For evaluation purposes, efforts were made to create some uniformity in service definitions across sites, but there are limits to uniformity—stemming both from local provider differences and from the sites' need to redefine service content to meet need. These variations point to the fact that standardized definitions and criteria for use of chronic care services are still being developed. It will be important to document which services are effective and efficient for which types of clients, in order to learn more about how best to structure and use the potential continuum of care.

In summary, the SHMO model has the potential to significantly expand the scope and span of authority for long-term care practitioners along lines that are parallel to but different from the physician's authority over acute care. As Austin (1983) suggests, however, such expansion of the case managers' roles will put these professionals in the middle of pressures from clients, administrators, and fellow practitioners. The "job burnout" phenomenon is a real hazard that cannot be ignored. In this situation, development of priorities and criteria for resource allocation is a pressing issue, not only for efficiency but also to give staff a more manageable decision-making structure.

Potential Models for More Uniform Norms of Chronic Care Practice. In a recent study of long-term care demonstration programs, Greenberg, Doth, and Austin (1981) noted that only one of these programs had attempted to develop a uniform set of standards for allocating services. The reliance on "clinical judgment" alone has been questioned in the few studies that have attempted to measure the consistency of assessment scoring among case managers in relation to care planning (Boyd et al. 1980; Austin and Seidl 1981). In order to make resource allocation decisions understandable and predictable, a certain level of standardization and routinization must be achieved. The argument that the uniqueness of every client makes it impossible to develop uniform criteria is suspect. Clinical judgment can never (and should never) be removed from care-planning decisions, but the standardization of norms should not only improve the consistency of care but also reduce some of the strain on case managers.

The efforts of several previous projects are relevant to the development of norms of practice in the SHMO, but the relevance is only fragmentary. For example, some of the state level-of-care certification forms and procedures (such as New York State's DMS-1 form) use numerical weights related to certain defined health problems or disability levels. At the moment, these criteria are used to define broad institutional levels of care (SNF/ICF). This is a beginning, and such tools might be refined to define narrower ranges of needed services.

It is a much more complex problem to define ranges of required services in home care, since the home environment and social situation (especially informal supports) are important variables to be considered, in addition to health and functional problems. These are interdependent variables, and their combined effects are difficult to measure. One example of a home care need–scoring tool was developed in the state of Washington's CBC program (Garrick and Moore 1979). The CBC assessment tool was developed for the population requiring chore services only. It yields scores for individual clients. Scores can be added up to form a functional ability rating (FAR), which indicates the maximum number of in-home service hours a client should receive.

A much more complex allocation system was developed by the Equity and Efficiency Project in northern California (Boyd et al. 1980). The goal was to develop a needs-scoring and prescription scheme that reflected the collective wisdom of the practitioners in county social service programs. During the project, each worker fed assessment data and prescription information for each case into a computer. The computer was programmed to compare client characteristics and services prescribed for them to corresponding data from other workers. The computer then provided feedback to workers about how their prescriptions compared to others for similar clients. The ultimate goal was to create some convergence. While the development and technology of such a model may be too expensive for the Demonstration, the idea of somehow pooling and learning from the collective wisdom of practitioners is relevant to the SHMO. Perhaps this function could somehow be performed by the case management director.

While there is no direct precedent for the type of chronic care practice that will be required in the SHMO, it is possible to list some elements that should perhaps be included in any method of regularizing case-management practice. They include:

Standardizing assessment instruments and processes. This increases reliability of the bases on which care plan decisions are made, as well as interassessor reliability. It provides a basis for accountability and determining effectiveness.

Defining service objectives in care plans. This increases specificity and accountability, while also providing a basis for determining effectiveness.

Development of criteria for care plan decisions. This might include defining expected types, frequency, and levels of services for clients at specific levels, or within specific client pathways.

Recruitment, socialization, training, supervision. This is another strategy for routinizing norms of practice. Workers with compatible approaches are hired, and their practice behavior is then molded through orientation, supervision, and in-service training.

Classifying clients. This might include defining clients in terms of "level of care need," "client pathway levels," "at risk of institutionalization or not," "assessment score thresholds," and other measurements. These methods facilitate screening for eligibility determination, as well as care plan decisions.

Descriptions of the sites' case-management norms as the Demonstration begins show that plans have been developed along some of these lines but that there is a long way to go.

Assessment Processes in the Demonstration

A necessary ingredient in the resource allocation process—in the targeting, prescription, and quality assurance stages—is assessment of the membership. Since the current sites are part of a national demonstration, there were requirements from HCFA, Brandeis, and the evaluators to standardize many elements of the assessment process so that resulting data for monitoring, research, and evaluation will be reliable across the four sites.

Aside from such external requirements, site clinicians also recognized that some level of standardization would be helpful to them. The site case management directors participated with Brandeis in the development of the two major assessment instruments for the SHMO: the initial Health Status Form (HSF) and the Comprehensive Assessment Form (CAF). This effort began as an attempt to define a minimum standardized data set, but it was thought that each site would further develop the form for its own purposes. However, through ongoing cross-site discussion and sharing of items and ideas, there was increasing consensus on the "best" items, and finally all the sites agreed on a completely standardized instrument for both the HSF and the CAF.

The Health Status Form

The HSF is mailed to each new enrollee immediately after the person is accepted for membership. It contains forty-four questions concerning the client's health and functional status, prior and current utilization of acute and long-term care services, and sociodemographic data. The HSF is thus a tool for proactive targeting and outreach efforts, since it provides an identification of possible need for chronic and acute care across the entire membership. However, since the HSF is a short, self-administered form, the more comprehensive CAF, administered face-to-face, is needed to confirm eligibility for chronic care benefits or need for other services. Thus, the assessment planning team had to devise criteria and procedures for using HSF information to select members for further assessment. The planners decided on three levels at which responses to the HSF may trigger further assessment:

> The CAF will always be administered to clients who indicate they are bedbound, or who have two or more ADL deficits. This is an administrative parameter that ensures comprehensive assessment of those who appear to be most frail, even though a CAF may show otherwise, and even though their informal supports may be so strong that they do not require additional chronic services from the SHMO. Use of the CAF ensures that there will be comprehensive information available on these clients.

> Certain responses to any of fourteen specific items will always trigger a telephone screen by the case manager.

> Certain responses to any of three specific items *may* trigger a telephone screen, based on the case manager's judgment of those questions in relation to other items on the form.

The Telephone Screen

This is a ten- to fifteen-minute telephone call in which the case manager asks the client about uncompleted HSF items, as well as any other item or issue that in the case manager's judgment requires further information. On the basis of this telephone screen, the case manager will use clinical judgment to decide whether or not the client should receive a comprehensive assessment. If the client does not need a comprehensive assessment at this time, this decision will be noted on the client's record, along with the reasons. If appropriate, the client's name will be placed on file for regular telephone monitoring. Note that the telephone screen is *not* a standardized instrument, but it is a follow-up to the standardized HSF, from which a uniform data base is obtained.

The Comprehensive Assessment

The CAF is a one to one-and-a-half hour interview conducted by the case manager in the client's home. The CAF collects detailed information on the client's current health status, past major illnesses, current and past utilization, functional level, mental and emotional status, informal caregivers, social interaction, environmental situation, and sociodemographic data. Using this information, the case manager will determine if the client is eligible for chronic care services and complete a level of care certification for chronic care eligibility. Since the sites are in four different states, one of the challenges in designing the CAF was to generate sufficient information to meet the level-of-care certification requirements of all four states.

Two concerns in developing the CAF were the validity of the items used and the reliability of the assessment procedures. Several steps were taken to meet these concerns. First, as far as possible, any assessment instrument should use well-tested and validated items and scales. A variety of these are described in the literature (see Kane and Kane 1981), and appropriate selections were made to suit the particular purposes of the SHMO assessment procedure. Second, uniform procedures for administering the assessment were developed and documented in a companion manual to the assessment instrument. Third, assessors were trained to use the assessment instrument so that reliability among assessors will be maximized.

An assessment manual for the SHMO CAF was developed by Brandeis staff, with input from the four sites and a consultant. Again working cooperatively with the four SHMO sites, Brandeis developed a generic training plan and standardized training materials including interview tapes, scripts for role playing, and other training resource materials, to be shared across sites. In this way, each site will have a similar basic approach to training and each site's resource materials will be enriched. A lesson to be learned from this cross-site cooperative process concerns the value of sharing related interests among similar projects. In relation to assessment procedures, it would have been extremely inefficient to reinvent the wheel at each of four different sites offering a similar program, aside from data and evaluation considerations.

Monitoring and Reassessment

Ongoing monitoring and periodic reassessment of clients who are receiving long-term care services actually comprise another phase of resource allocation. Elderly clients' conditions and problems change over time, and such change requires modification of the care plan. How frequently should a reassessment be done? There is no easy answer to this question. In a fixed-budget program oriented to timely downward substitution of services, the incentive is to reassess frequently so that prescription is kept to the minimum appropriate level. However, reassessment is a program cost that must be weighed in the decision. The SHMO protocols have proposed that the scope and duration of all long-term care plans be limited and defined. The duration ranges from one to four months.

Several phases and types of reassessment have been devised in the Demonstration. First, HCFA has required that nursing home certified status be reconfirmed every ninety days. Second, for data collection and evaluation purposes, HCFA also requires a full reassessment every six months of all enrollees receiving long-term care. A cost-effective yet comprehensive method of reassessment will require an instrument that collects sufficient information but involves a shorter, more streamlined process than repetition of the full assessment tool. Third, all members will complete the HSF annually, to update basic information for the entire enrollee population, and to identify previously able-bodied members who may now need social support services.

The above processes will be made easier if case managers frequently update client records. The MSSP case-management program established a system requiring that every client record contain a top sheet on which all update information was recorded for the past month. At a glance, the current status of the client at any time was readily available. While an efficient and adequate information system is essential for timely tracking and monitoring of clients, a caveat on reassessment is in order. Transfer of information from records is only part of a reassessment process. The essence of reassessment is to step back and take a fresh look at the situation in order to reevaluate the person's health and social circumstances. Reassessment should always involve a face-to-face interview with the client and an updating of all health or social factors that might prompt a reordering of services and priorities.

Description of Site Choices on Resource Allocation

The following descriptions of the four demonstration sites are organized to show the choices they made on the key issues discussed above. The descriptions begin with choices on chronic care benefits structure, continue with targeting and eligibility decisions, and conclude with the prescription norms that the sites have developed. The sites' choices on additional services beyond the core package were covered in the previous chapter and will not be repeated here. However, each of the four state nursing home certification processes and criteria is examined here in some depth.

An important caution regarding the following site descriptions is in order: The amount of detail and the areas emphasized differ markedly across sites. In large part this is probably more a reflection of what has been written down by the sites and made available to Brandeis than of what has and will be done at any particular site. Thus the site descriptions should be seen as illustrative, not as comprehensive pictures.

Elderplan

Chronic Care Benefit Structure. In terms of the aspects of chronic care benefit structure discussed in the introductory section, Elderplan is offering a gross benefit of $6,500 per year that is "intertwined"; that is, it can be applied to either institutional or noninstitutional care, or some combination thereof. Coinsurance is $10 per visit for home and community-based services, up to a maximum of $100 per month, and 20 percent of costs for nursing home care, up to a maximum of $200 per month. The benefit is fully renewable in either setting for each new "benefit year"; that is, the annual term of the benefit begins from the point when the member first obtains a long-term care plan, not from the point the member first joins the program. These structural characteristics were outlined in table 3–1 and are summarized in table 4–1, which also affords a comparison to structures at other sites.

The Elderplan benefit structure puts some specific constraints on case managers' resource allocation. Defining the benefit on the basis of a twelve-month benefit period with monthly copay limits makes it possible if not probable that heavy utilizers (more than five visits per week) will exceed the benefit well before the year is up. Members will then need to go to self-pay or Medicaid spend-down status until the benefit is renewable. The monthly copay limit will cause a somewhat faster use of benefits than an open-ended per-visit or percentage charge and thus restrict the case manager's ability to stretch benefits across the full year through higher monthly cost sharing. These limits will impose pressure on case managers to find ways of monitoring and stretching out available resources for members who do not

Table 4–1
Structure of Long-Term Care Benefits at the Demonstration Sites

Structural Characteristic	Elderplan	Medicare Partners	Medicare Plus II	SCAN Health Plan
Annual benefit maximum (gross)				
Institutional	$6,500	$6,250	100 nursing home days	$7,500
Home and community-based	$6,500	$6,250	$12,000	$7,500
Maximum possible total annual value	$6,500	$6,250	$12,000	$7,500
Renewability of institutional benefit	Fully renewable	$7,800 lifetime limit	Only for a new "spell of illness"	Fully renewable
Benefit period				
Institutional	By benefit year	By contract year	By contract year	By benefit year
Home and community-based	By benefit year	By contract year	By month ($1,000)	By benefit year
Cost sharing				
Institutional	20 percent of costs to maximum of $200 per month	20 percent of costs	10 percent of costs	15 percent of costs
Home and community	$10 per visit to maximum of $100 per month	20 percent of costs	10 percent of costs	$5 per visit to a maximum of $100 per month

easily qualify for spend-down eligibility. Finally, because of the renewable nursing home benefit, the plan does not have any financial incentives for encouraging institutionalization of costly home care cases.

Targeting

Prevention and Self-Care Programs. Elderplan's outreach efforts will be organized around a health education–self-care program. Both GMA and Elderplan are committed to a conscious effort to involve all providers in this program. They see health education and self-care as especially important in geriatric programs, since most elderly persons must learn to live with and understand chronic conditions. By learning to care for themselves, they can maintain maximum functioning and prevent further deterioration. The Elderplan health education program will address the concerns of both the well and the impaired elderly. It includes the following components (Glazer and Snyder 1983; Zimbalist 1983):

Health education modules on many aspects of self-care, such as how to handle common illnesses–conditions–emergencies; medications that help or hurt; listening to your body signs and symptoms; nutrition; exercise; psychology of aging; adapting the home to changing needs; managing household chores;

Instruction in self-care activities, such as administering tests, examinations, injections, weight control, stress management, and physical fitness;

Instruction for family caregivers in home care skills, specific illnesses and conditions, the aging process, and other areas;

Support groups for individuals or family caregivers who are coping with chronic illness and disabilities;

Preventive interventions such as comprehensive medical assessment of all new enrollees, selective high-risk screening, development of medical risk protocols;

Provider sensitivity training and orientation to the tendency of the elderly to under-report their illnesses and symptoms;

Teaching and support for the educator role of all providers.

Chronic Care Targeting. In order to qualify for chronic care benefits at Elderplan, the Elderplan protocol states that a member must be: (1) "assessed as moderately or severely impaired on the Comprehensive Assessment Form"[2] and (2) "meet state medical criteria for placement in an SNF or ICF." It should be noted that even though chronic care services are restricted to the NHC group, a broader group of members will be targeted for case management. All members who are found by the CAF to be moderately or severely impaired, or who have been determined after the telephone screen to be "at risk," will be assigned to a case-management team. (The term *at risk* may signify an unstable social or medical situation.) These clients will be given immediate help if required, and they will be placed on a monitoring list. The list requires the case manager to make a telephone call to the client or family at least every three months. This is the first light-contact level of case management.

New York State's established prescreening process employs an assessment tool (the DMS-1), which requires a clinician to document the client's condition and level of need in relation to physical and mental functioning, nursing therapies, sensory impairment, and major medical diagnoses. The clinician's assessment is then subjected to a numerical weighting system and summed. A total score of 180 or above indicates eligibility for SNF level of care: A score from 60 to 179 indicates ICF level of care, while a score below

60 indicates ineligibility. High scores are assigned for the following conditions listed in table 4–2.

Obviously, an individual with any one score of 60 or above would qualify at least at ICF level. However, most clients who qualify are likely to score on more than one of these items. For example, a client who cannot walk is likely to need help with other ADL functions and would probably score above 180. Similarly, a client requiring intensive skilled nursing therapy would probably also require assistance with ADL and would most likely score above 180. The severely mentally impaired, who are extremely difficult to manage, would in most cases qualify at ICF level.

Since the DMS-1 form was designed as an assessment tool for nursing home residents, it includes no assessment of living conditions or informal supports. This limits its usefulness in assessing need for home care, but it is the only state-accepted instrument available as the Demonstration begins. Currently, the state is working on a new set of assessment instruments, designed for both community and nursing home residents. It is possible that these will be incorporated into the NHC process when they become available. Although an inadequate tool, the DMS-1 form will certainly identify the most severely impaired.

Elderplan staff project that the entire 5.5 percent of the membership who will be severely impaired will also meet these state NHC criteria, and that about 70 percent of the 12 percent found to be moderately impaired will qualify, for a total of 13.8 percent of the membership.[3] The proportion of total eligibles is considerably higher than at the other sites. This reflects the conservative financial planning at Elderplan (revenue assumptions assume

Table 4–2
Examples of Scoring of New York States DMS–1 Form

	DMS–1 Score
ADLs	
Cannot walk at all	105
Total help—dressing	80
Total help—eating	80
Skilled nursing care	
Parenteral needs (nights)	60
Cath/tube irrigation (nights)	60
Oxygen	49
Suctioning	50
Tube feeding	50
Bedsore treatment	50
Mental status	
Assaultive all the time	80
Needs physical restraints	80
Regressive behavior	60

less than half the number of NHCs) as well as the uncertainty all sites face in predicting the results of applying state certification procedures to broad populations. It should also be noted that not all of those identified as NHC will actually need formal services, since some may be managing with the help of informal supports.

A summary of the Elderplan eligibility determination process and projected outcomes is found in table 4–3, which also affords comparisons to other sites.

Prescription Decisions: Care Plans and Monitoring. The case-management group at Elderplan has not yet developed systematic prescription guidelines. Rather, the group perceives this as a developmental task. In the beginning, there will be close monitoring and careful documentation of all care plan activity. As an experience base develops, case managers should learn how

Table 4–3
Eligibility Determination for Chronic Care Benefits at the Demonstration Sites

Features	Elderplan	Medicare Partners	Medicare Plus II	SCAN Health Plan
Definition of eligibility	Must be NHC	NHC or "at risk of becoming" NHC	Must be NHC	NHC or "at risk of reaching that stage"
State certification process and criteria	Structured form based on nursing and personal care needs	Essentially same as New York (Elderplan) form and scoring	Structured form based on nursing and personal care needs	Loosely structured form based on personal care and nursing needs
	No consideration of home supports or alternatives		Considers alternative and informal care	Considers alternative and informal care
	NHC status based on point score thresholds for SNF and ICF levels		NHC status based on "high risk" of nursing home placement using a defined scale	NHC status based on clinical judgment
Proportion of membership estimated to be eligible for chronic care benefits[a]	13.8 percent	8.5 percent	5 percent	10 percent

a. These estimates are likely to be affected by the HCFA limit on enrollment of NHC members.

better to categorize members and to project utilization, with the goal of devising more formal resource allocation guidelines.

The care plan format (following the Channeling model) is problem-oriented. For each identified problem, a desired outcome is stated, with a time frame. The plan specifies the type of help needed, whether it will be provided by informal or formal help, plus frequency, time, units, and copay. A care plan cost sheet identifies unit costs and per-month totals, including copays.

The case-management director will review every care plan. A monthly care plan certification form for each client will be sent to the finance department. The form will list the services used, the costs and copays, and the amount left in the client's budget. Thus, a running record will be kept of how fast the benefit is being used. The case-management director will maintain a close scrutiny of these monthly forms. Institutional care can be used only if the client's home environment is unsafe, or unsafe in the context of the client's condition, or if home care would cost more than 75 percent of alternative institutional care.

Guidelines in the case-management manual encourage use of informal caregivers. Also, the insurance contract signed by each member stipulates that Elderplan can "reasonably expect" informal support services to be provided by appropriate family members at no cost. The self-care–health education program will provide support to informal caregivers in skills training, as well as emotional support through support groups. Community resources (senior centers, volunteer programs, and so on) will be fully utilized. Elderplan is planning to develop its own volunteer program during the second year of operations.

In addition to the close scrutiny of case-management practice by the case-management director and one supervisory case manager, there are guidelines for systematic monitoring. In addition to the National Demonstration requirements for quarterly NHC reassessments and biannual CAF reassessments, the monthly certification form will require the case manager monthly to verify services given, at least by telephone. Any provider in the system (medical or long-term care) who identifies a new problem or situation will inform the case manager. Ongoing progress notes will be made on the patient's record. A detailed list of client status items that trigger a reassessment has been developed.

Medicare Partners

Chronic Care Benefit Structure.. Medicare Partners limits the non-Medicaid chronic care benefit to $6,250 per year, with 20 percent copayment (see table 4–1). There is no monthly benefit limit, so here too the case managers will be under pressure to impose some limits, in cases where the benefit could well expire before the year ends. Unlike Elderplan, Medicare Partners states no monthly limit on copays, so that Medicare Partners cannot pay more than 80 percent of chronic care costs at any time. This reduces the pressure on case managers somewhat as compared with the Elderplan situation. Also, Medicare Partners uses the "contract year" rather than the "benefit year," so that it would be possible for an enrollee to exceed the chronic care benefit within a twelve-month period.

For SNF–ICF care, Medicare Partners imposes a lifetime limit of $7,800 (with 20 percent copay) for Medicare-only clients, which contrasts with Elderplan's renewable benefit. This lifetime limit could provide an incentive to encourage expensive chronic care clients to enter nursing homes. On the other hand, the requirement for admission review and subsequent reviews at regular intervals of all SHMO nursing home residents may work in the opposite direction, encouraging movement back to community services wherever possible.

Two additional features of Medicare Partners' benefit structure should be noted. First, in developing a volunteer program, as well as a caregiver support program, Medicare Partners is working toward maximizing such low-cost and informal supports to augment formal chronic care programs. Such programs may prove cost-effective in maintaining frail enrollees in the community and in helping to spread the limited formal chronic care services over a larger number of clients and for longer periods of time.

Second, the site was able to negotiate an agreement with Hennepin County for Title XX funding of chore and homemaker services for income-eligible enrollees. The SHMO will deliver these services, and costs will be reimbursed by the County Community Services Department, up to a maximum of $175,000 for the first year. This will allow case managers to expand the benefits for eligible members, since the Title XX services do not count toward the chronic care benefit limit. (See chapter 6 for a more complete description of this arrangement.)

Targeting
Health Education. In early planning discussions, GHI's Health Education Department was highly interested in the SHMO concept and perceived it as an opportunity to design some new health education programs based on needs of SHMO enrollees. Although some of the existing programs were appropriate for the elderly, department staff decided that substantial new development was necessary to meet the special needs of seniors.

Chronic Care. The Medicare Partners protocol states that eligibility for the chronic care benefit may go beyond those assessed as NHC and include some moderately impaired persons "for whom, in the judgment of Social/HMO case management staff, earlier intervention could prevent deterioration to NHC status." How far the case managers go in extending chronic care benefits to those who are not NHC will depend on whatever bases and criteria are developed for resource allocation—and on case managers' skill in managing the chronic care budget. In its protocol, Medicare Partners states that its experience in serving the moderately disabled group is limited, particularly in terms of the cost of their care and the preventive character of service for this group. It is not known if prevention will add costs, or in the long run save costs. Therefore, provision of care to this group will be approached cautiously until specific guidelines can be developed through operational experience.

Procedures for documenting and verifying NHC determinations have been developed with the county agency that is currently responsible for preadmission screening (PAS) of nursing home applicants. The assessment tool used for PAS and NHC certification is a modified version of New York State's DMS-1 Form. The modifications tend to add complexity, especially to the mental health status section, but they do not add information about living arrangements or informal support systems. This modified form is thus just as weak as the DMS-1 when used to assess community residents.

The scoring for each item differs only slightly from New York's DMS-1 scores, and the cutoff points are the same—that is, 180 or more qualifies a client for SNF level and 60 to 179 qualifies for ICF level. Some items are refined into more categories (up to 6) than the DMS-1, which provides only three categories for each item. This accounts for slight scoring differences by category. However, as in New York, the client with severe ambulation difficulties is likely to qualify at least at ICF level, as is the client who needs substantial assistance in dressing or eating, or who is incontinent, needs intensive skilled nursing care, or has extremely disruptive behavior problems. Clients with severe depression score 120, and clients who have minor depression, with a treatment plan, score 60. In New York, clients with severe depression are referred for a psychiatric consultation, the result of which would be taken into account in placement determination.

Training in implementation of this assessment tool is being held jointly with Medicare Partners case-management staff and the county case-management assessors, so that there is consistency in PAS decision making within the county.

For capitation estimates, Medicare Partners projected that all of the "severely impaired" (4.3 percent of the membership) will use their maximum chronic care benefit. In addition, a quarter of the "moderately impaired" (17 percent of the membership) will use approximately 75 percent of the benefit. In all about 8.5 percent of community enrollees are expected to qualify for the chronic care benefit, which is lower than at Elderplan but higher than at the other two sites (table 4-3). It should be noted that these figures on the prevalence of impairment are higher than the site's projections of community averages. That is because an agreement with the Department of Public Welfare (DPW) calls for 20 percent of enrollees to be Medicaid recipients, twice the community average. Higher percentages of the Medicaid recipients are projected in the severe or moderately impaired categories. Finally, not reflected in these figures are 150 nursing home residents who will be enrolled at the request of DPW. Both the state and the site are interested in improving appropriateness and cost-effectiveness of medical and chronic care for this population.[4]

Prescription Guidelines

A Client Tracking Model. In their planning phase, Medicare Partners began to develop a resource allocation model based on their prior experience in working with impaired elderly clients. The model has these main features:

Identification of subgroups of enrollees by patterns of service utilization and social–environmental circumstances (to date, four subgroups, or client tracks, have been identified);

Identification of key indicators that will flag the need for closer case-management involvement (for example; change to another track);

Development of thresholds for each track;

Use of the HSF, telephone screen, CAF, and provider feedback–referral to identify enrollees in each track;

Provider feedback mechanisms to case managers to indicate client changes that require further monitoring, assessment, change in care plans, and moves to a different track;

Specification of sample packages of client services for each track;

Cumulative assessment over time through monitoring, reassessment and recertification procedures, specialized assessment (nutrition, financial, medications), and ongoing provider feedback.

The site's goal is to refine this model through operational experience, especially in relation to more detailed identification of projected service packages and cost per track. The four client tracks identified to date are detailed below.

Self-Management: Well Elderly. This group will receive primary and acute medical services, as required, and will have their care managed primarily by their GHI physician, who will be the main source of referral should there be any change in the client's health or social situation. This group will receive information-and-referral services from case managers, if required. Indicators for more case-management involvement include increased clinic visits (more than three per twelve months); frequent telephone contacts with clinic or case management staff; and change in housing arrangements, social situation, or informal supports.

Low Contact: Impaired Enrollees—Stable Condition. These are impaired enrollees in stable situations. They may have adequate informal supports or have the capacity and preference to manage by themselves. They will receive a CAF, and they will be monitored from time to time by the case manager. Care plans for this group are characterized by utilization of services such as personal care, homemaker, chore, day care, senior companions, and home-delivered meals. Maintenance of clients at the low-contact level is seen as potentially delaying movement into higher-cost services, and maximizing independence. This level includes providing support to caregivers and treating chronic health problems as required. Some clients may move into this track after more acute conditions have stabilized. Providers and case managers will monitor indicators of changes in health, functional level, or social situation that might require more case-management involvement.

High Contact: Short Term. These enrollees require increased services for a short term (up to two months) due to new traumatic medical diagnosis, hospitalization and need for postacute care, or traumatic change in living arrangements or informal supports (such as the death of spouse). These changes may create a temporary need for closer case-management involvement. After the two-month period, the client's situation will be reassessed, and he or she may be assigned to one of the other three tracks. Key indicators for closer case-management in this track include repeated hospitalization, continued instability of medical problems, slow progress in rehabilitation, poor coping abilities of client–caregivers, and change in living arrangements–social situation.

High Contact: Long-Term Frail Enrollees. This group is characterized by an ongoing need for increased medical and community-based long-term care services or institutional placement. Enrollees in this group will be NHC and will receive a CAF. Where possible, such enrollees will be maintained in the community with provision of appropriate long-term care services and support of informal caregivers. Key indicators for this track are increased or continued need for long-term care services after an initial two-month intensive period, recurring hospitalization, increased use of medical transportation, fatigue and stress on the part of the informal caregiver, and housing arrangements that are inappropriate in relation to the person's frailty.

It is anticipated that operating experience will help to further refine guidelines in terms of cost thresholds by client track, guidelines for service substitutions for institutional care, typical service packages per track, and so forth.

Additional Prescription Criteria. In addition to providing resource allocation guidelines through identification of client tracks, the Medicare Partners protocol specifies further general guidelines for care planning. These include the following:

Involvement of the primary physician in development of all care plans;

Problem-oriented service prescription, with specification of objectives and time, duration, and scope of all services, as well as caregiver (informal and formal);

Exploration of care options with client and family, with case managers providing reinforcement and supportive services to maintain family caregiving, as well as use of volunteer services unit;

Use of least restrictive location with most cost-effective mix of services within the benefit package constraints; if institutional placement is being considered for enrollees, several criteria will be assessed, including the safety of the client's home, need for a more protective environment, and relative costs of institutional care compared with comparable community-based services;

Availability of volunteer services, as well as support services to caregivers, which have the potential to free up the formal chronic care resources.

Monitoring and Reassessment. Recognizing the importance of monitoring and reassessment activities as methods of maintaining timely downward substitution and least-cost mix of appropriate services, the Medicare Partners' protocol spells out in some detail its monitoring requirements. Since Medicare Partners is expanding the chronic care benefit beyond NHC enrollees, more case-management resources will be devoted to reassessment activities. This in turn provides added incentive to streamline the initial CAF procedure and design a reassessment form that requires a shorter interview and that collects as much information as possible from client records and other sources. Efficient methods of ongoing documentation and updating can simplify the reassessment tasks, and considerable planning efforts have been dedicated to designing an efficient MIS for case managers.

In addition to the standard semiannual home visit for reassessment, Medicare Partners will maintain monthly telephone contact with impaired enrollees, with their caregivers, and with SHMO providers involved with the client. Reassessment may occur whenever a change in the client's health or social situation so warrants, in the case manager's judgment. Ongoing review of SHMO nursing home residents will be conducted by facility staff in consultation with case managers.

Medicare Plus II

Chronic Care Benefit Structure. Table 4–1 shows that Plus II has by far the deepest chronic care benefit of the four sites and that the benefit is structured differently at this site. A $12,000 annual benefit is allocated to $1,000 monthly maximums for home- and community-based services. Thus the resource coordinators do not need to worry about benefits lasting the whole year; they have more to offer than at other sites; and the small 10 percent copay reduces the impact of the member's resources on decision making. All of these factors decrease the likelihood of members' spending down while living in the community. Also, the monthly-verus-annual definition of benefits makes the benefit year–contract year distinction less important. Kaiser made the same choice as Medicare Partners in enhancing the value of home care by making its institutional long-term care benefit basically nonrenewable. The same types of safeguards against inappropriate nursing home use will be applied.

Targeting

Outreach, Prevention, and Health Education. Within the Kaiser system there are various health education programs that have outreach potential. First, intrasystem provider referral is emphasized at all the Kaiser sites. Second, the HSF will be used to identify any problems that might need immediate referral to the medical or resource coordination systems. Third, like Medicare Partners, Kaiser is developing a volunteers program, with major emphasis in (1) networking among elderly enrollees and (2) outreach by elderly volunteers to other enrollees living in their neighborhood. Such a network structure has a potential case-finding mechanism. Fourth, Kaiser developed an active member representative program during Medicare Plus I. As will be seen in more detail in chapter 5, the member representative will assist resource coordinators in evaluating HSFs, will refer to medical providers and resource coordinators, and will work closely with resource coordinators in monitoring service provision.

Targeting of Chronic Care Services. Early in the planning process, Kaiser formed the assumption that about 5 percent of Plus II members would use chronic care benefits. The basis for this figure is the Medicare Plus I enrollment, in which about 4 percent of the members had severe mobility limitations. In order to stay within the limits of this utilization assumption, Kaiser decided to restrict chronic care benefit eligibility to those "at high risk of nursing home placement, as defined by Kaiser-Permanente using criteria derived from the State of Oregon criteria for placement in an SNF or ICF." In other words, since Oregon's prescreening form does not have a numerical cutoff point on the DMS-1 model, Kaiser chose to define the cutoff at a point consistent with its planning assumption. The 5 percent eligibility assumption is the lowest among the four sites (table 4–3).[5]

Prescreening in Oregon is performed with an instrument called the Placement Information Base (PIB). The PIB is a twenty-five-item client assessment tool that has been used extensively by several demonstration programs in Oregon. It goes beyond the DMS-1 form in measuring IADL as well as ADL activities, plus items on social activities and orientation, emotional control, and informal support system. Scoring of items involves a two-step process. First, each of the twenty-five items is rated at one of five well-defined levels, giving the rater a range of choices to describe the functioning level of the client. Then, for each item, each of the five scale levels is assigned a risk level, ranging through five risk levels from (1) nursing home placement not likely to (5) very high probability of nursing home placement. Each of the five risk levels has a detailed definition, which includes some estimation of the extent and reliability of help available from the family.

Only eight of the twenty-five items have risk levels that result in a "high" or "very high" probability of nursing home placement, and Kaiser selected only those eight items for its NHC classification. The eight items are listed in table 4–4 and a Kaiser enrollee must meet the "high" or "very high" risk probability level on at least one of these eight items to be considered NHC.

It should be noted that qualifying on one of these items is a necessary but not sufficient condition for nursing home placement in Oregon. That is, a client would not qualify for nursing home placement if an appropriate substitute home (foster home, home for aged) were available; if unusual help from family, friends, or community were available (as indicated on the PIB form); or if the individual had strong desire and capacity for living alone, as

Table 4–4
Nursing Home Certification Criteria for Medicare Plus II

	Comparable DMS-1 Score
Cannot walk, needs continuous assistance	70 or 105
Needs total help with feeding or intravenous feeding	50
Dangerous, violent, abusive, or needs physical restraint	40 or 80
Frequently confused or physically wanders	(Not scored) (40 in Minnesota)
Highly impaired health status, bedbound, needs full-time nursing–medical care to maintain vital bodily functions	(Oxygen—49; sectioning—50; parenteral needs—60)
Cannot manage medications, needs daily help	(24 in Minnesota)
Needs total help to use toilet or cannot use	(7 or 14)
Incontinent 3 to 5 times per week, needs help 3 to 5 times per week, or total help	(20 or 40)

well as strong personal independence (as measured on the PIB scales). Thus, unlike New York and Minnesota, Oregon assesses the availability of alternative housing and informal support before resorting to placement in a nursing home.

Of the four state level-of-care certification procedures in the SHMO Demonstration, Oregon's assessment instrument provides the most detailed definitional guidelines for the clinicians' decision making, and the site's requirements for NHC designation appear to be the most stringent. If Medicare Plus II enrolls a representative population, it is not likely to find that more than 5 percent of its members meet these NHC criteria.

While Kaiser's eligibility guidelines seem strict, the restrictions allow deeper benefits for those who are eligible. The tight eligibility definition may also reflect Kaiser's caution in entering a field in which it has no experience. Even the long-term care sponsors know very little about the needs and demands of the moderately impaired. Kaiser planners did, however, leave the door open for some testing of that broader area of chronic care, if their budget allows. Resource coordinators may allocate services beyond the strict eligibility criteria by administrative decision, and if the budget allows they will likely begin to test out this broader area as operations proceed.

Prescription Decisions: Care Plans and Monitoring. At this time, Kaiser has not developed any guidelines for systematic resource allocation through the care plan process, beyond the type of care plan formats used by all sites. These specify amount, scope, duration, and objectives of each specific service. The director of the expanded care benefit program is responsible for management of the chronic care budget. In order to assist the resource coordinators in the required close monitoring, a computerized data base was designed, with constant updating required. Although care plans may be developed in consultation with a team of providers, resource coordinators are ultimately responsible for the authorization. If home care costs exceed $1,000 in any month, the care plan must be reviewed and approved by the director of the expanded care benefit program. Thus, review and monitoring are the initial tools for controlling resource allocation, together with detailed, updated computerized documentation.

Kaiser places much emphasis on continual monitoring of all enrollees who are receiving the expanded care benefit. The resource coordinator is responsible for updating the patient status codes on the computer data base. Enrollees who require SNF–ICF placement will receive an admission review within four to seven days (as at the other sites) and will be reviewed periodically as appropriate. The resource coordinator authorizes continued institutional stays. Reassessment of enrollees receiving home care will occur periodically as appropriate, while monitoring will be implemented through frequent but at least monthly telephone contacts with client and family, and at least monthly information feedback from providers. The data base to be built up from these close monitoring activities on utilization, service packages, and costs (by types of impairment) will be invaluable in future development of resource allocation criteria.

SCAN Health Plan

Chronic Care Benefit Structure. SHP's chronic care benefit is $7,500 per benefit year and is fully renewable in both institutional and noninstitutional settings. Coinsurance is 15 percent of costs for nursing home care and $5 per visit for home care (with a $100 per month coinsurance cap on home care). Thus, the benefit structure constraints on providing chronic care are similar to constraints at Elderplan (see table 4–1).

Targeting Chronic Care Services. SHP's definition of enrollee eligibility for the chronic care benefit goes beyond strict NHC guidelines and leaves the door open for some expansion of eligibility based on clinical judgment. The SHP protocol states that enrollees may receive chronic care services "if they qualify for admission to a SNF or ICF, or are at risk of reaching that stage." This definition is very similar to the one used by Medicare Partners (see table 4–3).

The state of California's level-of-care determination is based entirely on the assessment team's judgment, based on client information collected with an eighteen-item screening instrument. This instrument's items relate to medical conditions; need for assistance with medical treatments, ADLs, and IADLs; existence of an informal support system and whether or not it meets the client's needs; mental and communication problems; institutional days in the past twelve months; preference of client and family for institutional or noninstitutional placement; and reasons for requiring a higher than current level of care. No scoring mechanism is used with this instrument, nor are there any defined rating scales. The method, as used in the MSSP program, was accompanied by extensive case-manager training and ongoing checking by an outside evaluator of inter-interviewer reliability.

In addition to the screening instrument, the state has provided written regulatory criteria for determining admission to SNF and ICF care. Criteria for SNF care include the need for constantly available nursing services; the need for observation and evaluation; medications that cannot be self-administered; and the need for extensive care due to physical or mental limitations. Criteria for ICF care include a medical condition that requires protective living arrangements with twenty-four-hour supervision; intermittent skilled nursing or observation to abate deterioration; prevention of acute episodes of physical or mental illness; or minor assistance or supervision needed in personal care.

SHP projects that its enrollment procedures will yield a membership with 4 percent of the people severely impaired and 10 percent moderately impaired. The planners assume that all the severely impaired will be eligible for chronic care. Using Triage II data that showed that the severely impaired made up 40 percent of the high-risk population (Quinn 1982), the site is also assuming that 60 percent of the moderately impaired will qualify, for a total of 10 percent of the overall membership (see table 4–3). Similar to Elderplan, SCAN is being conservative in its estimate of utilization rates, since reimbursement assumptions project only 4 percent in the NHC category.[6]

Prescription Guidelines: Care Plans and Monitoring. SHP's criteria for resource allocation are contained mainly in a case-management protocol in the form of guidelines and procedures. A central tenet of the guidelines is a protocol developed in MSSP for priorities in service utilization. It calls for case managers to explore services in the following order:

Exploration of the informal support system, the level of these caregivers' current participation, and any potential for additional involvement;

Utilization of any existing community resources (Title XX, Title VI, nonpurchased);

Utilization of purchased services (that is, through the benefit package).

This protocol serves to conserve program service resources.

The care plan format is problem-oriented and for each identified problem requires (1) a statement of objectives and desired outcome, with anticipated target date; (2) type of service and providers recommended (including informal caregivers); (3) units of service and time frame (visits and hours); and (4) cost and copay amount. The above is divided into nonpurchased and purchased services. A follow-up chart identifies each problem resolved (yes or no), with date; each service delivered (yes or no), with date; and changes in care plan, with effective date.

Another guideline concerns discharge planning. Daily notification (via MIS) of current acute care admissions will expedite the involvement of the case manager, who will communicate promptly with the relevant providers (such as hospital nursing staff) and implement discharge planning in a timely and cooperative manner. All operating procedures for case managers, with flow charts, are spelled out in the case management protocol.

The medical group monitors the well elderly, by use of a utilization review (UR) system and ongoing contacts with enrollees and involved caregivers, as well as by feedback from the health educator.

For the chronically impaired, all service plans are reviewed by the case manager at intervals of no more than one month. There is ongoing documentation and updating (at least monthly) of the care plan follow-up chart, which indicates the disposition of the previously identified problems and keeps track of any service changes and unresolved needs. Telephone contact with the client at least monthly enables the case manager to stay informed of service utilization and changes in client status.

For ongoing, active clients, an at-home or in-office visit is scheduled with the case manager every three months. Documentation that follows a prescribed format is required of all client–caregiver contacts, including changes in an enrollee's health or social situation, provider feedback, any complaints or grievance procedures, and all progress notes. Institutionalized enrollees (SNF–ICF) receive an admission review by the case-management team within four to seven days of admission, and thereafter at appropriate intervals.

Quality Assurance in the SHMO

Measuring and monitoring quality in the SHMO are especially important because it is a prepaid program. Prepayment affects both providers and clients. Although there is an incentive for providers to maintain clients at their maximum functioning levels, there may also be an incentive for management to encourage prescription of minimum service. From the client's viewpoint, once the premium is paid, client demand may increase. If this possibility is kept in check by the use of such noneconomic factors as long waiting periods or obscure service authorization requirements, clients may feel they cannot gain access to services they have paid for—which may in turn lead to client dissatisfaction and grievances. Even more confounding is the fact that in long-term care, the formal service system must interact with the informal one, in which quality is especially difficult to measure.

For the last two decades, measurement of quality in health care has focused on structural standards, process standards, and to some extent outcome standards (Donabedian 1966). More recently, it has been argued that outcome standards may not be an appropriate measure of quality in health care because medical outcomes are not necessarily related to provider performance (McAuliff 1979). In acute care, process measures have received the most attention. For example, utilization review and professional service review organization (PSRO) programs for the most part have measured the service quality in relation to local best practice and peer review process standards.

In long-term care all the problems of outcome-based standards are multiplied because (1) recovery is often not the goal and (2) most long-term care clients have multiple chronic diseases, a fact that makes prognosis even more difficult. There have been some attempts to devise outcome indicators for patients in nursing homes (Schneider 1980; Woodson et al. 1981; Kane et al. 1982). There are no reports of similar attempts to measure outcome in community settings. The problems associated with quality assurance in, or even measuring performance of, social services are even greater than those encountered in medical care (Wood 1978). There are no widely accepted process standards for home care services. How often should a person be bathed? How often should the care plan for a given client with a given diagnosis be monitored? Translation of needs assessment into care plans is currently more of an art than a science, with no generally accepted objective criteria.

It should be clear from the foregoing that formally assuring the quality of long-term care in the SHMO will require a major developmental effort. The following section provides a summary of the basic requirements for quality in the Demonstration. As the sites become operational, careful documentation of the processes of assessment, care plan development, and monitoring will provide the basis for building an information base that could result in development of more objective criteria and standards for measuring quality in long-term care.

Basic Approaches to Quality Assurance in the SHMO

Structure. Each SHMO plan must assure that every provider included in the system satisfies all federal and state requirements for certification and licensure, and that all professionals practicing in the system meet professional and licensure standards. This includes the requirement that all facilities providing basic and supplemental health services are either (1) certified in accordance with Title XVIII of the Social Security Act, or by the state where Title XIX SNF facilities are used; or (2) in the case of hospitals, accredited by the Joint Commission on the Accreditation of Hospitals (JCAH). In addition, each site must describe its relationship with the local PSRO or with another federal quality assurance entity in their local system. Finally, each site must have a system of medical records and records of long-term care plans.

Process. Mechanisms are being established at each site for ongoing execution of the following activities, in both the medical and long-term care components:

Peer review;

Utilization review;

Audits of medical care records and long-term care plans;

A system to manage enrollee grievances.

Quality assurance committees will be established for both medical care and long-term care. Provider performance in both areas will be reviewed, based on systematic data collection. Procedures will be established for taking remedial action when peer review determines that inappropriate services have been provided or that appropriate services have not. Finally, accessibility as well as quality of care must be reviewed. One possible option for reviewing accessibility is to administer comprehensive assessments to a random sample of persons who were not identified in the proactive targeting procedures.

Site Choices for Assuring Quality

The discussion of site choices for quality assurance (QA) programs begins with the two sites that include established, federally qualified HMOs, which have their own QA requirements. These sites can build upon existing QA programs in medical care, with which they must integrate their long-term care QA programs. The discussion will then move to the two sites sponsored by long-term care agencies that do not include an established HMO. These sites have built on their existing QA programs in long-term care and have then integrated quality assurance of their medical components.

Medicare Plus II
Medical Area QA Programs. Medicare Plus II will build on existing Kaiser QA mechanisms, which integrate features inherent in prepaid group practice with formal QA programs. First, physicians practicing in a multispecialty group are constantly observed in their work setting. The professional performance of Kaiser physicians is regularly reviewed and evaluated by department chiefs and other medical managers. Availability of a comprehensive "unit record" enables perusal of the entire medical record by any physician who has contact with the patient. In addition, formal QA programs are required by JCAH, including documentation of health services delivery in both hospital and ambulatory settings, while all Medicare and Medicaid clients are subject to PSRO review. The PSRO coordinator (QA nurse) reviews records of all clients admitted to the hospital. Care must be certified to be medically necessary, to be provided in the most appropriate setting, and to be meeting accepted quality standards. Kaiser's home health agency conducts quarterly audits of home care clients.

HMO regulations require that accessibility, as well as quality, must be systematically reviewed and that QA programs must stress outcome as well as process measures. Furthermore, the internal QA program must be reviewed by an outside entity (such as PSRO).

Kaiser conducts both inpatient and outpatient QA reviews in close association with utilization review. For example, some of the inpatient medical audits have involved management of anticoagulation; monitoring of the time from arrival at the emergency room to admission to cardiac care unit of patients with suspected myocardial infarction; refinement of the management of patients admitted for alcohol withdrawal; and development of standards for administration of proper blood components.

Outpatient QA is more difficult to perform, and at Kaiser many of the outpatient reviews have focused on an illness episode where hospitalization provided a focal point for pre- and posthospital evaluation. Examples are reviews of patients with: diabetic ketoacidosis, drug overdosage, complications of hypertension requiring hospitalization, cataract extraction, and breast carcinomas.

Currently, new methods of evaluating ambulatory care are being explored, such as systems of computer-assisted chart abstracting that apply predetermined criteria to medical care data. Abstractors enter information about medical conditions, drugs, lab tests, and procedures prescribed by providers. The computer analyzes the chart information against the criteria and determines what further questions need to be asked. This system is currently being pilot tested and will be explored for its applicability to monitoring QA in long-term care settings.

QA Programs in Long-Term Care. The development of QA programs in the long-term care component will be ongoing during SHMO operations. These programs will build on the current system of quarterly auditing of home care patients and the extension of computer-assisted abstracting, as described above, related to chronic care plans. However, this will require the establishment by long-term care providers of some standards and criteria for long-term care service delivery.

Grievance Procedures. Kaiser follows the standard HMO member-satisfaction procedure. Information related to Kaiser services and procedures is provided to all new members, and each member is assigned to a health plan service representative. The service representative orients the member to the Kaiser system, guides and assists the member in obtaining appropriate services, and receives member complaints. On receipt of a written complaint, the service representative determines the action required and responds to the client within thirty days. The written response contains the resolution of the complaint, the basis for the resolution, and notification that if not satisfied the member may request a review. The supervisor of member services provides this review. Regular reports of this operation are made to the management, medical chiefs, and hospital administration.

Medicare Partners QA Programs

Medical Area Procedures at GHI. Group Health, Inc., as a federally qualified HMO, must comply with the same HMO quality assurance requirements as Kaiser. Each medical department has established a QA committee to develop standards for care. The internal medicine department, for example, is developing protocols for care of the more commonly diagnosed conditions, listing criteria for diagnosis, therapy, continuity, and outcome. An overall QA department, in cooperation with each medical department's QA committee, examines a valid number of client records for their compliance with predetermined standards. Recommendations concerning compliance and noncompliance are reviewed, with accountability and feedback mechanisms overseen by the department head and medical director.

Chronic Care QA Programs at Ebenezer.. At Ebenezer Society, QA activities are coordinated by a separate QA department, which has developed minimum standards for record keeping and other procedures, as well as protocols for treatment of chronic care clients. The QA department regularly audits nursing home client records, identifies problem areas, recommends strategies for correcting problems, and reports on resulting changes. The community service division has a fifteen-member advisory committee composed of clients, family members, professionals, and senior community residents. The committee's responsibility is to conduct an annual review of all community programs. The review identifies issues, problem areas, and unmet needs, and makes recommendations for changes and future decisions. In addition, a QA committee consisting of the director of the QA department (an RN), the director of rehabilitation (a PT), an administrative staff person, and a medical adviser reviews clinical records quarterly on home care nursing clients and annually on all other clients. Case managers review all client records monthly to identify unmet needs or changes in a client's situation, and to review the care process.

QA in the SHMO. The SHMO QA program will integrate the two QA systems described above and add a component specifically for SHMO enrollees. The Medicare Partners QA program will involve at minimum the directors of the QA programs at GHI and Ebenezer and the Medicare Partners medical and case-management directors. This committee will monitor the assessment process, the quality and implementation of care plans, and the implementation of a comprehensive prevention and wellness program. The process will involve peer review, utilization review, client record audits, systematic data collection of provider performance and results, and written procedures for remedial action when appropriate. Contract providers will be reviewed by the Medicare Partners QA program through a process of client record review, conferences with the enrollee and family members, as well as implementation of structural requirements for contractual agencies.

Grievance Procedures. Medicare Partners' grievance procedures are similar to those at Kaiser. Formal complaints will be made to the GHI member services department, which will acknowledge receipt of the complaint within five days. The director will prepare a file investigating the complaint in relation to policy issues, decisions required, and the person responsible for deciding the complaint, and will collect the information needed to evaluate the complaint. This information will be forwarded to the appropriate decision maker, who will recommend a resolution to the member services director, who in turn will respond to the member within thirty days of when the complaint was lodged. Failing resolution at this point, the member may go before an appeals committee of the GHI board of directors, which is composed entirely of GHI members. The Medicare and Medicaid appeals processes are accessible at any time for eligible enrollees, but they will be encouraged to first use the GHI procedure.

PSRO Review. Both Medicare Partners and Elderplan, as Demonstration projects, have negotiated the "focus out" option with their local PSRO's (that is, the PSRO will monitor and work closely with the project, but will not be required to certify SHMO enrollees).

QA Programs at Elderplan
Medical Area Procedures. Since Geriatric Medicine Associates (GMA) is a new medical group, it does not bring an established QA program to the SHMO. Elderplan's SHMO protocol delegates medical QA responsibilities to GMA and requires that GMA set up an audit committee consisting of the medical director, one other physician, the nursing supervisor, the medical records supervisor, Elderplan's director of professional affairs (who is medical director of MJGC's SNF–ICF), and the director of case management. GMA providers will develop written protocols for preventive care, specific illnesses, and injuries.

The review process is as follows: the medical records supervisor will select a topic and review the appropriate charts for compliance with criteria. Each client will be listed as justified or deficient, with reasons given, and the percentages of acceptable and nonacceptable charts noted. Audit committee members will then discuss audit results, analyze patterns across criteria, and decide on action to correct deficiencies. The final audit is approved by the GMA medical director and medical group manager and Elderplan's director of professional affairs. Provider staff will receive audit summaries, including problems identified and action taken.

In addition, GMA staff members will present specific cases of interest at monthly meetings of medical providers. From these activities and from comprehensive computer records, a variety of organizational and performance indicators will be developed, such as:

Number of visits per enrollee per year by age, sex, and impairment level;

Number of hospitalizations per 1,000 members, by age, sex, and impairment level;

Rates for common surgical procedures;

Percentage of enrollees not making visit appointments in a twelve-month period, by age, sex, and impairment level.

Chronic Care QA. Elderplan has established a case-management systems review committee, consisting of Elderplan's general director, director of professional affairs, director of case management, GMA's medical director, a GMA primary care physician, and a physician extender. Thus, there is overlapping membership in the medical and long-term care QA committees, which reflects Elderplan's closely integrated system. The case-management systems review committee will monitor both utilization and the quality of chronic care plans and services, in terms of appropriateness, continuity, coordination, acceptance, and accessibility. Regularly scheduled case conferences will be held to discuss and analyze chronic care cases and the interventions used. This committee will be responsible for developing protocols and criteria for chronic care. It is recognized that this will require extensive development, since accepted specific standards for home care and downward substitution are not currently available.

New York State HMO Requirements. In addition to the above internal QA systems, Elderplan will meet the following state HMO requirements:

Twenty-four-hour telephone coverage;

Provision or authorization of medically needed emergency services;

Urgent health services, to be available on the basis of need within seventy-two hours;

Basic ambulatory care services to be available within fifteen days;

Nonemergency, nonurgent referrals to specialists to be available within thirty days;

Baseline health status examinations to be provided within ninety days of request.

Grievance Procedures. Like those at the other sites, Elderplan's grievance procedure uses the member services representative as the receiver and coordinator of member complaints. Unsatisfied complainants can make appeals to Elderplan's general director and to a grievance committee consisting of Elderplan's executive director, general director, director of professional affairs, and at least one Elderplan board member. Final appeal may be made to the state insurance department. The director of marketing will maintain a log of all formal grievances and complaints and their disposition, and will prepare periodic summary reports.

SCAN Health Plan QA Programs

Medical Area QA Program. The medical QA program will build on the existing QA–UR procedures of the Harriman Jones Clinics. As a medical group practice, the providers are under constant observation. Their professional performance will also be reviewed and evaluated regularly by HJC's and SHP's medical directors. As at the other sites, the availability of centralized, comprehensive medical records enables scrutiny of medical prescriptions and procedures by any provider having contact with the patient. In conjunction with HJC, SHP will utilize written protocols for preventive care, illness, and injuries. Medical audits will be conducted periodically by an internal HJC review committee, which will report to the HJC and SHP medical directors. Audit summaries, including corrective actions recommended, will then be fed back to provider staff.

Chronic Care QA. Similar to Elderplan, SHP will establish a case-management systems review committee to monitor the chronic care component and develop protocols and criteria for care in this area. Within the case management unit, staff will conduct a monthly random audit of client records in order to identify problems in recording or clinical treatment. This review follows a prescribed documented format (as used in MSSP). If standards have not been met, recommendations in writing are made to the case-management supervisor, who will initiate corrective action and monitor as appropriate the client chart, client progress, and/or case-manager performance, to ensure that the problem is rectified and does not recur.

Grievance Procedures. SHP's grievance procedures are almost identical to Elderplan's. The member services representative receives and coordinates complaints, and the marketing director oversees the process. Appeal can be made to the SHP administrator.

Some Concluding Comments

A concluding discussion can touch on only a few of the decisions and issues raised in this chapter. The following points address three of the key outstanding questions. The first two relate to benefit levels and targeting, while the third relates to prescriptions and quality assurance.

First, the sites illustrate two (of many) potential models for allocation of long-term care resources through benefit levels and targeting. Kaiser stands out from the others in that it has chosen to target benefits to the most impaired group only (those at "high" or "very high" probability of needing to enter nursing homes). By doing so, Kaiser can offer a deeper benefit ($12,000 per year) at a similar capitation cost. Of course, the targeting decision means that on the average the elders served will be more dependent, and average costs per case will thus be higher. The other sites have adopted more liberal eligibility guidelines that extend to the moderately impaired (Elderplan), to those at risk of becoming NHC (Medicare Partners) or to both (SHP), but this in turn has required lower annual benefits ($6,250 to $7,500). Thus these sites will have less to offer their most impaired members but much more to offer the moderately impaired. It will be important to evaluate and compare these strategies in terms of overall costs, nursing home utilization (a difficult comparison), and member satisfaction.

Second, only experience will tell whether the state assessment protocols are consistent with the sites' care planning and capitation assumptions. The initial review of the site and state protocols seems to indicate that there is some congruence. Since the state protocols have never been administered on a survey basis to a population, and since they in fact were adopted as measures after capitation assumptions constrained the targeting assumptions, the agreement would be a fortunate coincidence.

Third, the development of detailed protocols for prescription of chronic care services and for quality assurance in that area has largely been left to the operational phase at all sites. Only Medicare Partners has initial protocols in these areas, and these need further development. Each site is likely to take its own approach to developing these protocols, which will probably differ in formality, level of detail, and specificity. It will be important for the National Demonstration to document and compare the products and to try to evaluate their effectiveness.

Notes

1. Demand induced by being insured.
2. The definitions for these impairment groups come from the queuing protocol. See chapter 5.

3. These estimates were made prior to August 1984, when HCFA issued a condition for waiver approval that initial enrollment could include no more than 5 percent NHC members. It appears that the limits will keep most of the sites from serving as many frail elderly as they had planned.

4. All enrollment projections in this paragraph were made prior to HCFA's limit on the proportion of NHC members to 5 percent.

5. The HCFA limit on the proportion of NHC members makes Kaiser's target figure an upper boundary.

6. The 5 percent limit on the NHC category will constrain the site's flexibility to raise reimbursement assumptions.

5
Marketing and Enrollment

This chapter deals with the development of marketing strategies by SHMOs. A good marketing strategy deals with much more than just promotion or advertising. It should encompass a series of decisions about variables that can directly and indirectly influence consumers to enroll and stay enrolled in a SHMO. Decisions regarding product, price, and target markets are just as important in the development of the marketing strategy as are promotional decisions.

In general, a marketing strategy is designed to answer three basic questions: At what point of development is the organization? Where does it want to go? How can it get there? Developing a marketing strategy thus involves three sequential planning steps: (1) the conduct of a situation analysis; (2) the development of marketing targets or objectives; and (3) the design of a marketing strategy that details a set of interrelated activities to be conducted in order to reach the objectives specified.

Before addressing these points in turn it is important to point out that the overriding goal of the SHMO marketing effort is to attract and maintain a relatively representative or balanced sample of the local population. The balance must include both functionally dependent and independent elderly as well as both Medicaid beneficiaries and those who have only Medicare coverage. This contrasts both with previous long-term care programs and with the HMO Medicare demonstrations. Prior long-term care programs have served only the impaired, with a clientele numbering in the hundreds. SHMOs will also serve the well, with initial overall targets of 4,000 members at each site, reached through an open enrollment process. The Medicare HMOs did not face special requirements to serve the functionally impaired, and some even excluded Medicaid eligibles from membership.

A balanced membership is central to the SHMO model for two reasons. First, by collecting premiums from a balanced membership, the SHMO creates an insurance risk pool from which much of the additional long-term care benefits offered are financed.[1] Second, a key objective is to learn how to manage the long-term care needs of a full spectrum of the population. By enrolling a microcosm of the population, the Demonstration will shed light on the effects of targeting and resource allocation decisions on the utilization and costs of the whole population.

The overreaching issue in attracting and enrolling a balanced membership is selection bias. That is, will the case mix of members actually enrolled be congruent with the membership projected, or will they be either "sicker" (reflecting adverse selection) or "healthier" (reflecting favorable selection) than the target? While most of the initial Medicare HMOs seem to have experienced favorable selection (Eggers, 1980; Eggers and Prihoda, 1982),[2] this does not mean that SHMOs will follow the same pattern. The expansion of Medicare benefits offered by the HMOs was modest compared to what is being offered by SHMOs. There is reason to believe that the SHMO will be especially subject to adverse selection in terms of impairment status, since it offers chronic care benefits that are not available elsewhere. If selection were to turn out unfavorable, the insurance pool would be put out of balance and the program would be in severe financial straits. There would be more impaired members to care for than could be financed through premiums and acute care savings.

Since adverse selection was such a dangerous possibility, the Demonstration developed a direct control on membership balance. Sites are allowed to enroll by quota or queues based on impairment status. Because the size of each quota proportionately represents the local population, queuing should protect providers from adverse selection and the government from favorable selection.

The remainder of the chapter is divided into two sections. The first is an introductory analysis of the issues and options faced by sites in developing marketing plans. The second consists of descriptions of the sites: the situation they face, their objectives, and their strategies.

Introduction to Marketing Planning

The Situation Analysis:
Where Is the Sponsor Developmentally?

Situation analysis should be the first step in the development of the marketing strategy. If properly conceived and executed, the situation analysis identifies key problems and opportunities that the SHMO will face in attempting to market various services to various markets. Put another way, if the entire marketing plan tells the organization "how to get there from here," then the situation analysis defines where "here" is. Specifically, this includes:

Key features of the market the SHMO serves (or is thinking of serving);

Characteristics of the organization itself;

Characteristics of the external environment, such as competition and other factors;

How all these factors relate to each other to form potential marketing problems and opportunities.

In developing the situation analysis, each sponsor faces (and will continue to face) a series of issues and decisions to be resolved. These include identifying the specific types of information that will be needed and the sources for this information; specifying how formal and detailed the analysis should be and who should do the analysis; and indicating whether the situation analysis should be a "one-shot" effort or an ongoing iterative process. Three of the four SHMO sites decided that the situation analysis was important enough to justify a formal market survey. Planners at the fourth site—Kaiser—felt they had sufficient market experience and knowledge to forego a survey.

Market Segmentation. It is important to realize that the SHMO's potential membership encompasses a very heterogeneous population group. Members of this group will, among other variations, live in different parts of the service area, hold different attitudes about HMOs, have different care needs, and be seeking different benefits from their health insurance. In order to achieve maximum effectiveness in marketing, the SHMO planners must recognize these differences and develop marketing strategies that target specific subgroups. Marketers refer to the development of these subgroups as segmentation.

Kotler (1976) describes an attractive market segment as one that possesses the following four characteristics:

The market segment is of sufficient current size.

The market segment has the potential for growth.

The market segment is not "owned" or "overoccupied" by existing competition.

The market segment has some relatively unsatisfied needs that the organization can serve well.

Segmentation criteria should identify distinct groups, for the purposes of product design (including location), pricing, and the development of promotional strategy. Market segmentation variables are often categorized as geographic, demographic, and psychographic. However, because of the importance of functional status levels in the SHMO membership, this factor must also be included as a segmentation variable.

Geographic Variables. Geographic boundaries can be used by a SHMO to help define its local service area. Each of the current sites segmented its market geographically. Two criteria used in making preliminary decisions about service areas were potential response (concentrations of elderly) and the cost of providing services.

Demographic Variables. Demographic indicators are essentially objective measures that are believed to correlate with consumer interest, behavior, and service needs. Demographic factors analyzed by the sites include:

1. Age
2. Sex
3. Marital status
4. Household composition
5. Education
6. Religion
7. Income
8. Social class

The selection of the demographic variables on which to segment the market should be a function of the strategic decision at hand. For example, if it is more expensive to provide formal services to an individual who lives alone, then this segmentation variable should be taken into consideration when pricing decisions are made. Similarly, demographics can be used to improve the target efficiency of promotional campaigns. For example, Burnet and Wilkes (1980) found that older blue-collar workers responded better than other segments to an HMO's promotional material when the material stressed a concern over fear of illness. The central goal when using demographic variables to segment the market is the identification of which of these factors are most predictive of purchasing and use.

Psychographic Variables. Psychographic variables describe what the individual knows, thinks, and feels about issues related to the services being offered (Sapienza 1980). Often the information that is most useful to a manager is also the hardest to obtain, and this is certainly the case with psychographic variables. This fact offered a powerful reason for sites to conduct formal surveys. Variables may include lifestyle, knowledge, perceptions, history of use of a similar product, "stage of readiness" in making a purchase decision, perceived health status, and benefits sought from the product. Haley (1968) argues that the researcher's knowledge about what benefits consumers seek from a product or service (such as economy, convenience, prestige, security) is the most effective predictor of future buying behavior.

Functional Status Variables. Measures of functional status describe the capacity of individuals to live independently in the community. Factors may include mobility; capacities to perform personal care tasks (bathing, dressing, eating, toileting); and ability to manage instrumental activities such as shopping, cooking, money management, and taking medications. Since the SHMO needs to attract and enroll a membership that roughly represents the larger community according to these variables, planners need information on where in the community to find individuals of different functional status and information on the various segments' relative interests in and motivations toward joining the SHMO. Rough data on the incidence and prevalence of impairment are available from national and local surveys, but few sites can count on finding such data on their particular local areas.

Analysis of the External Environment. A critical examination of the SHMO's ment includes a study of characteristics of the organization itself as well as its relationship with the external environment. Chapter 2 analyzed the internal organizational situation, in order to see if SHMO sponsorship was consistent with corporate mission and goals. Here the purpose of analysis is to develop a better understanding of potential marketing problems and opportunities. In this regard, sites focused their attention on the following internal environmental variables:

Comparative missions of the sponsoring organization(s) and the SHMO;

Program–service profile of the sponsoring organization(s);

Advertising and promotional campaigns used by the sponsoring organization(s);

Current staff and facility capacities;

Community image of sponsoring organization(s);

Future plans that will affect the SHMO.

Analysis of the External Environment. A critical examination of the SHMO's external environment is essential to the identification of preferred market segments and to the development of successful marketing strategies. It is through the juxtaposition of external factors, internal factors, and market segments that marketing problems and opportunities emerge. In addition to information on the market and its relevant segments, it is particularly useful for the SHMO to gather information on the following three types of external environmental factors: potential competitors, governmental–regulatory activities, and local economic–social conditions.

Potential Competitors. Who are likely to be the SHMO's major competitors?

The answer to this question will clearly depend on the segments to which the SHMO chooses to market. Therefore, information on potential competitors should be developed along the lines of market segments, whenever possible. As much information as possible should be gathered regarding the market shares of competitors, their capacities to compete with the SHMO, and client perceptions as to the strengths and weaknesses of the programs and services of these competitors.

Governmental Regulatory Activities. Are there current or proposed governmental activities that will significantly affect, either positively or negatively, the SHMO's competitive position in various market segments? Examples of such activities are existing or pending demonstration projects in the SHMO's marketing area, possible changes in laws or regulations, and governmental agreements with other providers.

State Medicaid programs are beginning to move rapidly in developing multifaceted approaches to cost containment. Each SHMO site should be in frequent contact with legislative staffs and Medicaid program personnel, in order to stay abreast of proposed changes that could affect the SHMO. In particular, sites should obtain copies of any section 2175 or section 2176 waiver applications submitted by their state Medicaid agency.

Local Economic–Social Conditions and Anticipated Changes. Certain changes in local economic and social conditions can have important impact on the SHMO's marketing position. Factors to examine include changes in the supply and cost of housing, social unrest in the target area, and major population shifts and trends.

Assessment of Problems and Opportunities. The situation analysis culminates in the development of statements of marketing problems and opportunities. The primary purpose of gathering information on markets and market segments, on the internal situation, and on the external situation is to aid in the identification of marketing problems and opportunities. Identified problems and opportunities can then be used to develop well-focused and realistic marketing objectives and strategies.

Setting Marketing Objectives: Where Is the SHMO Going?

Although first-year enrollment targets represent important marketing objectives, it would be short-sighted to set only enrollment objectives, and to set enrollment objectives only for the first year. Some areas of the SHMO's business activities may not have substantial impact on first-year enrollment but may have impact on future enrollment. For example, lack of understanding regarding lock-in may affect satisfaction, retention rates, and image, which in turn will directly affect future enrollment. The specific marketing objectives to be discussed in this section are:

1. Selection of market segments;
2. Enrollment targets by segment;
3. Retention rates and member satisfaction;
4. Maintaining or strengthening image in the community;
5. Acquisition of better marketing information.

Selection of Market Segments. One of the most critical marketing decisions that each SHMO faces is choosing segments on which to focus its marketing efforts. These decisions can be thought of as hierarchical. For example, the first segmentation variable used by most sites was geographic location (for example, by certain ZIP codes). Once these decisions are made, each geographic area can be segmented by another variable, for instance housing type (senior high-rise, cooperative housing, public housing). Clearly, the extent to which a site chooses to continue such segmentation analyses will depend on the level and accuracy of its segmentation data and the size of each subsegment.

Enrollment Targets by Segment. Once the market segments are identified and quantified, it is useful to establish enrollment targets by segment. Once again, the situation analysis should provide useful information regarding: what motivates individuals to select certain health plans; the perceptions of each segment toward the SHMO's sponsoring organization(s); the size and nature of the competition; and the likely impact of the site's decisions about benefit package, price, and location.

Although little segment-specific enrollment data are publicly available from the Medicare HMO demonstrations, their overall rates suggest significant market penetration. With the exception of three of the Minneapolis sites (MedCenter, Nicollet-Eitel, and HMO Minnesota) all of the sites met or surpassed initial enrollment targets. There is some evidence to suggest that all three of the Minneapolis sites that did not achieve significant penetration rates had not pursued vigorous marketing campaigns (Greenberg 1983a).

It is also important when making enrollment projections to examine the SHMO's capacity to serve each segment. Experience at many of the Medicare HMO demonstration sites suggests that capacity is often a limiting factor (Galblum 1982). It makes little sense to expend resources on marketing to a segment that the organization cannot serve—or cannot serve well.

Retention Rates and Member Satisfaction. The long-run success of a SHMO will largely depend on how satisfied its members are with the plan.

Thus, high retention levels and member satisfaction should be considered important marketing objectives. Preliminary data from the HMO demonstrations suggest that SHMO planners can be very optimistic regarding reenrollment rates: Between August 1980 and June 1981, Kaiser had a 4.5 percent voluntary disenrollment rate and a 2.5 percent death rate; between April 1980 and September 1981, Fallon had a 5 percent voluntary disenrollment rate and a 2 percent death rate; and between July, 1980 and February, 1981, Marshfield had a 3.5 percent voluntary disenrollment rate and a 4.9 percent death rate. Data were not available for the Minneapolis sites (Galblum 1982). Although SHMOs can expect higher death rates (reflecting an older, more disabled population), there is little reason to suspect that their voluntary disenrollment rates will be any higher.

Maintaining or Strengthening Image in the Community. The more positive the image of the sponsor and its partners in the community, the more successful the SHMO is likely to be in meeting its future enrollment and retention targets. *The community* as an undifferentiated concept is not particularly useful for the purposes of developing image-strengthening objectives. What is needed instead is an understanding of the decision making of the members of the various market segments that the SHMO is attempting to penetrate. Once this is accomplished, the situation analysis can be used to identify major concerns that these groups may have about the SHMO concept or about the particular organizations involved with its development. The sponsor should also identify groups and organizations that favor the SHMO concept. The same type of analysis and objective setting applies to various governmental bodies who directly or indirectly can influence the future success of the SHMO.

Acquisition of New Marketing Information. The SHMO sites discovered that most of the information they wanted was not available. They decided to use market surveys only after a careful review of secondary data on market segments and potential competition. In the future, certain aspects of information acquisition would be ideally suited for multisite collaboration. This is particularly true with regard to information about how the elderly make insurance and health plan decisions and about what their perceptions are toward current health care coverage and delivery systems.

Elements of a Marketing Strategy

This section reviews six strategic decisions that a SHMO faces in developing a specific marketing strategy or plan. These decisions are:

1. How to enter the market;

2. What price(s) to charge;
3. What product to offer;
4. How to promote that product;
5. How to acquire better marketing information;
6. Whether or not to control case mix directly through queuing.

Market Entry Strategies. Market entry refers to how or in what form the sponsor enters the SHMO market. Organizations have three general options regarding how to enter a market (Hughes 1978):

1. Acquisition
2. Internal development
3. Collaboration

The Demonstration sites' choices on these options have been detailed in previous chapters and need not be repeated here. However, it is important to highlight some of the marketing implications of various organizational development strategies.

The major marketing considerations involved in an organization's decision to acquire a certain service capacity are its location, the attractiveness of its facility, and its image in the community. The key marketing consideration with regard to internal development is whether or not prospective clients in the relevant market segments believe that the sponsoring organization has the ability to meet their service needs. For example, Kaiser-Portland is not now heavily involved in the delivery of social and long-term care services. Nevertheless, it is well-known for the delivery of medical services, has experience in caring for an expanded elderly population, and over its forty-year history has been profiled often in local newspapers as providing innovative services. Kaiser hopes that it can expand its favorable reputation and image to other elements of care. Finally, collaboration is an ideal marketing strategy when two or more organizations within a geographic area have positive community images regarding separate parts of the service package or business. Collaborative strategies are being pursued by Medicare Partners and by SCAN Health Plan.

Price. The determination of price should not be simply a matter of "costing out" the service package. Cost-based price setting is conceptually flawed because it contains the implicit assumption that the average cost of providing a particular service package is not significantly related to the size of the member group. The method also fails to recognize the real possibility that price will influence demand (enrollment) in the SHMO. Nor should price setting necessarily be based only upon the average local cost of Medicare supplemental insurance plans. This cost may *not* be a good index of "the price to beat." Even combining these two methods (service costs and prices of local competition) will probably fall far short of an optimal pricing strategy, for the following reasons:

It ignores corporate objectives and strategies.

It ignores corporate financial position and attitudes toward risk.

It assumes rather than examines the reasons that people will join a SHMO.

It fails to recognize major differences in market segments.

Price is a factor that cuts across more functional areas of planning than does probably any other variable or element. Although this discussion will primarily focus on price setting as a marketing decision, the analysis will also attempt to show how these decisions must be balanced with other corporate objectives and constraints.

Corporate Objectives and Position. One of the most important short-run marketing objectives of the SHMO is likely to be enrollment targets or penetration rates, and one of the most important financial objectives will likely be to break even by a certain target date. A major financial constraint may well be the maximum "down-side" risk (that is, the maximum potential loss) that the organization is willing to face. The price level will directly affect achievement of each of these objectives, and it will *be* affected by the organization's attitude toward risk. For example, a sponsor that feels it is crucial to obtain a large market share quickly, and that is willing and able to absorb significant initial losses to do so, will set a different price than a sponsor that is cautious about the SHMO line of business and that has smaller reserves. The latter sponsor will likely give break-even objectives a higher priority than it gives enrollment targets.

Why Will People Enroll in the SHMO? If the sponsor cannot answer this question, then it does not really know what business it is in; it does not know who its potential members are; and it does not know who its *real* competition is. This makes it very difficult to properly determine a price that will help meet established corporate objectives. A Revlon corporate executive is credited with saying that "Revlon manufactures lipstick, but it sells hope." The SHMO sponsor is clearly producing health and social services, but what is it selling? Is it selling a better, less confusing form of health insurance? Is it selling easier access to quality medical care? Is it selling security against being inappropriately placed in a nursing home? The answer is probably yes to *all* of these and more, but for *different people.*

Before the SHMO establishes either price or benefit packages, the sponsor should begin to identify which of these needs it is primarily filling and how many elderly in the target area fall in each relevant service segment.

Initially, the Demonstration sites took rather conservative approaches toward projecting motivations to enroll and toward pricing the private premium. They priced close to costs; they viewed the medical insurance market as the competition; and they targeted segments and prices accordingly. Over time, SHMO sites should attempt to determine whether an individual's concern about being institutionalized correlates strongly with a subsequent need for large amounts of service on his or her part. If this correlation proves not to be significant, then marketing to those concerned about the problem may not result in serious adverse selection. Here again, having case-mix targets by distinct market segments is critical.

Differences between Medicaid and Medicare-Only Market Segments. A comparative examination of price and motivation to enroll is particularly important with regard to the Medicaid and Medicare-only segments of the market. The government's decision to allow the SHMO to enter the Medicaid market will be based on price, but the decision to enroll will not be based on price (unless the Medicaid program has established a significant cost-sharing program). That is, the Medicaid agency will be concerned with price, subject to benefit and quality constraints, while the Medicaid recipient will be solely concerned about product. Furthermore, the recipient's concerns or wants regarding product may be very diffierent from the non-Medicaid population. This may be particularly true of the "categorically needy"—that is, those eligible for cash benefits. These differences are important when considering case-mix targets by segment.

In establishing Medicaid prices, the SHMO does not have to be concerned about the price sensitivity of demand. Rather, it becomes an issue of establishing likely costs and bargaining on price. Clearly, the "trading region" over which the SHMO is willing to bargain should be a function of objectives and constraints as discussed above as well as the risk-sharing agreements that Medicaid is willing to entertain. From a marketing perspective, Medicaid price setting is an all-or-nothing variable. This is very different than price setting for the Medicare-only market segment.

Product. To a certain extent, the determination of product and of price must be done simultaneously. Hence, talk of product often creeps into the discussion of price. Nevertheless, there are certain product decisions that must be made without regard to the ultimate level at which price is set. The aspects of product that will have important marketing implications include the following elements:

1. Structure of the benefit package;
2. Facility location;
3. Hours of service.

Inherent in these elements is a *positional* strategy with respect to competitors.

Structure of the Benefit Package. Other chapters discuss benefit structure from the standpoint of service delivery and finance, but marketing must also be considered. When planners address the issues of the loading of the service mix, they must pay attention to the specific benefits that potential SHMO members are seeking. This is particularly true with regard to trade-offs between non-Medicare acute benefits and long-term care benefits. If there is a significant, nonimpaired segment of people who are really seeking greater protection from the economic consequences of functional dependencies, the SHMO could market a benefit package that is more heavily loaded toward services that are geared to these needs and still avoid adverse selection.

At another level is the question of shallow versus deep coverage for long-term care. The sites' long-term care benefit packages for Medicare-only enrollees currently consist of first-dollar coverage (with copays) up to a maximum level. An alternative to this would be a very large deductible (such as $3,000 to $5,000) with much deeper coverage (possibly the full cost of nursing home care). Important empirical issues are involved in determining the exact nature of the marketing, service, and financial trade-offs of shallow versus deep coverage. These issues should be systematically studied.

Another option is to market the SHMO to more than one segment of the Medicare-only population, perhaps by offering more than one benefit package. These different benefit packages could be the same price with a different benefit mix, or they could have different prices. Such multiple offerings present great marketing advantages, but they also present potential financial problems. These problems could occur if members were permitted to switch between high and low options each time their contracts were renewed. One possible solution to this dilemma would be to require some form of health screening if the member wants to switch to a higher option plan.

Location of Facilities. Research and demonstration findings suggest that facility location is an important factor in the decision to enroll in or disenroll from an HMO. InterStudy found that, of the people they surveyed who joined an HMO through the Medicare demonstration project, 64 percent claimed that convenience of clinic location was an important factor in their decision to join. Of the people who did not join, approximately 22 percent reported that *inconvenient* location was an important reason for *not* joining (InterStudy 1981). According to Wolfson and Diamond (1981), lack of convenient clinics was a reason why some seniors left the Fallon Community Health Plan. HMO planning guides suggest that a clinic should be located within a ten-mile radius of the target population. However, before using this rule of thumb, SHMO planners should attempt to convert mileage into expected travel time and travel convenience, with special attention paid to public transportation routes.

Another locational issue is whether to "mainstream" SHMO members, set up separate departments within existing facilities, or develop altogether separate clinics. Although this decision must be made in the context of financing, service delivery, and the larger mission of the sponsor, its marketing implications should not be ignored. Do the targeted market segments of the elderly population prefer to feel a part of a larger health system that serves multiple age groups, or would they prefer to have their own special center or unit?

Hours–Extent of Coverage. If the sponsor hopes to attract large numbers of the "young old" who are still working and have private transportation, then providing night and weekend clinic hours may be important. For the retired elderly, evening clinic hours are probably unimportant. However, what will be important to all market segments is the perception that when an emergency arises, the SHMO will respond to their needs rapidly and efficiently. Along the same lines, waiting time for nonemergency appointments will be an important criterion in the individual's decision to join and retain membership (InterStudy 1981).

Promotional Strategies. Perhaps the most familiar aspects of a marketing plan are the methods to be utilized to promote the product—in this case to enroll the target number of members across the segments selected. This part of the marketing plan is more than a set of sales techniques, however. It also includes activities needed to "raise the consciousness" of the local market with respect to the SHMO service system. It is therefore useful to separate the discussion of promotional efforts into educational strategies, product information strategies, product persuasion strategies, and member-retention strategies.

Educational Strategies. The first step in persuading someone to accept an innovation is building awareness. Recent studies reveal much ignorance and misinformation about Medicare, Medicare supplemental plans, and HMOs (Titus 1981; Greenberg and Doth 1982; Lambert 1980). It will therefore be essential to the success of the SHMO's marketing efforts in most areas to increase elders' knowledge about Medicare and Medicaid coverage, and their knowledge of prepaid comprehensive care.

These educational strategies can take the form of articles in newspapers, articles in state and local health journals, discussions with elected officials and local senior organizations, public meetings, and public testimony. Because credibility is essential when building awareness, the sponsor should rely on as many "trusted sources" as possible to aid in sending its educational messages. The sites have thus taken a community organization approach, by lining up support from the most reputable elderly advocacy and trade organizations in the community. This is a two-phased approach. First the sponsor provides information to those people and organizations to whom senior citizens typically turn for information, and the educational message is in turn delivered to seniors by these trusted sources.

Product Information Strategies. Once awareness is increased, the sponsor can develop more effective product information strategies. The objectives of these strategies are to convert awareness into interest, and to get people to consider the SHMO. This can be done by presenting the important elements of the model and showing how this option compares to the alternatives available. The sponsor should avoid the temptation to turn these strategies into instruments of persuasion. The long-run success of the SHMO will depend on the enrollment of individuals who understand the concept, its benefits, and its limitations. Product information strategies should pay special attention to areas that are of particular concern to seniors, such as the relationship of the model to existing Medicare and Medicare supplement coverage, the new chronic care benefits, as well as such potential disadvantages as the lock-in requirement. Information vehicles used by the Medicare HMOs (Galblum 1982) include brochures, speaker programs, open houses, health fairs, direct HCFA mailings, and discussions with employer groups. The SHMO sites are using similar approaches.

Product Persuasion Strategies. The next phase of the promotional strategy is intended to persuade people to join. Here the emphasis shifts from the straight presentation of facts to the presentation of images—positive images of the SHMO and perhaps negative images of the alternatives. Four persuasion strategies that the current sites are either considering or using are paid advertising, direct mailings, sales promotions, and endorsements.

Paid advertising is viewed by many as the mainstay of a promotional campaign. Indeed, many people get so carried away with its importance and glamour that they fail to put it into proper perspective. Advertising, when viewed as just part of an overall marketing strategy, becomes a matter of goals and decisions. Decisions that must be made include the following:

1. What message(s) and mode(s) of presentation should be used?
2. Which media should be used?
3. How should the strategy be phased?

4. How much should be spent on each element?

Many elders read local newspapers regularly and are also heavy television and radio users. Advertising through these media will reach a good portion of the local market.

Endorsements are another valuable persuasion strategy, but endorsement is really not a substitute for other persuasive strategies. Rather, it is a complement to them. The selection of whom to seek endorsements from should ideally be based upon segmentation analysis.

Direct mailing is another approach. If the sponsoring organization of the SHMO has a built-in constituency, that group should be reached by a "personal" letter from the president or chairman of the board. These mailings can either be directed at the elderly themselves or friends and family members of elderly persons. In addition, letters announcing the availability of the SHMO can be sent with benefit checks to all area Medicare and Medicaid eligibles over age 65 by HCFA and local welfare offices, respectively. However, this approach has its limits, since many Medicare eligibles use direct deposit systems for their Social Security checks and may not receive this mailing. Should sites prefer, they can arrange with HCFA to obtain a mailing list of all Medicare-covered persons in the target area and can then send letters directly, once the text has been approved.

Sales promotions were used by at least one of the Medicare HMO demonstration sites as a device to get seniors to try their plan. In 1981 SHARE, Inc., offered seniors three months of free care on enrollment. In 1982 the same organization began giving a guarantee of satisfaction in the first three months, or the premium for these months would be refunded. SHMO sites are not starting out with any such promotional efforts, but some have considered special rates for family enrollment and for groups, such as residents of large housing complexes and elderly fraternal or trade organizations.

Member Retention Strategies. Marketing does not end when enrollment begins. Once an individual is enrolled, the marketing strategy must change to a client satisfaction approach. Retention rates will be high if the member feels that the plan is living up to expectations and providing better service than its competitors. High rates of satisfaction will also mean lower promotional costs in the future, since fewer new members will be required. Also, word-of-mouth endorsements from existing members will lessen the need for paid advertising.

Several potential problems may lead to dissatisfaction with the SHMO. Among the more important are:

Lack of clear understanding about benefits and benefit limits;

Misunderstanding about lock-in and the use of Medicare cards;

Lack of clear understanding about out-of-area coverage and claims procedures;

Perceived (or actual) difficulty in getting appointments and long waiting time;

Feelings that there is a lack of concern on the part of the clinic staff.

Some possible strategies to preclude these problems include the following.

New Member Education Services. Problems of confusion among members about procedures, unauthorized out-of-plan use, and members' perceptions of a lack of concern can be minimized if special attention is paid to the development of new member services. Taking a cue from Kaiser's successful Medicare Plus I new member entry program (Galblum 1982), all the SHMO sites have given their marketing–enrollment representatives responsibility for providing newsletters, member handbooks, open houses, and telephone information services to new members. Some of the Medicare HMOs made special mailings about lock-in and telephoned out-of-plan users.

Use of Medicare Cards and Plan Cards. A major reason for the problem of out-of-plan use is that enrollees maintain their Medicare cards during their period of enrollment with the SHMO. HCFA will not allow provider organizations to take away the Medicare card or to laminate the identification card over the Medicare card.[3] According to Wolfson and Diamond (1981) there are several strategies for dealing with Medicare cards that are acceptable to HCFA:

Print the Medicare number on the member's enrollment card, and educate members not to present their Medicare cards.

Place a temporary clear plastic cover over the Medicare card with the SHMO identifiers.

Issue holders in which members can place their identification card *and* Medicare card.

Strategies to Systematically Monitor Member Satisfaction. Waiting until annual reenrollment rates are counted is a costly way to see if new member strategies have worked. The SHMO sites have considered developing one or more "early warning" systems to evaluate member satisfaction with the plan, including analysis of complaints, written member surveys, monitoring waiting times at the clinic and the time it takes to get an appointment, and making random calls to members to ask how they are doing and how the plan can serve them better.

Information Acquisition Strategies for Developing a Marketing Plan. There are a number of informaton acquisition strategies available to SHMOs. The decision as to which strategies to use should be based on the plan's information objectives, available funds, when the information is needed, how important the information is, and the required precision of the information.

Formal Market Research. Formal market research studies are useful strategies for developing better information about the needs and perceptions of members and potential members, and for improving understanding of important differences among market segments. Such research is ideal for attempting to identify and quantify new market segments. Activities can vary from reviewing published studies and conducting secondary data analyses on existing data sets, to conducting surveys or doing test marketing.

In regard to market surveys, some experts (Flexner, McLaughlin, Littlefield 1977; Leonard 1975) argue that the identification of issues or questions, and the wording of these questions, should be done by the consumers themselves and *not* the researcher. Thus, they suggest that prior to developing a survey (a quantitative technique) the researcher should use qualitative techniques to establish question content and wording. One popular method for obtaining this qualitative information is the "focus group discussion." The basic steps of a focus group are as follows:

A small but representative group of consumers is assembled, and a facilitator encourages consumers to express their feelings about the subject of discussion.

Discussion is on a focused question (desired benefits).

The elements or phrases coming out of the discussion form qualitative operational definitions of desired benefits and can be used for further investigation into priority of benefits.

Interpretation of the results involves transforming the phrases obtained into statements or judgments about each particular issue.

These statements then form the foundation for a follow-up quantitative survey (Flexner, McLaughlin, and Littlefield 1977).

The Elderplan and SCAN sites both used focus groups to develop survey questions.

Sites that do not have staff experienced in market research may wish to contract with a market research firm to conduct a marketing survey. This was the choice at three of the sites. Although prices vary widely, the experience of the sites suggest that sponsors can expect to pay $40 to $60 per fifteen- to twenty-minute phone interview, with a sample size range of 200 to 500. The above price range includes the cost of sampling, questionnaire design, data collection, data analysis, and write-up. In-person interviews are considerably more expensive, and mail questionnaires are considerably less expensive. If a sponsor chooses to do its own design and analysis, it can expect to pay a reputable survey firm $15 to $20 for a fifteen- to twenty-minute interview.

Data from the Management Information System. One point that is often overlooked is that a great deal of marketing information can be obtained on a timely, ongoing basis from a good management information system. The MIS can be used to compare actual segments to targeted segments; to track complaints, waiting times, unauthorized out-of-plan use; and to uncover other signs of member dissatisfaction. However, this type of information-generating capability must be designed into the MIS if it is going to be cost-effective. Therefore, the marketing staff should work with MIS staff when the MIS system is being developed.

Queuing. The goal of the SHMO marketing effort is to enroll a balanced membership on a first-come, first-served basis. Such open enrollment is mandatory on the part of the sites, and planners hope to achieve their desired case-mix through the traditional marketing strategies described above. However, since the SHMO is an untested entity, site planners fear that traditional strategies may not be sufficient. Therefore a queuing mechanism has been devised for the Demonstration to help sites ensure the proper mix of enrollees. To protect sites against adverse selection (and also to protect third-party funders against favorable selection), sites will be allowed (at their discretion) to queue applicants based on their level of functional disability and/or personal care needs. The distribution of these categories by functional level within the enrolled SHMO population will be representative of their distribution within the community, according to the best available data on the community distributions. Selected items from the application form will be used to accept or queue applicants by impairment group.

The queuing process will be conducted using a protocol devised by Brandeis and approved by the sites and HCFA. The specific queuing categories being used are as follows:

1. *Severely impaired:* needs assistance in activities of daily living (ADL) (bathing, dressing, eating, toileting, transferring) or is bedbound.

2. *Moderately impaired:* does not need ADL assistance and is not bedbound, but must stay in the house most or all of the time, needs the help of another person in getting around, needs a device (a cane or wheelchair) to get around, or has trouble getting around freely.
3. *Unimpaired or mildly impaired:* does not have trouble getting around freely.

The impact of queuing on marketing is not known. Since questions about health status on insurance applications are common, the queuing questions may not discourage the elderly from applying. Because of the marketing unknowns, the sites would prefer not to use queuing. In fact, two sites (Kaiser and Medicare Partners) will not use queuing unless selection departs significantly from projections.[4] If the initial enrollment period shows that queuing effectively controls case-mix and does not have an adverse effect on marketing, queuing could be an attractive option for future SHMOs to consider.

Some of the issues faced in choosing queuing questions and categories deserve mention. First, the queuing questions were used previously in national surveys of the elderly that related to mobility limitations (1972 Health Interview Survey; 1977 Current Medicare Survey) and ADL limitations (1977 Health Interview Study; Nagi 1976). Here it should be noted that these surveys were not large enough to allow an analaysis of local variations in the prevalence of impairment. However, the regional variations reflected in these surveys suggest that proportions of the total for the three queues will range from 3 percent to 6 pecent for the severely impaired, from 13 percent to 17 percent for the moderately impaired, and from 77 percent to 82 percent for the unimpaired or mildly impaired. By using the figures that apply to their regions, site planners hope that their targeted queue sizes will closely approximate local distributions. While local populations may differ in their impairment characteristics, small errors are not important in setting the sizes of the queues. It is much more important that the queues be consistent with the population assumptions in the capitation.

Second, in order to avoid a cumbersome queuing process, and also because of the goal of reflecting community distributions, the number of queuing questions had to be strictly limited. Adding more criteria would be difficult, since for each question the population distribution must be known. While some inaccuracies in the classification of individual enrollees will therefore be inevitable, it is expected that the queuing process will still be reliable on a population basis; that is, that errors will cancel each other out. The Demonstration staff will closely monitor and refine the process during the initial period of the Demonstration.

Third, the queuing system is not a health screen. Queued applicants are not rejected, they are only classified and (perhaps) asked to wait. The intent is not to "cream," but rather to represent the community.

Fourth, questions about acute care were also considered for use as queuing items. Fairly recent county-level Medicare data are available on such indices as hospital days, hospital admissions, and admission diagnoses. It was decided, however, that queuing on both acute and chronic care items would be too cumbersome for the Demonstration, and such queuing was not acceptable to HCFA.

Descriptions of Sites' Marketing Plans

The remainder of the chapter summarizes the marketing plans actually devised by each of the four sites. Attention is paid to the issues discussed above, and the descriptions follow the three-stage analytical framework already suggested: situation analysis, objective setting, and strategy development. To the extent possible, comparative information has been gathered and displayed in tables.

Elderplan

Situation Analysis. Elderplan is situated in southwest Brooklyn, New York City's largest borough and the home of nearly 280,000 elderly persons. Early in the planning process Elderplan decided to focus its marketing efforts on seven nearby ZIP code areas with a total of 82,017 elderly persons who are eligible for Medicare. The target area consists of elders who are on average somewhat older and wealthier than these in the borough at large. Forty-two percent are over age 75, as compared to 38 percent in the borough, and 11.5 percent are on Medicaid, as compared to 21 percent in the borough. Many white ethnics have been moving out of central Brooklyn into the southwest section, where the elderly population, though declining slightly, is becoming increasingly middle class. These target area characteristics can be compared to other sites in table 5–1.

In creating Elderplan, MJGC's objective is to reach out to the general senior citizens market. MJGC itself intends to continue providing care to the chronically impaired, while Elderplan will be the coordinator of a broad range of services to both the well and the impaired. If the SHMO proves to be successful, the long-term goals for it include increased membership, an expansion of acute and long-term care coverage, a broadening of the market area (perhaps into noncontiguous areas), an increase in the number of ambulatory patient clinics, and a role as service provider to other home care providers.

The site planners view the external environment as generally favorable

Table 5–1
Characteristics of SHMO Site Market Areas

	Elderplan	Medicare Plus II	Medicare Partners	SCAN Health Plan
Market area	7 ZIP code areas in Brooklyn, New York	Multnomah County, Oregon (Portland)	Hennepin County, Minnesota (Minneapolis)	27 ZIP code areas in Orange and Los Angeles counties surrounding Long Beach, California
Number of elderly in market area	82,000	78,000	100,000	85,000
Proportion of elderly age 75 and older	42 percent	44 percent	46 percent	44.3 percent
Proportion Medicaid eligible	11.5 percent	N.A.	9 percent	20 percent
HMO penetration in elderly market	N.A. (but less than 5 percent)	17 percent (almost all in Kaiser)	16 percent (and growing fast)	10 to 15 percent (and growing)

to the development of Elderplan. The governmental bureaucracy is complex and highly regulatory, but MJGC has experience in negotiating it. The strongest health care competition comes from standard insurance supplements to Medicare, with monthly premiums of $20.27 (1982) for the low-option Blue Cross–Blue Shield (that is, a buy-out of Medicare copays and deductibles only), $50 or more for high option plans (including drugs and other extras, but not long-term care). HMO competition is essentially limited to the large Health Insurance Plan of greater New York (HIP), which serves more than 80,000 elderly in the New York area in a cost contract (largely age-ins), and another 11,000 persons in a Medicare 95-percent-risk contract. However, the HIP risk contract is a low-option, low-premium ($15) plan; its activities in the market area are limited; and HIP has a relatively weak reputation in the area.

In summary, the site's initial assessment of its situation includes both pluses and minuses. Among the perceived advantages are MJGC's positive experience and reputation, its good relationships with governmental and community organizations, the development of a quality geriatric medical group with a Cornell affiliation, relatively good benefits, a shortage of physicians in the target area, and good relationships with the media. Potential marketing problems include MJGC's image in non-Jewish communities, MJGC's lack of experience with acute care, the novelty of HMOs in New York City, the strength of fee-for-service medical establishment and possible hostility from fee-for-service physicians, and Elderplan's status as a demonstration project. Additionally, the initial assessment identified a variety of gaps in the MJGC's knowledge of the local elderly population's health care consumption patterns and preferences. This provided the motivation for the market survey, which will be described below.

Marketing Objectives. Prior to conducting its market survey, Elderplan set some basic objectives for the enrollment of particular market segments. First, it segmented the Medicaid and Medicare-only markets. It set the objective of enrolling more than the local share of Medicaid elderly by choosing the overall Brooklyn average of 21 percent. This target was agreeable to the state and city Medicaid officials, who wanted to see their beneficiaries served in the SHMO system; and it was agreeable to the site, since the Medicaid market contains a greater proportion of the impaired, and the Medicaid rate is designed to cover their full costs of care. (See table 5–2 for impairment segmentation data by Medicaid status.) The city Medicaid agency had some data concerning beneficiaries' service use that indicated that Elderplan might be attractive to this segment. The data showed that very few elderly Medicaid beneficiaries were enrolled in HMOs but that 30 percent to 39 percent of them in the targeted ZIP code areas used hospital outpatient departments. Elderplan should be able to capitalize on these preferences by offering the credibility of a full-service clinic but with easier access to physicians because of scheduled appointments.

Elderplan's targets for the Medicare-only segment of the market were initially based on the experience of the Medicare HMO demonstrations. Data from these programs showed that the best targets for enrollment were males age 65 to 74, in part because they were most likely to be married, to be in fairly good health, and to have adequate income to pay the premium. Data also showed that the Medicare-only elderly were less likely to be functionally impaired (see table 5–2). The next step in segmenting the Medicare-only market was to identify ZIP code areas where the most likely enrollees resided and to analyze the public transportation systems connecting these areas with the clinic site. Elderplan will be queuing both Medicaid and Medicare-only segments according to the case-mix targets in table 5–2.

The site viewed the data from the Minneapolis HMOs as the best source from which to project enrollment and disenrollment rates. The similarities in terms of demographics and urban setting were deemed important, although clear differences were noted in terms of how established the HMO concept was in each area, provider reputations, and the availability of word-of-mouth marketing through younger members. In any case, the site had three projections as to when the full enrollment of 4,000 members would be reached, ranging from "cautious" (sixteen months based on non-SHARE HMOs), to "prudent" (twelve months adjusting "cautious" for seasonal

Table 5–2
Case-Mix for Medicaid and Medicare-Only Segments[a]

Site and Impairment Groups	Number and Percentages of Members					
	Medicare-Only		Medicaid		Total	
	Percentage	Number	Percentage	Number	Percentage	Number
Medicare Partners						
Severely impaired	3.4	109	8.9	58	4.3	167
Moderately impaired	13.6	435	33.7	219	17.0	654
"Well" or mildly impaired	83.0	2,256	57.4	373	78.7	3,029
Totals	100.0	3,200	100.0	650[b]	100.0	3,850[b]
Elderplan						
Severely impaired	4.2	134	10.2	86	5.5	220
Moderately impaired	7.7	243	28.2	237	12.0	480
"Well" or mildly impaired	88.1	2,783	61.5	517	82.5	3,300
Totals	100.0	3,160	99.9	840	100.0	4,000
Medicare Plus II						
Nursing home certifiable	5.0	195	c	c	c	c
Noncertifiable	95.5	3,325	c	c	c	c
Totals	100.0	3,500	c	500	c	4,000
SCAN Health Plan						
Severely impaired	4.0	128	4.0	32	4.0	160
Moderately impaired	10.0	320	10.0	80	10.0	400
"Well" or mildly impaired	86.0	2,752	86.0	688	86.0	3,440
Totals	100.0	3,200	100.0	800	100.0	4,000

a. The 5 percent limit on the proportion of NHC members at enrollment may reduce the proportions of impaired at most sites below the figures in this table.

b. Medicare Partners will also enroll 150 Medicaid eligibles who reside in nursing homes.

c. Kaiser distributions have not been established.

factors), to "optimistic" (ten months). Disenrollment was cautiously projected at 6 percent for deaths and 6 percent voluntary (the Medicare HMO voluntary rates cited above ranged between 3.5 percent and 5 percent). These figures can be compared to other sites in table 5–3.

In addition to enrollment targets, Elderplan set a series of other objectives. Several of them related to establishing and maintaining good relationships with media, community groups, and public officials. Most of them concerned the development of operational systems, such as queuing, MIS, marketing materials, enrollment, member relations, and satisfaction monitoring.

Table 5–3
Enrollment and Marketing Data

	Elderplan	Medicare Partners	Medicare Plus II	SCAN Health Plan
Monthly enrollment rate	333	233	400	300
Annual disenrollment rates				
Death	6 percent	N.A.	2.6 percent	N.A.
Dropouts	6 percent	N.A.	5.3 percent	N.A.
Total	12 percent	4.8 percent	7.9 percent	
Monthly private premiums (1984)	$29.89	$29.50	$47.00	$40.00

Elderplan Marketing Strategies. Elderplan describes its marketing strategy as both "geographical and segmental." Entering the market through Geriatric Medicine Associates is expected to be plus in southwest Brooklyn, where there is a physician shortage. Site planners expect that the population will recognize the value of being served by geriatricians in a high quality system.

The segmentation analysis is based on identifying and responding to the elderly's perceived needs and dissatisfactions with current care and coverage. In the marketing plan, special attention is paid to obtaining psychographic information, which will be used to support a "positioning" of Elderplan in the competitive market along ten dimensions:

> (1) core benefit diversity; (2) size of ambulatory care center and range of subscribers served; (3) image distinctiveness of Elderplan; (4) price competitiveness; (5) convenience for subscribers; (6) service quality; (7) innovativeness of Elderplan; (8) lifestyle awareness regarding our market segments; (9) Elderplan dependability; and (10) community identification (i.e. the definition of Elderplan as a community-based organization) (Salisbury 1983).

In general terms, the Elderplan marketing plan compares the program's intended image to that of

> other high quality retail merchants who provide a comprehensive product line for a specific market segment. . . . We are trying to provide the best in health care services at a lower cost in money and time for our subscribers. Health care is a non-profit *business* for Elderplan and the analogy to retailing is apt because successful retailers respect and cherish their clients (Salisbury 1983).

Like the other SHMO sites, Elderplan contrasts its basic marketing approach to the mass media approaches used by most of the Medicare

HMOs. The Elderplan marketing effort will be locally oriented and aimed at groups and individuals. Resources to be used include:

The influence of board members who represent important senior citizen organizations (for example the commissioner of the New York City Department for the Aging and the chairperson of the Brooklyn Borough-Wide Inter-Agency Council on Aging;

Video and slide presentations to local groups (Eli Wallach, the actor, narrates a ten-minute video);

Direct mailings using lists obtained from HCFA, Medicaid, the motor vehicle bureau, and other sources;

Health fairs and open houses;

Advertisements in local newspapers.

The marketing staff is headed by a director of marketing and member services, who has experience in private sector marketing to the elderly. He will be assisted by an enrollment representative and trained volunteers.

The Medicaid marketing effort has been developed jointly with city and state agencies. The general approach will be: (1) Medicaid will mail an announcement on the availability of Elderplan (including a special brochure); (2) Elderplan will train Medicaid caseworkers to present the program; and (3) the Elderplan marketing team will follow up on both efforts.

The intent for all segments is to market in small groups and to establish personal contact with each enrollee. This will allow informed, nonpressured decisions to join and will also allow early identification of impaired applicants. All applications will be initialed by a member services representative to certify that all program features have been explained to the member. In these presentations as well as in mailings, Elderplan will distribute a basic brochure (laid out clearly and set in large type) on the decision process the elderly person should follow in weighing the alternative to join. The brochure will include questions and answers and will explicitly outline the program's pluses and minuses. The marketing themes include "Elderplan takes the worry out of Medicare and adds health to your years." "Elderplan is your partner in good health." "Medicare is good as far as it goes, but it doesn't go far enough." Marketing to Medicaid beneficiaries will emphasize personal attention and six months of guaranteed eligibility. The emphasis concerning long-term care will be on extra home support and prevention services, not nursing home benefits. Once applicants have joined, Elderplan will conduct a new member orientation program.

Survey Findings. Elderplan's market survey was conducted in the summer of 1983 by a private firm. Survey questions were developed through focus groups. The firm used a reverse directory method to scientifically locate 589 eligible elderly, 410 of whom agreed to be interviewed over the phone (amounting to a 70 percent response rate). The sample was demographically similar to the market area, but data were weighted for analysis, for an even closer fit.

In general, the survey found some dissatisfaction with current insurance coverage as well as a strong market for the SHMO. The most common areas of dissatisfaction with Medicare (on a three-point scale) concerned high hospital and physician costs (expressed by about 30 percent of those with opinions). The most frequent dissatisfaction with supplemental coverage concerned the cost of monthly premiums (expressed by 30 percent).

When the survey researcher explained the SHMO and outlined premium options ranging from $30 to $40 per month, 19 percent of the respondents said they would join under at least one of the options outlined, 14 percent were uncertain, and 67 percent said they would not join. Fourteen percent said they would be willing to take at least one option *and* change their physician and insurance coverage. Among the interested and uncertain, the strongest identified market was for a premium below $30 per month (hence Elderplan's $29.89 premium). The segments of the elderly population that showed the strongest relative interest were the younger age groups, those with incomes above $10,000 per year, the less impaired, and those who were "relatively more healthy" on an index constructed by the survey analysts. It should be noted that a discriminant analysis determined that the relationship between interest and health status was an artifact of the correlations between interest and age and income. (The Elderplan marketing survey can be compared to other site surveys in table 5–4.)

Elderplan planners believe that these survey findings point to the market feasibility of the plan. The 14 percent who would join and change current arrangements represent 11,000 people in the target area, and the undecided represent an additional market. Research that is under consideration for the future includes finding out what people dislike about their Blue Cross coverage, what separates the interested from the uninterested, and what special needs exist among the 13 percent of the sample who said they were functionally impaired.

Medicare Partners

The Situation in the Twin Cities Area. The outstanding feature of Minnesota's Twin Cities area is its highly developed and highly competitive HMO market. Four HMOs have been in the elderly market since early to mid-1981 under the first round of the Medicare HMO demonstration, and two more (including Group Health) entered more recently in the second round.

Table 5–4
Selected Results of Site Marketing Surveys

	Elderplan	Medicare Partners	SCAN Health Plan
Type of survey	Telephone	Telephone	Mail
Eligibles contacted	589	352	20,852
Completed surveys	410	309	1,200
Response rate	70%	88%	6%
Areas of dissatisfaction with Medicare			
Hospital costs and coverage	30%	6%	n.a.
Physician costs	30%	10%	n.a.
Paperwork	15%	8%	n.a.
Areas of dissatisfaction with supplemental coverage			
Costs	30%	14%	n.a.
Proportion of respondents who would join SHMO under at least one cost or benefit option outlined	19%	27%	60% (18% in telephone follow-up)
Proportion who would join under at least one option *and* change insurance and physician	14%	8%	38%
Demographic and health status characteristics that distinguish those more interested in joining	Younger; Higher income; Less impaired; Relatively more healthy (on an index)	Slightly greater interest among relatively more healthy (on an index)	Younger; Moderate income; Higher out-of-pocket costs for insurance and expenses; Males

Among them, these HMOs had enrolled nearly 30,000 elderly persons as of March 1983, for a penetration rate of 15.6 percent in the Twin Cities area and 16 percent of Hennepin County's 100,000 elderly persons.[5] In addition, the SHMO faces acute care competition from standard Medicare supplementation insurance.

The HMO market is also highly competitive in terms of costs and promotional efforts. All plans offer a basic and high-option benefit package, with the high option structured to be significantly more attractive (for example, covering 365 as opposed to ninety days of hospital care, routine and preventive physicians visits, immunizations, eye exams) at an additional premium of only a few dollars a month. High-option premiums at all plans ranged between $18.50 and $21.95 for 1983, the exception being $32.84 for membership in an independent practice association (IPA) that allows members to keep their own physician. The SHMO has a benefits advantage over all the other plans in that only one of them includes prescription drugs (at an additional $6 premium) and none includes long-term care. The HMO plans have used extensive radio, television, and newspaper advertising, open houses, endorsements, and in some cases promotional gimmicks such as money-back guarantees and free initial premiums.

A wild card in the market is the fact that HCFA has allowed these HMO plans to use health screening in offering their high option benefits. This arrangement was negotiated by Interstudy, the local initiator and coordinator of the HMO demonstration in the Twin Cities. The health screening means that the HMOs may not only have siphoned off a large proportion of the healthier elderly interested in HMOs, but may have also left a substantial group of relatively unhealthy elderly still waiting to join a plan without such health screening. The HMO health screening has created some controversy in the well-organized Twin Cities senior citizens community, and Medicare Partners' initial assessment was that GHI was wise from a public relations standpoint to have steered clear of the initial round of the HMO demonstration.

However, since GHI's entry into the prepaid elderly market in April 1984 was through the InterStudy demonstration, GHI is also following the high-option–basic-option model and is using health screening for the former. As was pointed out in chapter 2, this has created some tension between the partners, since staff at Ebenezer fear the screening will create adverse selection for the SHMO. The variable selection accord (see chapter 2) will shift more of the risk to GHI if this turns out to be the case, but this will still leave substantial risk for Ebenezer, and Ebenezer will have no chance to share in any savings that GHI may realize through favorable selection on the 95 percent risk business.

In addition to these complications in the acute care market, there are uncertainties in the chronic care sector. For many years, Ebenezer has had a long-term care counterpart in St. Paul (Ramsey County) called the Wilder Foundation. Concurrent with Ebenezer's efforts to develop the SHMO, Wilder has for the past two years been organizing the Senior Health Plan, a prepaid joint venture with acute care providers that will offer a full medical package plus case management for long-term care. While Senior Health Plan will thus offer fewer contractual long-term care benefits than will Medicare Partners, a significant amount of free chronic care will apparently be available from Wilder providers, since the Foundation is very well-endowed.

The opportunities for expansion and more stable and substantial financing through comprehensive prepaid systems obviously offer some attractions for these long-term care agencies, but there are also clear dangers and uncertainties in this highly competitive and fluid market. Since being left out of new developments is potentially the greatest danger of all, both are going forward.

Despite the competition and uncertainties, Ebenezer and GHI feel that the SHMO can be sold in the market (but "not easily," according to the site market plan). The plan assumes that the value of basic Medicare benefits will continue to decline, that the prepaid market will continue to grow, that there are needs unmet by the competition, and that the two sponsors can draw on a lot of goodwill, based on their long histories and fine reputations in the community.

Medicare Partners Marketing Objectives. The largest target segments for the Medicare Partners market are within the Ebenezer and GHI networks. The marketing plan calls for GHI to convert 600 cost contract members. Ebenezer plans to enroll 550 through its constituencies, including its sponsoring churches. Projections are that another 800 will come through Medicaid, and the remaining 2,050 are expected from the general public. The sponsors expect some conversions from other HMOs, but there are no specific projections or plans for reaching this segment. It should be noted that the GHI conversion and internal constituency projections have become problematic with the delay in SHMO start-up and GHI's risk contract marketing.

Table 5–2 shows that Medicare Partners makes assumptions similar to Elderplan's about the impairment case-mix of its Medicare-only and Medicaid segments. Medicaid beneficiaries are assumed to be much more likely to be impaired than are private-pay members. Medicare Partners also plans to enroll Medicaid eligibles in greater proportions than reside in the community (for reasons similar to those cited for Elderplan). Furthermore, Medicare Partners plans to enroll 150 Medicaid beneficiaries residing in nursing homes. The site plans to be very cautious in soliciting these members from its own nursing homes, to avoid jeopardizing relationships that its staff have developed with physicians willing to practice in the facilities.

Queuing will be applied to Medicaid and Medicare-only members in different ways. Medicaid applicants will not be queued, since the impairment-based Medicaid reimbursement formula protects against selection risk (see chapter 6). Medicare members will not be queued during the first four months of enrollment, unless the severely impaired category reaches 9 percent or the moderately impaired category reaches 20 percent. After four months, queuing will be employed (if necessary) to reach the targets in table 5–2.

The figures in table 5–3 show that Medicare Partners projects a relatively slow enrollment rate (233 per month) and a low disenrollment rate (4.8 percent per year). The enrollment rates are based on Medicare HMO rates in the Twin Cities (apparently the slower ones), as well as an analaysis of the site market survey. It should be noted that the enrollment rate cited is an average of a somewhat staggered pattern projected by the site owing to seasonal fluctuations and the availability of conversion enrollees.

Apart from segmentation and enrollment goals, Medicare Partners has set two additional goals. The first is to develop a marketplace for long-range enrollment growth and to develop methods of maintaining a representative case-mix. A second is to maintain member satisfaction and minimize disenrollment. Strategies for achieving these goals are discussed below.

Medicare Partners Marketing Strategy. To achieve its segmentation and enrollment goals, Medicare Partners plans to orient its initial marketing efforts toward internal constituencies. Messages will include a mix of educational product information and promotion. The campaign will employ such means as organizational newsletters, direct mail, endorsements by influential individuals, and open meetings. To support the internal effort, Medicare Partners will launch appeals to the general public through media advertising, a mailing to Medicare beneficiaries on the HCFA list, distribution of promotional materials through banks, and various attempts to attract media coverage of both the plan and the general needs and problems of the elderly vis-à-vis health and long-term care.

Like Elderplan and the other sites, Medicare Partners is preparing a short flyer and an informational brochure that explain the various features of the program and create an image for the plan. An initial draft of the flyer to be mailed emphasizes the sponsors' "90 years of combined experience" and the comprehensiveness of the coverage. It also introduces the theme of "a health care plan so complete it follows you home." The brochure picks up the same themes and also highlights choice among a large number of GHI physicians, taking "the wait out of waiting rooms," "encouraging healthy lifestyles," and an endorsement from the powerful Metropolitan Senior Foundation. The brochure seeks to put the demonstration aspect of the program in a positive light by making it seem "exclusive." That is, it points out that the comprehensive SHMO benefits are available at only four sites around the country.

Marketing to the Medicaid segment of the market will be done in cooperation with the county welfare department. Details of the effort are still under negotiation as of this writing, but the intent is to have the Medicare Partners staff train the county staff to present the program as part of their normal, ongoing procedure. A separate informational brochure is being prepared, and planners also hope to conduct mailings and hold special meetings with slide-tape or video presentations to both new and current beneficiaries. The appeal will stress the plan's quality and access as well as the additional waivered services not otherwise available in the state plan.

There are three strategies for achieving the objective of long-term and balanced enrollment growth. First, the site will develop systems for evaluating the outcomes of promotional efforts, especially in terms of different market segments. Second, the site will monitor the marketplace for changes in demographics, competition, regulations, and the like. Third, the sponsors want to create an image of Medicare Partners as an advocate for the elderly and an expert regarding their care. They will do this by being active in community affairs, by courting media attention, by publicizing research, and other means.

Strategies aimed at ensuring the satisfaction and retention of members will consist of the development of a comprehensive system of applicant and member services. As is true at the other sites, the goal is to have pre-enrollment contact with individuals and small groups, to assure consumer understanding of the program. A telephone bank will be set up to answer inquiries, and a new member entry program will provide orientation. Staff and volunteers in the volunteer services unit will assist in these efforts. After enrollment, staff will maintain communications through a newsletter and monitor member concerns and satisfaction through periodic member surveys. The marketing and member services staff of the SHMO will consist of a marketing supervisor, three marketing representatives, and a member services director.

Survey Findings. To test the potential market for the SHMO, a telephone survey of Hennepin County elders was conducted by a private firm in the winter of 1983. A scientific sample was selected using a reverse directory method; 352 senior citizens were contacted; and 309 interviews were completed (representing a response rate of 88 percent). The low refusal rate supports an interpretation that the sample is representative.

In general, the survey found some dissatisfaction with current health care coverage and a relatively strong market for the SHMO. Views toward current coverage were solicited through an open-ended question asking what respondents like and do not like about Medicare (all had it), Medicaid (3 percent had it), and supplemental coverage (77 percent had it). Two-thirds to three-quarters of the respondents in each category could cite nothing they disliked about their coverage. The most common dissatisfaction with Medicare was poor coverage of doctor bills (expressed by 10 percent of respondents), paperwork (8 percent), and poor coverage of hospital bills (6 percent). The major dissatisfaction with supplemental coverage was with costs (14 percent), and only negligible dissatisfaction was found with Medicaid.

The survey presented four different cost-and-benefit options from the

SHMO, with costs of $30, $45, and $60 per month, and with benefits ranging from $5,000 to $10,000 on chronic care, and from no coverage to full coverage of dental, hearing aid, and eyeglasses. A total of 27 percent of the sample said they would subscribe to at least one of the benefit–premium options offered. Interest was strongest in the $30 version, but both of the $45 versions received significant interest. However, willingness to join fell off significantly (to 8 percent) when respondents were asked whether they would take one of the options *and* change doctors and join an experimental program. (See table 5–4 for a comparison to other site surveys.)

Medicare Plus II

Kaiser's Situation in Portland. In marketing Medicare Plus II, Kaiser differs from the other sites in three significant ways. It has experience in mounting prepaid Medicare demonstrations; it has very high penetration of the elderly market; and it has no significant prior experience in long-term care. These differences have given Kaiser some advantages over the other sites in mounting its marketing and enrollment efforts, but they have also created some difficulties and barriers.

Kaiser's experience in marketing Medicare Plus I and in serving the members of that program should help the site in marketing the SHMO. Plus I has been very favorably received by the elderly, the media, public officials, and senior citizens' organizations. The Plus I marketing effort made Kaiser Research Center staff aware of the issues that surround the design of marketing literature for the elderly, and the logistics of inducting elderly members into the plan. The staff also learned about the preparations that need to be made with provider staff in order to serve a new group of elderly members with new benefits. Furthermore, the success of Medicare Plus I, both as a demonstration and afterwards, should mitigate the fear on the part of the elderly of joining an experimental demonstration program. Because of this prior experience, the site did not feel it was necessary to perform a formal market survey.

While Kaiser is serving a five-county area in Medicare Plus I, it decided to limit marketing of the SHMO to Multnomah County (Portland). Multnomah is the largest and most urbanized of the surrounding counties, and Kaiser planners felt that it would be most practical to develop the new chronic care service component in a more limited geographic area. Kaiser's challenge in marketing Plus II in Multnomah is to increase an already high penetration rate: 17 percent of the county's 78,000 elders are already enrolled in Kaiser. Marketing plans for the SHMO call for increasing the penetration to almost 20 percent. The Kaiser staff feel confident they can attract new members, in part because of their positive experience with Plus I and in part because of the superiority of their product to those of the competition. While several new managed systems (mostly PROs and IPA HMOs) are now mounting challenges to Kaiser's market share, HMO competition in the seniors market is negligible in Portland. The Medicare supplement market has a large share, but price and benefits compare poorly to Kaiser's. Blue Cross, for example, offers a low option that covers only part A deductibles, for $20 per month, and a higher option that also covers part B deductibles, for $34 per month.

Kaiser's recent enrollment of large numbers of new elderly members is probably more of an internal than an external problem. As was discussed in chapter 2, the Research Center staff have had to overcome certain concerns on the part of Kaiser's corporate management and the medical staff. These concerns centered on the risk associated with the SHMO's long-term care benefits and on the implications of absorbing a substantial number of new elderly members so soon after the expansion from Plus I. Risk-sharing and internal conversion limits were designed to meet these concerns, however, and the involved parties decided that the concerns were outweighed by the potential learning and market advantage that could be gained if the SHMO is successful. If the program turns out to be attractive to the elderly and manageable from a cost standpoint, the Research Center staff would like to see the SHMO benefit package become the standard Medicare supplement offered by Kaiser. Considering the size of the Kaiser system nationally, the replication potential is substantial.

Kaiser's third difference from the other sites lies in its inexperience in long-term care. Planners at the three long-term care sponsors have worried somewhat about whether their images as chronic care providers would hinder their credibility as acute care providers and open them to adverse selection. Kaiser may have some cause to worry about whether the public will see it as a credible chronic care provider. Of course, this issue is sharpened by Kaiser's choosing an internal development strategy for market entry. But this is an issue only to the extent that Kaiser wishes to develop an image as a chronic care provider, which is a question that will be addressed below in the section on strategy.

Medicare Plus II Marketing Objectives. As does Medicare Partners, Kaiser states its general enrollment objectives in terms of major market segments. The intent is to obtain half of the 4,000 members internally from cost contract conversions. This number of members (2,000) is a compromise between HCFA (which wanted fewer) and the medical staff (which wanted more). It is projected that another 500 will come from Medicaid beneficiaries, and the remaining 1,500 from the general elderly public outside the Kaiser system.

The Plus II enrollment target for the impaired segment (5 percent of membership) is significantly lower than at any of the other sites (see table

5–2), which is a reflection of both the definition of the segment and prior Kaiser experience. Rather than stating enrollment targets in terms of both the moderately and the severely impaired, Kaiser has limited its targeting to the severely impaired, as defined by nursing home certifiability under strict Oregon definitions. The 5 percent figure represents a slight increase over Medicare Plus I, where an initial health status survey showed the prevalence of severely impaired members to be just under 4 percent. Like Medicare Partners, Kaiser does not plan to use queuing in Medicare Plus II enrollment unless patterns depart significantly from case-mix projections.

The site has set the objective of reaching full enrollment within ten months, which is the fastest enrollment rate of all the sites (see table 5–3). The rate is still far slower than that of Medicare Plus I—more than 1,000 a month—but the staff felt the lower rate would provide a more orderly process for taking in new members, especially in light of the need to perform comprehensive assessments of impaired SHMO members. The disenrollment rates projected for Medicare Plus II are the same as the actual rates of Plus I.

As was noted in the introductory section of this chapter, Kaiser's objectives for education, induction, and orientation of new members have served as models for the other sites. Kaiser learned of the importance of these activities the hard way, during the initial months of Medicare Plus I, when there was signifidant unauthorized out-of-plan use. The arrangements for these activities will be discussed below.

Medicare Plus II Marketing Strategies. Kaiser's marketing strategy for Medicare Plus II will emphasize the same themes and images as Plus I in selling the product, but it will use a very different approach in reaching the market. Whereas Medicare Plus I was promoted broadly with television and newspaper advertising, Plus II will be promoted through a direct-mail campaign supported by a community organization approach. The primary emphasis will be on reaching the segment of elders outside the Kaiser system. Because of Kaiser's already high penetration rate, site planners expect that they will have to reach virtually every eligible senior citizen in the county to meet their enrollment objectives. The primary mailing list will be the HCFA tape of Medicare beneficiaries (excluding current Kaiser members), supplemented by lists of seniors with driver's licenses or bus passes.

The Area Agency on Aging, the County–City Commission on Aging, and many senior groups have been supportive of the new program, and the site has an advisory committee composed of these and other constituencies. The committee will advise on the marketing campaign and provide liaison to community groups. Direct mailing will be supported by group presentations and poster displays in the network of community groups and organizations. The 2,000 conversion members will be recruited through separate direct mailings in specified geographic areas.

The choice of the name *Medicare Plus II* is a reflection of Kaiser's choice to build on the name recognition and positive image of the prior local demonstration. The direct-mail flyer that has been drafted also emphasizes the medical aspects of the program and downplays long-term care. The flyer announces "a bright idea in health care coverage from Kaiser-Permanente" under the image of an umbrella. The themes are "Bigger Coverage—Better Protection—Greater Peace of Mind." The text starts out with emphasis on comprehensive coverage of doctor visits, hospital charges, lab tests, "and more." It continues by stressing simplicity of paperwork, "no surprises" (no unplanned expenses), personal relationships with physicians, "and more." At the very end it announces "a new benefit that could help you stay in your home . . . if you become eligible for nursing home care." Thus, Kaiser is not trying to develop an image as a long-term care provider, and its market entry strategy of internal development, it is hoped, will not be a problem.

The marketing brochure is patterned very closely after the one produced for Plus I. It clearly explains benefits and repeatedly reviews the advantages and disadvantages of joining. The text emphasizes the personal choice of each beneficiary, urging the reader to review the material carefully, and asking in bold type, "Is this special program really for you?" Concerning the new "expanded care benefits" (that is, long-term care), the brochure is very explicit about the advantages, range of services covered, and limitations. Again the emphasis is on services in the home, "where most people are happier, stay healthier, and fare better than they do in nursing homes." Family support is also mentioned, as is "short-term nursing home care when you need it."

Kaiser planners expect to reach many Medicaid elderly through these efforts, but they are also working with state staff in designing a specific marketing and enrollment effort to take place in welfare offices. Details are not available as of this writing, but the intent is to have state caseworkers advise beneficiaries of the availability of the plan and hand out marketing materials. The caseworker will also handle enrollment.

The final aspects of Kaiser's marketing strategy are its plans for enrollment and new member services, and the site takes both processes very seriously. The stated goal is to enroll as many members as possible face-to-face, working with individuals and small groups, to ensure consumer understanding of the program. All applicants who mail in their applications will be telephoned so staff can verify that the person understands the program. The new member entry program developed in Medicare Plus I will be continued to help new members learn to cope in the "new and uncertain environment of a large and complex HMO." The program will be supported through a line item in the capitation of $1 per member per month, which will cover the costs of special personnel. They will be available throughout the Demonstration to respond to member requests and questions, to produce written materials, and to provide special programming. Components of the new member entry program include:

Development of an orientation program;

Assistance in the administration of the Health Status Form, including necessary referrals;

Hiring and overseeing of "special project representative(s)" with responsibilities in ongoing member education and as ombudsman for members in understanding and obtaining services and resolving enrollee–staff problems.

SCAN Health Plan

The Situation in the Long Beach Area. SCAN is located in Long Beach, an urban center on the coastal edge of the Southern California sprawl. SCAN sees its market as the areas whose ZIP codes begin with the digits 907 and 908, encompassing ten cities and towns in two counties: Los Angeles (mostly) and Orange. The area is home to 85,000 elderly Medicare beneficiaries. About 44 percent are over age 75—a proportion similar to that of the other sites' target markets. About 9 percent are members of minority ethnic groups, mostly hispanics.

The three partners in the SCAN Health Plan (SHP)—SCAN, Harriman Jones Clinics, and St. Mary's Medical Center—all hope that the SHMO can become the basis for their own long-term survival and growth. SCAN stands to gain firmer financing and the chance to expand to the private-pay market. St. Mary's sees SHP as a way to survive in a very competitive hospital environment where occupancy rates are only 70 percent to 75 percent. St. Mary's has given SCAN substantial financial support since the time of SCAN's formation, and the hospital is assuming large financial risks in the Demonstration. Harriman Jones is less a financial partner than a clinical one, but it does stand to gain increased shares of the elderly HMO market. The three orgnizations bring good reputations to the venture. Harriman Jones and St. Mary's are well known for quality care, and SCAN has developed constituencies among providers, opinion makers, and the poor.

The site sees the external situation as generally favorable. SCAN has good relationships with elected officials at all levels of government and has worked with state agencies through the MSSP project. Medicare insurance supplements currently hold the bulk of the elderly market. However, as of this writing, no data are available on market shares, premiums, or benefits.

The major HMO competition is the Family Health Plan (FHP), which began operations under the second round of the Medicare HMO demonstration in August 1983. Using an intensive, four-month media marketing campaign, FHP enrolled about 8,000 seniors by the end of 1983, and enrollment may have risen substantially since then. It offers a very low-option plan at no premium (essentially Medicare coverage, with very little more) and a high-option plan for $35 per month (including most everything in the SHMO package except long-term care). No data are available on what proportions of FHP enrollees have selected each of the two options.

Site planners believe that SHP can position itself well vis-à-vis FHP, in terms of price and benefits (long-term care for only $5 more per month) and in terms of quality and choice of physicians (Harriman Jones's size and reputation are considered superior to those of the FHP physicians group). Two other HMOs whose images in the community are stronger than FHP's (Pacificare and Maxicare) are not yet in the elderly HMO market, but both are expected to enter as soon as the TEFRA regulations receive final approval.

SHP Marketing Objectives. As at the other sites, SHP's first-level objectives were stated separately for Medicaid and Medicare-only segments. The site plans to enroll 800 Medicaid beneficiaries (the 20 percent proportion is similar to that which prevails in the local population) and 3,200 private-pay members. No specific objectives have been set for recruitment from internal constituencies on the part of any of the providers in SHP. It is expected, however, that SCAN's provider network will be helpful in attracting the necessary Medicaid members. Significantly, the medical director of the county health care center (which serves many Medicaid eligibles) is on the SCAN board of directors.

The site projects that the best source of private-pay members will be the same population segments who were attracted by the Medicare HMOs—that is, the younger, healthier, and higher-income elderly. As will be seen below, the site's initial goal is to attract "older adult opinion makers," and planners believe these are to be found among the higher-income groups as well as among couples. The SHMO will initially target its marketing efforts to geographic areas where there are significant concentrations of such elderly persons.

As can be seen in table 5–2, the site's targets for the impaired segments (4 percent severely impaired and 10 percent moderately impaired) are similar to Elderplan and Medicare Partners. However, the site projects that relatively few of its members (4 percent) will be nursing home certifiable, a level even lower than Kaiser's projection. SHP's projection seems to be based more on a desire to estimate revenues conservatively than it is on a projection of the results of the nursing home prescreening process. Like Elderplan, SHP will be queuing both Medicare-only and Medicaid applicants from the start of enrollment, according to the proportions in table 5–2.

The site plans for the full enrollment of 4,000 to be reached in thirteen months. Table 5–3 shows that this pace translates into an average of about 300 per month, one of the slower rates among the sites.

As have the other sites, SHP has set objectives toward assuring that applicants and new members are fully aware of the limitations as well as the benefits of joining the SHMO, and it too has adopted strategies to serve these ends.

Marketing Strategies at SHP. The overall marketing strategy at SHP is to create a positive image of the plan and to convince individuals to "pass the word" to others. The image sought is similar to the one Elderplan hopes to achieve. SHP wants to create the image of a "high-quality, up-market program that is unique and effective." The theme under consideration is "The SCAN Health Plan—A Better Way." The theme, planners feel, is simple for people to remember and repeat. It also invites comparisons to other plans—comparisons from which SHP should emerge looking good.

The site is also considering a second strategy to supplement the "pass-the-word" approach. This second phase would consist of approaching (1) the management of large housing complexes for the elderly and (2) large employers who offer good retirement benefits. The general goal in both cases would be to enroll concentrated blocks of members, perhaps at special rates.

One "better way" that SHP will stress is its better way for "older persons to decide whether to enroll or not, without a lot of pressure." The SHP planners think that FHP's expensive media and enrollment effort was too "high pressure" and that as a result some elders enrolled without fully understanding the program. Apparently there is a relatively high disenrollment rate at FHP. The site contrasts its slow, steady enrollment buildup to the blitz of the HMOs; its word-of-mouth confidence building to the pressure of insurance sales; its waiting to be asked by groups to make presentations to the intrusion of large-scale, blanket campaigns.

The site will use a coordinated direct-mail, media, and community organization approach to promote the plan. Using the HCFA tapes, mailings will be sequential by ZIP code area and will be supported by newspaper advertisements, targeted ads (such as billboards, buses, cabs), community presentations, teas, and media coverage. SCAN already has a half-hour radio program twice a month and can obtain time on cable television.

As of this writing, SHP's plans for producing marketing materials and for enrollment and orientation of new members are still only in general outline form. Since SHP's plans are patterned after the other sites, they need not be repeated here. The plan calls for a marketing staff consisting of a director of marketing, a marketing specialist, a health educator, and member services representatives.

Market Survey Results. The SCAN marketing survey was conducted by a private contractor in August 1983. A four-page survey was mailed to 20,852 elders who were selected through a reverse telephone directory method. SCAN chose a mail rather than a telephone survey in the hope of promoting consumer awareness of the plan and with the intent of building up a list of interested prospects. The return rate was a little less than 6 percent, lower than had been anticipated. A telephone follow-up was conducted to assess how representative the sample was. It was found that the respondents to the mail survey were about three times as likely to be interested in joining the SHMO as were the telephone respondents (more than 50 percent as opposed to less than 20 percent). Additionally, the mail respondents were nearly twice as likely to be male (59 percent versus 36 percent), and they tended to have somewhat higher income levels than did the telephone respondents. Qualities that correlated positively with interest in the SHMO were being male and tending to have high income.

A somewhat disturbing finding of the mail survey is that respondents were apparently sicker than would be expected. First, they report relatively high hospital utilization: 9,200 hospital days per 1,000 persons per year. The telephone survey did not ask hospital utilization questions, but this compares to a community average of about 3,300 days per 1,000 elderly per year. However, physicians visits were relatively few: about five visits per person per year (compared to HMO figures of six to eight visits; see table 6–5). Perhaps the low physician use reflects poor physician ties, which may in turn prompt interest in the plan. Second, rates of impairment were relatively high. Only 91 percent of males and 80 percent of females said they could "handle most daily tasks."

In conclusion, both the mail and telephone surveys found a sufficiently large market for SHP. However, if SCAN's marketing efforts lead to selection that is as adverse as what the mail survey reflected, the plan will be in trouble. These findings also call into question the site's desire to use the list of survey respondents as an initial target market.

Conclusions

In summary, the four sites show both contrasts and similarities in their marketing and enrollment situations and plans. The markets at all four sites are similar in size, target segments, and urban setting, but their competitive environments are very different. The particular internal and external situations of each sponsor shaped their approaches to market entry, but each sees the SHMO as a vehicle for a more stable and perhaps growing future base in the elderly health care market.

All have set enrollment targets quite cautiously, and all are committed to developing an informed population of applicants and new members. The slow enrollment buildup may not be ideal from the standpoint of cash flow, but it is probably a very good choice on the part of the sponsors, for reasons above and beyond the time needed to perform comprehensive assessments. While a big media blitz would probably produce the same flood of applicants that the HMOs have received, such a response could create serious problems if the new members do not understand both the advantages and the limitations of the program. Furthermore, even with the findings from the market surveys, no one yet knows what the market for the SHMO will be and how the different population segments will respond to marketing efforts. A slow approach that stresses high interaction with applicants will allow midstream assessment of outcomes and techniques, and leave time for adjustments.

The market surveys tend to support the sites' choices in terms of price, product, and public image. The most common concerns of the elderly over health care are gaps in Medicare coverage and the costs of Medicare supplements. Poor long-term care coverage is a less frequent concern, but this may be because of misunderstanding about coverage. This supports the educational approach adopted by the sites, but it does not support the notion that there is an immediate market for a plan offering high long-term care benefits at a high premium. The sites' choice to compete in the acute-care supplement sector of the market in terms of both price and product seems prudent.

While each of the sites enters its market with a different organizational configuration, most will be trying to convey a very similar image of the SHMO and the benefits of joining. All are playing up quality, ease of access, and the history and reputations of providers. Those with large medical groups are emphasizing choice of physicians. None is hiding its long-term care benefits, but none is selling the SHMO as a long-term care program, most especially not a nursing home program. Rather, long-term care is being billed as an extra and as a unique benefit.

The surveys support the notion that there exists a private market for the SHMO, and the market appears to be large enough, as well as broad in terms of age, sex, income, and health status. More people are interested in the SHMO than are willing to give up their current medical and insurance arrangements, but that is to be expected. The adverse selection issue, however, remains unresolved. The two most scientific market surveys show that interest in joining varies little by health or impairment status. In fact, favorable selection on these characteristics would appear somewhat more likely. However, the high response to the SCAN survey by heavy utilizers of health care gives one pause.

Perhaps the greatest unknown is the response of the Medicaid market. The surveys did not reach sufficiently large numbers of Medicaid beneficiaries to allow planners to draw conclusions about their interest in the program or their concerns about their current arrangements. Will they give up their freedom to shop around, in return for membership in a closed system operating under cost constraints? Will marketing efforts through welfare offices and welfare workers be effective? Will the community organization approach to marketing to the broader community reach enough Medicaid beneficiaries to make the direct effort through the welfare department unimportant?

These questions cannot yet be answered, and the sites have spent somewhat less time on them than on the private marketing effort. The questions are extremely important, however, because three of the four sites have plans for serving large and disproportionate shares of the Medicaid segment. Given that the Medicaid segment is where full benefits will be tested, achieving this penetration is central to the sites' plans and to the success of the Demonstration as a public policy initiative.

Notes

1. As will be seen later, in the finance chapter, some of the financing for these benefits also comes from savings achieved on acute care services—again on the entire population. Thus, there is little direct financing for long-term care services.

2. Although some dispute Eggers. See Greenlick (1983) and Marks (1983).

3. Medicaid cards can, however, be taken back by Medicaid.

4. The 5 percent limit on the proportion of the NHC members increases the likelihood that queuing will be used by all sites.

5. It should be noted that the Group Health enrollees included in these figures are age-ins under their cost contract. The risk contract, which will be discussed further below, did not start until April 1984.

6
Finance Planning

This chapter examines issues related to the preparation of a finance plan for the SHMO. The issues are addressed primarily from a provider perspective, but the concerns of government are also examined when appropriate. The finance plan should provide sponsors and third-party funders with some of the crucial "bottom-line" numbers they need to justify going ahead with the project. The numbers come in stages: If initial gross estimates are favorable, they justify more work. It is hoped that each stage brings increasing accuracy and detail in what is very much an iterative process.

At the most general level, the finance plan should answer two questions:

How much will individual enrollees and third parties pay the program for the benefits to be offered?

How much will it cost the SHMO to provide these benefits to members?

A third and related question is, What happens if costs and payments do not balance? This will be addressed in the next chapter, which focuses on risk. The present chapter describes the various aspects of the two general questions in detail, and it also discusses some basic ways to analyze and make decisions on them. Also described are the ways in which the Demonstration sites are dealing with these questions. The chapter is not, however, a detailed planning guide for any of these issues. Rather, the analysis concentrates on the points where the SHMO requires going beyond existing methodologies, data sets, and policies.

Revenue Analysis

Given the iterative nature of the finance planning process, it is a somewhat arbitrary decision to start the analysis with revenues. One justification is that Medicare reimbursement—the major component of revenues—can be estimated quite accurately in advance, since there is an established and tested Medicare policy. Revenues from Medicaid, private premiums, and private coinsurance, however, are more difficult to estimate. Medicaid agencies generally do not have established policies or formulas. And predicting potential revenues from private premiums and coinsurance levels is difficult because the market for long-term care insurance is untested. The interaction among price, produce (benefits), costs, and selection risk creates a fluid situation.

Revenue at the Demonstration sites will have four basic components, each of which will be addressed here in turn:

Medicare payments for all enrollees;

Medicaid payments for those eligible;

Private premiums from those not eligible for Medicaid; and

Direct cost sharing (that is, copayments, deductibles) from those who use particular services.

SHMOs could be organized using only one or some of these components (such as Medicare and Medicaid, Medicare and private, or even Medicaid only). However, each of the four revenue sources offers SHMO planners particular opportunities for testing the SHMO model and maximizing its potential. Medicaid participation allows a test of full long-term care benefits, while inclusion of the private-pay group gives a chance to learn about long-term care insurance. Without Medicare, integration with acute care would be more difficult, and the savings generated by the model would be lower. HCFA was insistent from the start that all parties should be in the Demonstration.[1]

Funds from these sources will be pooled within the SHMO, but in order to estimate the size of the pool, each individual revenue source must be calculated separately. To make these estimates during the planning process, it was often necessary to go beyond existing models and methodologies. It was not simply a matter of "plugging in" numbers to existing formulas. Rather, in order to determine how much to expect from each source, planners had to identify and evaluate the possible options concerning a second level of issues. These issues include:

The approach to the question. That is, what general methodology, concept, or policy will be adopted to answer the question?

Accommodating case-mix effects. How does the approach take into account the fact that subgroups of the population have significantly different costs?

Data and implementation. What are the data requirements of the approach, and how can these requirements be met?

These issues and options will be discussed below, and the initial choices made on these questions by Medicare, Medicaid, and the individual sites will be described. However, future sponsors should be aware, as the Demonstration partners are, that early experiences will modify some of the choices, that new data will alter some of the formulas, and that changes in revenue by source will eventually result.

Medicare Revenues

The Approach to Medicare Rate Setting. Both the concept and the basic elements of prospective, capitated Medicare reimbursement were established prior to the SHMO Demonstration (Trieger, Galblum, and Riley 1981; Kunkel and Powell 1981). The established methodology is called the adjusted average per capita costs (AAPCC). The idea behind the AAPCC is to reimburse a program according to what it would have cost Medicare to serve the enrolled population in the fee-for-service sector. More specifically, AAPCC includes Medicare's share for part A and B acute care services (that is, allowable costs minus beneficiary payments for copays, deductibles, and expenses after benefits are exhausted). Medicare is paying SHMOs 100 percent of AAPCC, 5 percent more than it pays HMOs. The "bonus" is intended as an incentive for SHMOs to offer additional long-term care services.

The Case-Mix Adjustment Process. The current AAPCC methodology begins with the estimate prepared for the Medicare trustees of Medicare's national per capita costs next year. Second, the method estimates Medicare's per capita costs next year in the program's target county. This is called the area prevailing costs (APC) and is obtained by multiplication of the national figure by a five-year unweighted average of the ratio of national to county costs. Third, the formula estimates how expensive the enrolled population is in relation to the county population, according to a table of underwriting factors. The current underwriting factors (table 6–1) are based on a statistical analysis of Medicare's fee-for-service costs in relation to beneficiary characteristics. The factors adjust reimbursement according to sex, age, whether or not a person is eligible for Medicaid, and whether or not a person resides in a long-term care institution. The formula adjusts the APC by multiplying it by the ratio of the program membership's weighting of the underwriting factors to the county population's weighting. Thus, if the members are more frequently in the high-cost cells than are county residents, the AAPCC will be higher than the APC, and vice versa.[2] It is important to reiterate that these factors represent differences in acute medical costs and to understand that Medicare payments are meant to pay primarily for these acute costs rather than for long-term care costs.

The current formula poses serious problems for the SHMO as it is now

Table 6–1
AAPCC Aged Underwriting Factors

Age–Sex	Institutional	Community Welfare	Community Nonwelfare
Part A			
Male			
65–69	2.05	1.35	.70
70–74	2.15	1.55	.80
75–79	2.35	1.95	1.00
80–84	2.35	2.30	1.20
85 and over	2.35	2.60	1.35
Female			
65–69	1.65	.90	.60
70–74	1.90	1.15	.70
75–79	2.20	1.50	.70
80–84	2.20	1.80	1.10
85 and over	2.20	2.15	1.25
Part B			
Male			
65–69	1.75	1.20	.85
70–74	1.90	1.40	1.00
75–79	1.90	1.55	1.10
80–84	1.90	1.70	1.15
85 and over	1.90	1.70	1.15
Female			
65–69	1.55	1.10	.70
70–74	1.60	1.15	.80
75–79	1.70	1.25	.95
80–84	1.70	1.25	1.00
85 and over	1.70	1.25	1.05

Source: Trieger, Galblum, and Riley (1981).

being used to reimburse programs that are not long-term care programs. This problem relates to institutional underwriting factors, whereby reimbursement for an individual approximately doubles when the individual enters a long-term care institution. Since it is a major goal of the SHMO to increase the proportion of seriously impaired individuals who can be maintained in community settings, a perverse incentive is created here for the SHMO: A seriously impaired individual who is maintained in the community is reimbursed at the low resident rate. Assuming for a moment that community-based and institutional benefits are about equal in value, and thus of equal cost to the plan, it would make financial sense for the SHMO to encourage the member to enter an institution.

Because of this undesirable incentive, and because analyses of data from the 1977 Current Medicare Survey show that extremely impaired beneficiaries are just as costly to Medicare as are nursing home residents (Gruenberg and

Stuart 1982a), the SHMO planners explored alternatives to the current AAPCC formula. After considering the options, they decided to ask for a different application of the current formula. Under the modification, SHMO programs will be reimbursed according to the institutional underwriting factors for enrollees who meet state certification requirements for placement in nursing homes but who remain in the community. This nursing home certifiable (NHC) formula will give SHMOs incentives to maintain their impaired enrollees in community settings.

In order to incorporate a factor for NHC into the AAPCC, it was necessary to modify the current AAPCC underwriting factors for community residents. This is because the expensive NHC group's costs are included in the community resident group's costs in the calculation of the current AAPCC underwriting factors. The modification of the factors was calculated by Brandeis using the 1977 Current Medicare Survey. The Medicare costs of community beneficiaries who were in bed or at home most or all of the time because of a disability, or who needed the help of another person in getting around in the community (about 5 percent of the community sample) were removed from the community groups, and the factors were recalculated. The modified community factors displayed in table 6–2 are on the average about 5 percent lower than the community factors in table 6–1. This is consistent with the fact that the NHC beneficiaries who were removed are about twice as costly as the average.[3] The underwriting factors in table 6–2 will be used to reimburse SHMOs. (The institutional factors are the same as table 6–1.)

Maintaining some such adjustment in the reimbursement formula for level of impairment is an important issue for the SHMO program. However, it must be acknowledged that the NHC methodology is imperfect. The shortcomings include the assessment issues discussed in chapter 4, and issues related to data and implementation.

Data and Implementation for the AAPCC. Obtaining the data to implement the AAPCC methodology is a rather cumbersome process. This is because the methodology requires placement of every individual (both in the program and county populations) into one of the discrete underwriting cells. While HCFA can supply information on the age and sex of both members and county residents (and update this information automatically), it is more difficult to estimate accurately data on welfare status and nursing home status, both at the county and program levels.

Starting with the denominator of the formula, until recently, the estimate of the number of elderly in nursing homes at the county level was based either on data from Medicaid agencies or more frequently on surveys of nursing homes. HMOs were required to supply HCFA with the names and addresses of all long-term care institutions in the target county, and HCFA

Table 6–2
Revised AAPCC Underwriting Factors for Aged

Age–Sex	Institutional or Nursing Home Certifiable	Community Welfare	Community Nonwelfare
Part A			
Male			
65–69	2.05	1.32	.67
70–74	2.15	1.51	.76
75–79	2.35	1.92	.95
80–84	2.35	2.29	1.14
85 and over	2.35	2.63	1.29
Female			
65–69	1.65	.85	.58
70–74	1.90	1.07	.65
75–79	2.20	1.39	.81
80–84	2.20	1.71	.99
85 and over	2.20	2.14	1.12
Part B			
Male			
65–69	1.75	1.17	.83
70–74	1.90	1.35	.96
75–79	1.90	1.52	1.07
80–84	1.90	1.68	1.10
85 and over	1.90	1.68	1.10
Female			
65–69	1.55	1.07	.69
70–74	1.60	1.10	.77
75–79	1.70	1.15	.90
80–84	1.70	1.16	.93
85 and over	1.70	1.16	.96

staff conducted the survey and analyzed the responses. To implement the TEFRA HMO program, HCFA has changed the way the institutional population is estimated. First, the use of surveys and Medicaid data has been abolished in favor of data from the U.S. Census. Second, the entire process of analyzing census data, data for the Medicaid underwriting cell, and age–sex data, has been contracted to a private firm. As of this writing, the changes have created a great deal of dissatisfaction among HMOs and SHMOs, since neither HCFA nor the contractor has been willing to reveal what census groupings are being included in the definition of the nursing home cell or more generally how data are being analyzed. The long-run acceptability of the AAPCC methodology to providers is likely to rest in part on HCFA's opening of these "black boxes."

In the numerator of the formula, it has been very difficult to estimate the numbers of members who will be certifiable for state nursing home placements but who will be maintained in the community through home care services. County data were not available on the distribution of such individuals in local populations (and thus no county estimate of these individuals has been included in the county population distribution). National data sets, including the Health Interview Survey and Current Medicare Survey, were therefore used instead (Gruenberg and Stuart 1982b, 1983). Sites are initially projecting ranges between 3.5 percent and 5 percent NHC members.[4] An important item on the developmental research agenda is an improvement of the whole process by which members are classified NHC.

Once the county population data are compiled, the HCFA contractor will calculate what is known as a "rate book." This is a listing of the actual dollar amount Medicare will reimburse the program for an enrollee in each of the sixty underwriting cells. To estimate reimbursement, financial planners should work with marketing planners to project what the membership characteristics will be according to each of the underwriting indices.

Once enrollment projections are set, expected reimbursement per capita can be easily calculated by multiplication of rate-book rates by the expected number of enrollees in each cell. The average reimbursement for the membership is what can properly be called the program's AAPCC. HCFA's preferred approach to reimbursement is what is called a "full rate book." Under this method the program is reimbursed at the projected AAPCC for the first month's enrollees, but the rate is adjusted monthly to reflect the characteristics of the actual enrollees as new members are accreted (enrolled) and deleted from the rolls each month. During Medicare Plus, Kaiser-Portland negotiated a "hybrid" approach to the rate book. Under this approach, monthly per capita reimbursement is agreed on in advance for the duration of the contract, and adjustments (either up or down) to reimbursement because of membership AAPCC characteristics are made out of a "benefit stabilization fund." Kaiser will continue this approach in Medicare Plus II, and other sites have negotiated somewhat shorter periods of stabilized rates. More detailed analyses of rate-book calculations and other AAPCC reimbursement mechanics are available elsewhere in the literature (Kunkel and Powell 1981; Trieger, Galblum, and Riley 1981; Leutz and Hannon 1981).

Site Choices. Most of the Demonstration sites predicted that membership will reflect county distributions of age and sex. Kaiser projected that its population will reflect the Medicare Plus enrollment on these factors, and the enrollment in that program was very similar to the elderly in the county at large. Medicaid enrollment projections were set on the basis of negotiations with state Medicaid agencies at all sites. In chapter 5 it was seen that most of the sites and states chose to enroll a slightly larger proportion of Medicaid members than the proportion of such beneficiaries in their counties.

The effects of these estimates are illustrated in table 6–3, which shows the demographically adjusted 1984 county per capita Medicare spending by site—the adjusted APC[5]—in column 2, and the programs' average estimated per capita Medicare reimbursement—the AAPCC—in column 3. The fact that some of the AAPCCs are slightly higher is a reflection of the higher-than-prevailing rates of Medicaid enrollment.

Medicaid Revenues

Establishing the basis of the Medicaid rate has been one of the most problematic aspects of the Demonstration. Even though the participating states are among the most sophisticated about long-term care and prepayment, the SHMO is a big departure from business-as-usual for all of them. None of the four states had ever capitated long-term care or pooled funding with Medicare. Only two of the four (California and Oregon) had ever capitated acute care for the elderly. Only California had ever shared risk.

While participating states and providers had limited experience with capitating Medicaid long-term care, there has clearly been an interest on their part in learning more. The SHMO offers a vehicle for learning, but the planning period shows that learning does not come easily. Good solutions require an investment of staff time and budgets, when both are already stretched tightly.

Furthermore, Medicaid rate development is not merely a technical process; perhaps just as important it is a political and educational process that can develop into a complex set of negotiations and communications among the provider and varous government agencies. Since the SHMO takes a consolidated approach to services and finances, it can be construed as falling within the regulatory domain of many branches of state and local government. In the more regulated states in the Demonstration (particularly New York), it seemed at times as if the entire bureaucracy was involved in

Table 6–3
1984 Medicare Area Prevailing Costs (Adjusted for County Demographics) and AAPCCs by Demonstration Site

Site	Adjusted Medicare APC (per capita per month)	Medicare AAPCC (pmpm)
Kaiser	$241 (Multnomah)	$224
Elderplan	$269 (Kings)	$289
Ebenezer-GHI	$220 (Hennepin)	$226
SCAN	$290 (Orange) $300 (Los Angeles)	$283 $294

the negotiation and approval of rates. The frequent corollary was that no single entity seemed to be in overall charge of the process.

This section should help sponsors and state agencies work out a process for establishing Medicaid rates. It will analyze the same second level of issues addressed in covering Medicare: (1) the approach to rate making; (2) data needs; and (3) case-mix adjustments. The section concludes with detailed descriptions of the choices each site and state made in initial implementation.

Approaches to the Medicaid Rate

Policy Considerations. In establishing pooled funding systems for third-party payers, it is important that each pay its fair share of costs. Pooling removes all of the current system's constraints on what services are reimbursable under what circumstances and thus leaves third parties wide open to cost shifting. If one third party thinks that its contribution is actually paying for the costs of another, the long-run viability of the pooled funding system is questionable.

Brandeis recommended that the concept of *fair share* could most easily be incorporated into third-party rates if Medicaid based its rate on a concept of fee-for-service equivalency similar to that of the Medicare AAPCC (Leutz 1982). That is, Medicaid would calculate what it would have spent for Medicaid services for its SHMO enrollees in the fee-for-service system and then pay the program a similarly high proportion of projected spending.

In practice, this turned out to be a difficult concept to implement for both practical and political reasons. Practically, limited data made it difficult for state Medicaid agencies to calculate what they would have spent for enrollees in the fee-for-service system. Some states were able to make the calculation, but others used a cost-based concept—that is, rates were based on the expected costs of their services in the program. Politically it was difficult to "sell" the Demonstration to state agencies unless at least some savings could be figured into the rate from the outset. Thus, it will be seen below that the principle of fair share has been violated to some degree in Medicaid rates at all of the sites. How Medicare policymakers will accept this approach in the long run remains to be seen.

Rate Elements. Some of the most important ingredients in establishing the basis of the Medicaid premium are definitions of the actual cost elements included in the Medicaid rate "build up."[6] The choices made in this area again varied from site to site, but the general idea has been that Medicaid should pay for the same service and cost areas it pays for in the fee-for-service system. These include:

1. Medicare part A and B copays and deductibles, plus costs beyond lifetime reserves;
2. Drugs, eyeglasses, dentures, and other ancillary services covered by Medicaid, but not Medicare;
3. Chronic care—institutional, in-home, and community-based services (including those covered in the state plan as well as additional ones in states with limited community coverage).

Legitimate arguments can be made that Medicaid should also pay for any and all of the following in proportion to costs for Medicaid members:

1. Case management;
2. Administration;
3. Provider reserves.

Most of these items are self-explanatory, and the cost estimate section of the chapter will provide more detail. The question of how much Medicaid should pay for its enrollees' long-term care services requires a little more explanation here, since the model based on a fee-for-service equivalent for rate setting is more difficult to implement. This is because states have never purchased a full range of long-term care services for a representative population.[7] States do not know how many of their beneficiaries would qualify for long-term care services in the program, nor do they know how many of them would have entered nursing homes in the absence of SHMO services. If the state pays the program at the nursing home rate for NHC members, this may be too high. But since many would have entered and others *will* enter (and the SHMO will be responsible), the rate needs to take these costs into account. The site examples will show that the actuarial approach can accommodate these uncertainties by (1) making explicit assumptions about utilization of institutional and noninstitutional services and (2) basing the rate on expected costs. The approach based on fee-for-service equivalent, however, cannot accommodate these unknowns so directly.

Spend-Down Issues. In addition to addressing rate elements for current Medicaid beneficiaries, sites and states need to address the spend-down issue. There are two aspects to spend-down that must be considered: first, arranging for Medicaid coverage of those enrollees who spend down while in the SHMO, and second, compensating the SHMO for helping private-pay members avoid spend-down. Both of these issues are complex. Only two of the Demonstration sites have taken care of the former, and none has even begun to address the latter.

First, the two sites with spend-down arrangements are Elderplan and Medicare Partners. The arrangements have some similarities but also some important differences. The similar features are as follows:

Members whose spending on premiums and copays for Medicaid-covered services brings them below income eligibility guidelines will be eligible for Medicaid reimbursement for their care.

The SHMO will be responsible for collecting the premiums and copays required to meet the spend-down threshold and for documenting the member's income and spending status for the state.

The key difference between the two arrangements is that New York will pay Elderplan on a fee-for-service basis for additional member costs after the spend-down amount is paid by the member, while Minnesota will pay Medicare Partners according to the established Medicaid rate structure for the member (see below), minus the required spend-down amount. The Minnesota arrangement is clearly simpler from the standpoints of administration and record-keeping, and it also maintains savings incentives through the prepaid reimbursement structure. Both systems, however, are basically incompatible with the HMO concept of prepayment, since they essentially amount to a huge, continuing copayment. A more workable approach may lie in solving the second issue.

Second, a strong case can be made that Medicaid should pay SHMOs for preventing spend-downs among private-pay members. Spend-down will be reduced both in the acute care area, where hospital costs are fully covered for unlimited days, and in the long-term care area, where prepaid benefits will prevent many private-pay enrollees from entering costly nursing homes and eventually spending down. The spend-down issue was discussed in negotiations with Medicaid agencies. However, it was not possible to incorporate a spend-down element into rate making, due to a combination of tight state budgets and states' skepticism owing to past broken promises of savings. However, it was generally acknowledged that these savings may turn out to be significant, and an attempt will be made to identify and quantify them during the course of the Demonstration.

Case-Mix Adjustments. A case-mix adjusted rate is a direct way of accommodating the unknowns about prevalence and incidence of long-term care need in the population. Establishing a sound method for balancing reimbursement and case-mix is more crucial for Medicaid than for Medicare. This is because Medicaid's major cost item—long-term care—is a much more potent differentiator of costs than are Medicare's underwriting factors. In the Demonstration states, Medicaid elderly who receive long-term care services in nursing homes cost Medicaid about ten times as much as do regular beneficiaries. If Medicaid were to prepay programs without regard to how many enrollees require long-term care services, serious over- (or under-) payments would likely result.

As has been outlined above, establishing a Medicaid reimbursement formula that takes long-term care needs into account is not easy. Since the SHMO seeks to prevent unnecessary nursing home admissions, such admissions cannot be the only measure of need—if they should be a measure at all. Functional assessments of members are another option, but the data available during the planning phase were contradictory as to what levels of costs are associated with what levels of functioning (see below). The site examples show that two states, Minnesota and California, have established case-mix adjusted formulas.

Since data were so limited for establishing and implementing a rate book based on impairment, the Elderplan site chose another option: Rather than adjusting reimbursement to match the enrolled population, it will seek to adjust the enrolled population to match the reimbursement. In its cost buildup, Elderplan assumed a Medicaid membership with a particular distribution of impairment levels that is thought to represent the Medicaid population. Individuals at each level were assumed to use particular amounts of long-term care services, which were incorporated into the rate buildup. To match the membership to the rate assumptions, Elderplan will use the queuing process (see chapter 5) to enroll Medicaid applicants according to preestablished quotas for each impairment level.

Data. Whether the approach to the rate is fee-for-service or cost-based, and however the rate methodology incorporates a case-mix adjustment, it is necessary to determine how much Medicaid is currently spending on particular services for the types of Medicaid beneficiaries who will be joining the SHMO. Most of the sites are enrolling only Medicaid beneficiaries who are (1) not in spend-down status, (2) community residents, and (3) eligible for Medicare. Medicaid beneficiaries without these characteristics must thus be excluded from the analysis of spending data. This is important because beneficiaries who are in spend-down, who do not have Medicare coverage, or who reside in long-term care institutions are generally more costly than the categorically eligible recipient.

It has been extremely difficult for most state Medicaid agencies to isolate these categories of individuals in their reporting systems, and the national data that are available offer no assistance. Only California was apparently able to calculate spending relatively painlessly by aid category, place of residence, and Medicare status. The word *apparently* is used because neither the site nor Brandeis staff were involved closely enough with the analysis to independently confirm validity. The Ebenezer–Group Health site has made the greatest effort in working with Medicaid staff to make a thorough and accurate analysis of Medicaid spending data, but this has been a very time-consuming process.

Implementation by Site[8]

The Kaiser-Portland Approach. Kaiser-Portland used a cost-based approach in establishing a rate proposal to the Oregon Medicaid agency. The overall methodology was to calculate a Medicaid adjustment to its adjusted community rate (ACR). Kaiser began with utilization information gained in its Medicare Plus I program and first assumed that SHMO members would use 20 percent to 30 percent more services than Plus I members in the areas of home health, claims and referrals, and SNF care. Next, they used the ratio between AAPCC factors for welfare recipients and those for community members, to derive Medicaid adjustment factors. The resulting factors were 1.70 for part A services (hospital, SNF, and home health) and 1.40 for part B services (physicians visits, ambulance, and other). Claims and referrals were assumed to be about 60 percent higher for welfare members. The welfare population was assumed to have a 40 percent greater rate of impairment than the private-pay population, which is a somewhat lower differential than that derived by the Brandeis analyses (Gruenberg and Stuart, 1983); and expected long-term care utilization was correspondingly adjusted in the Kaiser Medicaid rate buildup. An additional element of the Medicaid rate was a "buyout" of copays and deductibles.

These adjustment factors were applied to the cost estimate for members not on welfare to derive an expected per capita cost for welfare members. The final derivation of the Medicaid dues rate followed a series of steps in the Kaiser capitation. In essence, though, the Medicaid rate proposal was derived by subtracting AAPCC reimbursement for Medicaid members (about 60 percent higher than for members not on welfare) from total expected Medicaid enrollee costs. Thus the Medicaid rate proposal was reduced below "fair-share" costs in that the expected "savings" on the costs of delivering Medicare-covered services (about 25 percent of the AAPCC) were applied toward costs usually covered by Medicaid.

Table 6–4 shows that the proposed 1983 Medicaid rate was $67 PMPM, which was about 70 percent higher than the 1983 private premium. However, Oregon Medicaid decided not to accept the long-term care portion of Kaiser's rate proposal, since the impact on the state budget could not be determined. Instead, the rate and service elements include only the Medicare Plus I package of acute and expanded medical services. The new rate proposal is based on costs, less Medicare reimbursement (at 95 percent of AAPCC for these members), and the 1984 premium is about $29 PMPM.

The Elderplan Approach. Elderplan's rate proposal to Medicaid followed an

Table 6–4
1984 Medicaid Premiums at the Demonstration Sites

Site	Rate Element	Monthly Rate (pmpm)
Medicare Plus II (Oregon)	Proposed rate with LTC	$ 67[a]
	Accepted rate—acute only	$ 29
Elderplan (New York)	Core package	$ 164
	Excess chronic care and medical	$ 155
	Total premium	$ 319
Medicare Partners (Minnesota)	Nursing Home Residents	
	Acute	$ 152
	Chronic	$1,658
	Total	$1,810
	Community NHC	
	Acute	$ 101
	Chronic	$1,575[b]
	Total	1,676
	Community non-NHC	
	Acute	$ 107
	Chronic	—
	Total	107
SCAN Health Plan (California)	Categorically needy (SS1)	
	Aged	$ 66
	Blind and disabled	$ 84
	Medically needy (nonspenddown)	
	Aged	$ 49
	Blind and disabled	$ 44
	Nursing home certifiable	
	Aged	$ 749
	Blind and disabled	$ 794

a. 1983 rate proposal.
b. Maximum, not necessarily average.

approach that is a hybrid of fee-for-service equivalent and cost-based. The methodology has some similarities to Kaiser's, but its population assumptions are significantly different. First, the similarity between the Kaiser and Elderplan approaches is that both used adjustment factors to estimate utilization by Medicaid members and by enrollees not on Medicaid. Elderplan's factors were somewhat different, however. The ratio between the total Medicaid and non-Medicaid AAPCCs (1.68) was used to factor all Medicare-covered services, Medicare copays and deductibles, and plan administration. Supplemental medical benefits were factored by the part B ratio (1.40).

Elderplan also assumed that its Medicaid membership would as a group be significantly more impaired than would the Medicare-only enrollees. Following the Gruenberg and Stuart (1983) analysis, Elderplan staff assumed that the Medicaid group would include more than twice as many severely impaired members, and three times as many moderately impaired, as would the Medicare-only sector. These estimates contrast with Kaiser's overall assumption of a 40 percent differential. Elderplan's assumptions resulted in an adjustment factor of 2.85 on long-term care costs for Medicaid enrollees. Finally, Elderplan also estimated that hospital costs above and beyond Medicare coverage are twelve times higher for the Medicaid elderly than for non-Medicaid elderly. The differential can be attributed to the fact that in New York City as in many other areas, Medicaid spending on "alternative level-of-care" days is significant (American Association of PSROs 1980). However, only a third of the fee-for-service costs of alternative level-of-care days were requested, since it was assumed that most or nearly all of such stays would be eliminated in the SHMO.

The staffs of Elderplan and Brandeis made a concerted attempt to use New York City Medicaid data to estimate current spending in all areas of the SHMO service package. Insufficient data did not allow isolation of particular types of spending for particular types of Medicaid beneficiaries, but the analyses tended to support the Elderplan estimates. The state carried out its own analysis but faced similar limitations.

Elderplan followed Kaiser's process in the final calculation of the Medicaid rate proposal. The Medicare AAPCC for Medicaid members was subtracted from expected service costs to these members. Thus, "savings" on the Medicare AAPCC (in this case, only about 15 percent of the AAPCC) were applied toward reducing the Medicaid rate share. Table 6–4 shows that the resulting Medicaid rate is more than five times higher than the private premium of $29.89.[9] As was noted above, this contrast with Kaiser stems largely from the significantly different Medicaid populations the two programs plan to enroll. Another difference between Elderplan and Kaiser is that the former included additional rate factors to provide Medicaid members with full long-term care benefits. This additional coverage almost doubles the Medicaid premium proposal. The Kaiser proposal was unique among the sites in that it included the same package for both Medicare-only members and dual eligibles.[10]

The Medicare Partners Approach. Medicare Partners and the State of Minnesota agreed to use a pure fee-for-service equivalent approach to the Medicaid rate. Their approach required a detailed analysis of current Medicaid spending, since their goal was to develop rate cells similar to those of the Medicare AAPCC underwriting formula.

The analysis of state data was carried out over the course of two years in a cooperative effort by site and state staff. The analysis was handicapped from the outset by the lack of data on what is perhaps the most important variable in such a ratebook: impairment status of beneficiaries. Still, the staff developed a number of other rate cells and devised an ingenious method for managing reimbursement by impairment status. As of this writing, the final data analysis for first-year rates was not yet complete, and the rates reported here are thus subject to change. Because the final data run will take some time to complete, the state and site agreed to proceed with interim rates.

Separate rate cells were established for acute and chronic care. Acute care rates were established for fifteen separate underwriting cells. First, beneficiaries were divided into two categories, either community or institutional. The community category was in turn divided into (1) aged and blind and (2) disabled; and the institutional group was divided into SNF, ICF I, and ICF II. These five resulting categories were then cross-referenced by three age groups: age 65 to 74, age 75 to 84, and age 85 and over. The resulting rates were higher for the institutional groups than for the community groups, but they showed a somewhat peculiar inverse relation to age. The highest rate was for SNF beneficiaries age 65 to 74 ($259 PMPM), but SNF beneficiaries age 85 and over were much lower ($135 PMPM). Community residents were similar in cost whether aged and blind or disabled, but again older beneficiaries showed lower costs, for example, $130 for disabled persons age 65 to 74 as opposed to $92 for age 75 and over. These rates represent 95 percent of current Medicaid spending levels.

Long-term care rates were established to cover a variety of contingencies and health status conditions. First, the state agreed to continue to pay full per diem costs for 150 Medicaid members who were permanent nursing home residents at the time of enrollment. Since the state was interested in learning more about how to manage acute care and nursing home care for these beneficiaries, not in trying to move them out of nursing homes, there was no justification for putting the site at any risk for their nursing home costs.

Second, a sliding chronic care rate structure was established for community Medicaid beneficiaries assessed as nursing home certifiable at admission to the SHMO. If 10 percent or fewer of these enrollees are NHC, the state will pay 95 percent of the average metropolitan area nursing home rate of $1,658 PMPM. If that proportion is higher than 10 percent, rates will fall for those NHC members above 10 percent of enrollment: The state will pay 80 percent of the nursing home average for the 11th to 20th percentile; 70 percent of the rate for the 21st to 30th percentile; 60 percent of the rate for the 31st to 40th percentile, and so forth. The sliding fee schedule was adopted as an alternative to queuing: It is assumed that as proportions of NHC members increase, the likelihood that the members actually would have entered nursing homes will be less.[11] Finally, since there is no experience with these rates and the effectiveness of community services with this population, a separate fifty-fifty risk-sharing arrangement between the site and the state will apply to the losses and gains on long-term care for this population. This risk sharing will be calculated before other third-party risk-sharing arrangements are (see chapter 7).

The third component of long-term care reimbursement applies to community Medicaid members who are not assessed as NHC at admission but who later need to enter nursing homes. There will be no prospective chronic care rate element for these members, but the state will provide an 80 percent stop-loss coverage after ninety days residence in a nursing home. In other words, the site pays for the first ninety days and 20 percent of costs thereafter. Reclassification of members into new rate cell categories will be done only once a year, at each member's enrollment anniversary.

Table 6–4 shows a summary estimate of the Medicaid rate structure based on expected enrollment distributions by age, and assuming less than 10 percent NHC members among community Medicaid enrollees. Obviously rates are substantially higher than the private-pay premiums of $29.50.

Medicare Partners was the only site to develop a reimbursement arrangement with a third party other than Medicare and Medicaid. Under Title XX Block Grant funds, Hennepin County has agreed to contract with the SHMO for homemaker and chore services for income-eligible members. These services will be provided in addition to services covered under the Medicare Partners long-term care benefit; that is, homemaker and chore services received will not be counted in calculations of the amount of benefits available to these members. This will expand the benefits available to the poorest members of the program, and it should also reduce coinsurance requirements for them. One restriction on member eligibility is that nursing home certifiable Medicaid enrollees will not be eligible for the Title XX coverage, although noncertifiable Medicaid enrollees will be eligible. Planners project a total of about 100 eligibles during the first year of the contract.

The contract will be paid on a fee-for-service basis at Ebenezer costs, with total spending per eligible capped at a maximum of 90 percent of current average spending per eligible member in the county ($87 per month). Any surplus will be returned to the county, but the site will be at risk for costs above the cap. The site does not expect its average cost to exceed the cap, since Ebenezer's track record of per person costs in serving Title XX eligibles is more than $20 below the county average. A further protection for the site is an agreement from Medicare and Medicaid to include the costs and reimbursement for the Title XX contract in the overall risk-sharing arrangement for the site (see chapter 7).

The SCAN Health Plan Approach. Unlike the other states in which Demonstration sites are located, California has a good deal of experience with prepayment. A basic approach to formulating rates was established in the PHRED and PHP programs (McHolland 1982). The methodology represents yet another hybrid, in this case a provider bid model (based on previous provider experience), with bids limited by a cap (based on some percentage of fee-for-service equivalent spending—always less than 100 percent). When SHP and the state began negotiations, the state had no prior experience in prepayment for long-term care services, although one model based on the existing medical methodology had been proposed (Harrington, Newcomer, and Newacheck 1982).

Because of the state's history in using a fee-for-service equivalent model, the state chose a similar approach to set rates for SHP. First, the site and state staffs worked together to specify the types of Medicaid beneficiaries who would and would not be eligible to enroll in the SHMO (excluding most importantly beneficiaries without Medicare coverage and those who were in spend-down). Then the state analyzed spending data through its MIS to develop separate rates for the categorically needy (the SSI population), the medically needy (but not those in spend-down), and the NHC group. Each of these groups was further categorized into (1) aged and (2) blind and disabled, creating six separate rate cells in all.

While California was able to make its data runs considerably faster than Minnesota was, the analysis was still quite complex because of the need to take into account a variety of changes in the state plan and procedures that had occurred since the most recent available data were compiled (1981). These changes include provider rate increases, changes in payment criteria, benefit cuts, utilization controls, inflation, and other factors. The resulting rates, shown in Table 6–4, represent 95 percent of the estimated fee-for-service spending for the six groups (less withholds for $15,000 individual stop-loss insurance; see chapter 7). The rates for categorically and medically needy include no nursing home costs, while NHC rates include both acute and chronic care.

It should be noted that the rates for the NHC group, like the corresponding Minnesota rates, are apparently based on 95 percent of estimated nursing home costs, not the costs of alternative community care. However, the great disparity between the two states in both the NHC and the acute care rates raises questions about how comparable the two methodologies are. While California may have a more limited state Medicaid plan and does have lower per diem charges in its nursing homes, it seems unlikely that these differences would produce such disparate rates. Further investigation into the rate-setting methodologies in the two states is indicated during operations.

Revenues from Private Premiums

The chapter on membership and marketing has shown that a premium high enough to cover the full expected costs of the membership could easily lead to adverse selection—that is, a membership more costly than the population used in making reimbursement assumptions. On the one hand, chronically impaired elderly might view even a high premium as a bargain, given their known, ongoing needs. On the other hand, most "well" elderly persons may choose not to join, gambling that they will either not become impaired or will be able to join later if they do become impaired. Thus, in the Demonstration, the approach to setting the private premium was based on marketing analyses rather than financial ones, and all sites decided to set private premiums just marginally above acute insurance premium levels— far below the level needed to insure for full long-term care coverage.

Revenues from Private Cost Sharing
for Long-Term Care Services

Chapters 4 and 5 have already described the models available to sites in structuring cost sharing for long-term care. While these discussions concentrated on the implications of different cost-sharing structures for service delivery and marketing, they also included financial impacts, which need only be highlighted here. From the standpoint of revenue analysis, the most important point is that the more sites use cost sharing as a revenue source, the more they can raise the level of the chronic care benefit. This is because high coinsurance levels will dampen demand for services (thus leaving more capitation dollars left over for those who do use) and also increase the proportion of costs paid directly by low and moderate users. Another point is that revenues from cost sharing will be reduced by the costs of billing and collection. Relatively low coinsurance requirements will probably not result in net revenue to the plan. With these two points in mind, it is clear that the Demonstration sites are not making significant use of chronic care cost sharing from the standpoints of either demand-control or revenue. The 10 percent to 20 percent levels of coinsurance at the sites (table 4–1) will probably cover the costs of collection, but little more.

Estimating Costs

As was mentioned at the outset of this chapter, SHMO cost estimates are quite strictly bounded by revenue estimates, and these estimates differ for the two types of SHMO members. On the one hand, revenues for Medicaid members can probably be negotiated to cover nearly full benefits, both acute and chronic. On the other, revenues for Medicare-only members are not sufficient to cover the full long-term care needs of the private-pay membership. Furthermore, the allocation of these revenues into acute and chronic care is largely predetermined. Medicare requires full part A and B coverage, and both marketing considerations and HMO policy require coverage of extra services (such as drugs), as well as a buyout of most copays and deductibles. Funds for chronic care are, to a large extent, residual.

This section will describe the issues and choices sponsors face in moving through this process, which ends with the estimation of the long-term care benefit level and structure. The process the Demonstration sponsors followed generally had these steps:

1. Choosing among methodologies;
2. Finding and interpreting data;
3. Estimating acute and related medical care costs;
4. Structuring the residual into chronic care benefits.

Once again, this was an iterative process in planning, and it will continue as such during the operational phase.

Choosing Appropriate Methodologies

The choice of methodologies is in part determined by the sponsor's organizational type and experience and in part by the type and amount of information available. Three basic models will be discussed below, but it is important to understand that they are flexible. None of the sites used a single or pure approach, and, on occasion, all had to innovate.

No matter what methodology is chosen to estimate specific costs, there is a common format used to present the costs of prepaid plans. This format is the "capitation," in which all costs of the SHMO entity are broken down and expressed in terms of dollar costs per member per month (PMPM). Included are not only service costs, but also costs of administration, out-of-plan utilization, reinsurance, and credit from direct enrollee cost sharing.

The Actuarial[12] Approach. The most frequently used method to estimate capitation costs is called an "actuarial" approach (Project PHRED, undated; USDHEW 1973). To calculate capitation costs, one first estimates the general membership's utilization of each service (usually expressed in units per 1,000 members per year); then one multiplies utilization by a service cost per unit. The product is divided by 12,000 (12 months times 1,000 members) to yield costs PMPM.

One of the advantages of the actuarial approach is that it lends itself to an analysis of the costs of different case-mixes. This is a crucial feature in estimating costs for SHMO long-term care services, where particular subgroups of the population (such as the severely impaired or those certifiable for nursing home placement) will be using disproportionate shares of services. Since the available data on chronic care utilization come largely from programs that serve only the impaired, the data must be statistically manipulated by assuming that each known subgroup will comprise a particular proportion of the enrolled population. This is easily done using the actuarial approach, at least from the stand points of calculation and explanation. However, there are major problems with developing assumptions for the calculation, since the SHMO will differ significantly from previous programs in terms of benefits, service system, population, and many other factors.

The Adjusted Community Rate Approach. The adjusted community rate (ACR) methodology can be used by sponsors that are established HMOs. This methodology modifies components of an HMO's costs by using adjustment factors that reflect the costs of serving elderly enrollees versus the costs of the HMO's under-65 membership. Factors of time, complexity, and volume have been established in the HMO Medicare Demonstration (Greenlick et al. 1983), and additional adjustment factors have been proposed by the SHMO sites. Only the latter will be discussed here.[13]

HCFA has looked favorably upon the ACR methodology (since it is derived from an analysis of market-tested rates), but this approval should not necessarily make the approach acceptable to every HMO. Deriving an ACR is dependent upon the program's allocation of its costs into categories that are consistent with Medicare service coverage. Administrative and other costs must also be calculated and expressed. The question is whether the HMO's accounting system can express such costs accurately. For example, to derive expected SHMO costs for medical encounters, the HMO will need to calculate the total costs of medical encounters in a particular period, and then divide these costs by the total number of encounters in the period. This cost per encounter will then be multiplied by the established time and complexity factors, to yield an estimated cost per SHMO encounter. The problem is that if the accounting system is not accurate, the HMO (and the SHMO) will not know whether the organization is making or losing money on this business. SHMO sites will need to establish better data and cost-accounting systems, and then monitor their experience. Accuracy in these systems will be especially important in establishing fair internal risk-sharing arrangements among SHMO partners.

This is not to say that SHMO sponsors should not use an ACR approach. But sites should realize its limitations and try to improve the approach. Also, it should be clear that the ACR methodology works only for services and costs currently covered. HMO sponsors can use an actuarial approach for services that they do not cover, especially in the long-term care area.

The Best Guess Approach. To acknowledge the many unknowns in the SHMO cost estimation process, it is important to include a "best-guess" approach under methodological options. For several service areas and cost items (especially in chronic care), the existing data and experience are so limited that it is only fair to call the estimates best guesses. Planners should note the items where this "methodology" is used—if only to avoid being lulled by the aura of reality that numbers acquire when they reach the printed page.

Finding and Interpreting Data

For most of the sites, the most time-consuming aspect of finance planning was searching for and attempting to interpret data. This section will help make the task easier for future sponsors by examining:

1.   Types and sources of cost and utilization data.
2.   General issues regarding data interpretation.

Types and Sources of Data. In order to assemble data about costs and utilization, finance planners must first define each service component of the benefit package as well as other capitation costs. Once this is done, unit costs are by far the easier of the two factors to estimate, since they can be directly obtained, negotiated, or budgeted in the sponsor's planned service system. It is important that finance planners work closely with staff who are developing the organizational and delivery systems, since all parties must be aware of what services are being covered by whom, for what costs, and on what basis (such as capitation, per diem, cost). For example, whether or not a provider agreement has a risk provision may influence the utilization estimate. Or more obviously, the exact listing of ancillary services included in a medical or hospital agreemenet must be the same as the list in the cost buildup.

Utilization data are more difficult to obtain, but an overall guideline is that the more data examined, the better. This allows a "triangulation" approach of looking for the central tendencies in diffuse data from different programs. Attention should always be paid to variances, however. Besides using the data listed below, which are available from demonstration programs in acute and long-term care, finance planners should tap local sources. This process should begin within the sponsor's own planned service system. Such internal data require the least amount of interpretation, and it will probably be worthwhile to "dig them out" if these data are not readily available. Other local sources include the PSRO, health department, and provider organizations.

Also to be considered in finance planning are data from studies of the characteristics of the population. The Medicare Partners planning team, for example, was able to locate several studies of the local elderly population and even have special runs made from data tapes. The studies were conducted by other providers, a vocational rehabilitation agency, and the Area Agency on Aging.

Interpreting Data—General Guidelines. Very early in the data search, it will become clear that experience varies widely for almost every service. How does the new sponsor select a point in the spectrum? A number of general guidelines should be followed. Data from other programs must be weighed in light of:

Similarities and differences with the sponsor's or sponsors' programs (such as case management structure, risk status, size);

Population differences (such as age, sex, impairment status, extent of informal supports);

Eligibility differences, both for entry into the program and for receipt of particular services;

Differences in local professional practice or patterns of care (such as lower hospital utilization in the western United States);

Degree of comprehensiveness and integration of services as compared with the SHMO.

All assumptions made in interpreting data and choosing an estimate should be clearly and explicitly stated. Assumptions and data that have been considered but rejected should also be recorded. This will provide a reference for future interpretation of actual experience.

A final issue here concerns the overall strategy for making assumptions in an initial capitation estimate. Should assumptions be liberal (that is, toward the low end of the data scale), or should they be conservative (toward the high end)? Liberal assumptions might include an optimistic estimate of possible hospital savings, a low estimate of the number of enrollees who will use long-term care benefits, or a low estimate of utilization per user in the long-term care benefit area. Such assumptions allow a program to offer a richer benefit and/or a lower premium, but they increase the likelihood that actual figures will exceed projections and thus result in a deficit. Conservative estimates are more likely to put the program on a sounder financial footing, but they decrease the consumer appeal of the benefit package. The Demonstration's consulting actuary advised sites that the choice of a liberal versus conservative approach must in part be influenced by the risk-sharing arrangements available to SHMO sponsors. If a sponsor must risk a considerable sum in the start-up year, it would do well to err on the conservative side. A final factor is the financial position of the plan: Can it afford to take the risk?

Another consideration in assessing the conservative approach versus the liberal approach is the amount of protections available against selection risks. As has been mentioned, the SHMO Demonstration has devised a system for queuing applicants on the basis of impairment. Future sponsors should determine the availability and reliability of these queuing procedures before making final cost and utilization estimates.

Making Cost and Utilization Estimates in the Acute Care and Medical Areas

This section provides a service-by-service analysis of cost and utilization data for the SHMO's full range of acute and related medical services. Also included is a discussion of administrative overhead and out-of-plan emergency costs. (Long-term care data are discussed in the next section.) The utilization data examined during the planning process include local fee-for-service experience, the HMO Medicare Demonstration programs, national survey data, and the sites' own experience. It is impossible to convey all the data, analyses, and estimates generated in the planning phase, but the core of the information for major SHMO services is in table 6–5. This table shows the range of utilization in Medicare HMO demonstrations for major services in one column and the range of estimates by SHMO sites for these services in the other. Included also are estimates of other capitation costs, such as case management, administration, and out-of-area/out-of-plan emergency services.

To illustrate some of the issues and choices sponsors face in deciding where their site might actually fall in the range of data in table 6–5, following are comments on each of the major service areas, using examples from the Demonstration sites. But first, a few words are in order on the general issue of comparing SHMOs to the Medicare HMOs. It appears from the table that the SHMOs are estimating higher costs and utilization for most capitation items. This is true and it is also understandable, since two of the sites in the table (Elderplan and SCAN Health Plan) do not have past HMO experience. But the differences suggested in the table may be exaggerated. Regional differences are probably a factor in terms of traditional patterns of practice, the structure of the home care industry, and other areas. For example, Minneapolis and Brooklyn are relatively high-use areas, as contrasted with the low use in the Marshfield and Portland areas. Second, even though the table may exaggerate differences, the higher SHMO figures are in part a legitimate result of differences in populations served. SHMOs will be serving many more Medicaid eligibles, and probably older members, than the HMOs have served. These SHMO members in general will have higher levels of impairment than the HMO members, and thus higher medical utilization. Given this background, the issues and options in interpreting specific items in table 6–5 are as follows.

Hospital Services. Perhaps the most important utilization estimate that capitation planners make is in the area of hospital services. This is the major cost item in the capitation, and the hospital savings the SHMO achieves over the fee-for-service system provide the major funding for expanded benefits. The choices made by sites on some of the key issues include:

Can a new medical group count on savings similar to that realized by established HMOs?

The answer is probably not—at least to start. The high estimate in table 6–5 is from a long-term care agency sponsor, and it is based on local fee-for-service experience. The fee-for-service utilization rates are modified by a 15 percent reduction in admissions and a 9 percent reduction in average length of stay. The site is assuming that a mandatory second-opinion program and risk incentives to the medical group will reduce unnecessary hospitalization. Length of stay will be reduced by virtual elimination of alternative level-of-care days. Staff- and group-model HMOs should be able to project SHMO hospital utilization levels somewhere within the range of the Medicare HMOs.

Should HMO sponsors use the ACR or an actuarial methodology to estimate hospital costs?

The Demonstration's HMO sites split on this issue: Kaiser used the ACR; Group Health used an actuarial adjustment to their data on current over-65 members. However, both of these sites factored in the effect of the older SHMO membership. Kaiser's rates are based on the ACR in its Medicare Plus I program, which now has a relatively old population. GHI had experience only with a relatively younger elderly membership that aged into the plan, and payment was through cost contract.

Will hospital savings on members known to have highest hospital costs (that is, the very old and the very impaired) be proportionally greater or smaller than savings on the younger, healthier elderly?

This question is hard to answer, since HMOs have had relatively few extremely old or impaired members. Sites have not assumed that they will realize greater savings on these high utilizers, and one HMO site initially assumed no reduction in fee-for-service utilization levels for the age-85-and-over group. These are conservative assumptions, since it is anticipated that the availability of comprehensive case-managed services will make hospital discharge planning easier and may even reduce admissions.

Nursing Home Care—Medicare Type. It is important to understand that the Demonstration SHMOs offer two types of nursing home benefits: (1) a postacute benefit under which stays that meet criteria similar to Medicare's skilled care criteria are virtually fully covered, and (2) a chronic nursing home benefit under which custodial stays are covered. Thus, the sites faced two issues concerning nursing home costs: first, where to draw the line between the two types of stays; and second, how to predict costs for each. The first issue will be addressed here, as will issues in estimating Medicare-type utilization. Chronic nursing home costs will be discussed presently along with the long-term care benefit.

Table 6–5
Annual Service Utilization and Cost Ranges for HMO Medicare Demonstration Programs and for SHMO Demonstration Sites
(*in units per 1,000 members per year*)

Service or Cost Area	Initial Experiences of HMO Medicare Programs[a]	Initial Estimates of SHMO Sites
Institutional services		
Acute hospital (unlimited days)	1,700–2,880 days per 1,000	1,600–3,700 days per 1,000
Skilled nursing facility (Medicare-type or rehabilitative)	180–650 days per 1,000	670–1,560 days per 1,000
Medical and related services		
Outpatient medical (includes preventive office and home visits)		
Physician	5,730–5,875 visits per 1,000[c]	4,880–5,760 visits per 1,000[d]
Nonphysician	1,890–2,300 visits per 1,000[c]	1,860–2,000 visits per 1,000[d]
Total[b]	6,790–8,180 visits per 1,000	6,740–8,600 visits per 1,000
Home health (unlimited visits)	300–450 visits per 1,000[d]	566–1,267 visits per 1,000[d]
Laboratory	5,470–6,920 tests per 1,000[d]	6,900–7,600 tests per 1,000[d]
X-Rays	1,130–1,490 tests per 1,000[d]	1,130–1,640 tests per 1,000[d]
Pharmacy	9,010–10,730 scripts per 1,000	10,730–13,600 scripts per 1,000
Refractions or eyeglasses (one set every 2 years maximum)	560–660 sets per 1,000	500–550 sets per 1,000[e]
Hearing aids (one unit every 2 years maximum)	106[c] per 1,000	103–106[d] per 1,000
Ambulance and other medical transportation	$1.00–$2.60 PMPM	$3.10–$5.65 PMPM[e]
Copay and deductive revenue		
Acute care and other medical copays	Varied but minimal	$4.00–$10.00 PMPM[e]
Long-term care copays	—	$5.00–$11.00 PMPM[e]

Table 6–5
Annual Service Utilization and Cost Ranges for HMO Medicare
Demonstration Programs and for SHMO Demonstration Sites
(*in units per 1,000 members per year*)

Service or Cost Area	Initial Experiences of HMO Medicare Programs[a]	Initial Estimates of SHMO Sites
Administrative and out-of-area		
In- and out-of-area emergency services	$1.00–$13.00 PMPM	$7.00–$10.64 PMPM
Administration	$2.60–$7.00 PMPM (2–12 percent of capitation)	$17.50–$29.58 PMPM (7–14 percent of capitation)
Case management (included in administration line)		$4.00–$10.00 PMPM[d]
Reserves and other special funds		$6.28–$10.31 PMPM[f]

a. HMOs included in the table are Fallon, Marshfield, and Kaiser-Portland.
b. This estimate excludes inpatient, home health, and mental health visits, but it is based on reports from all three HMOs and all SHMOS.
c. Data based on one HMO or SHMO only.
d. Data based on two HMOs or SHMOs only.
e. Data based on three SHMOs only.
f. Based on the three SHMOs that established such funds.

Where should sponsors draw the line between Medicare-type and chronic-care stays?

This is obviously an important issue for both sponsors and members, since the former type of care is fully covered and the latter is not. Medicare intermediaries are quite strict and somewhat inconsistent (Smits, Feder, and Scanlon 1982) in reimbursing for SNF care, and all sites want to develop distinctions that are consistent with care patterns. They also want to liberalize definitions somewhat (besides eliminating the three-day hospitalization requirement) to fully cover short postacute stays. As of this writing, specific criteria are not available.

Will SHMO utilization of Medicare-type SNF care differ from fee-for-service experience? From Medicare HMOs?

Liberalized eligibility will be one factor that may make SHMO SNF utilization greater than that under the fee-for-service system. Also, in some areas of the country, SNF utilization is low simply because SNF beds are scarce. Since most sites plan to contract for or "buy" beds, access should not be a problem. Accessibility may also account for part of the expected higher use of SNFs in SHMOs than in HMOs, which do not always contract for beds (see table 6–5). For example, Fallon Clinic initially projected more than 1,000 SNF days per 1,000 persons, but achieved only 177 days. In its second year, Fallon leased beds in an SNF adjacent to its primary hospital. SNF use increased to 515 days per 1,000 persons in year 2 (Fallon 1981, 1982). Sites have made one other choice that should cause increased Medicare-type SNF use. Medicare Partners and Elderplan are both establishing subacute or "hospital step-down" units in their nursing homes, which provide care for acutely ill patients who no longer need the intensity of hospital care. This is expected to reduce hospital utilization. Elderplan is also considering creating a hospital "step-up" unit in the future, which could prevent hospital admissions from the community.

Outpatient Medical. As in the hospital and Medicare-SNF estimates, sponsors face both programmatic and methodological issues in estimating outpatient medical costs.

Programmatically, what will be the division between physician visits and other medical visits?

There appears to be some consistency here in table 6–5: A little less than three-quarters of the outpatient visits are to physicians, while the rest are to nurse practitioners and physician's assistants, optometrists, and others.

Methodologically, should an ACR or cost-buildup approach be used by HMOs?

Kaiser and Group Health followed the same path here: Both used the ACR. However, Group Health again adjusted for the older SHMO membership, while Kaiser used the same estimates as in their current HMO demonstration, again for good reason, given their experience and older population.

Inpatient Medical. Inpatient medical visits are excluded from table 6–5. Most programs calculate one visit (or a little less) per acute hospital day.

Mental Health. Mental health utilization numbers are not reported in table 6–5 since utilization was reported only by one HMO and one SHMO. The predominant opinion among staffs at the sites and at Brandeis is that the elderly will not use mental health services unless they are encouraged to do so. The issue is, How important do staff members see these services as being? Utilization has been very low at the HMOs: One reported only about 35 visits per 1,000 members. The highest SHMO projection is 200 visits per 1,000 members.

Home Health. The major issue here is similar to that relating to the SNF item: Where does one draw the line between fully covered Medicare-type care and limited-benefit chronic care? Sites largely maintained Medicare's skilled care eligibility criteria for these services, but they projected higher utilization than the HMOs because of more impaired membership. Home health care under the chronic care benefit is discussed below.

Other Medical. With a few exceptions, all the "medical-and-related" benefits in table 6–5, from laboratory services through ambulance and other medical transportation, show a good deal of consistency both in definition of benefits and in utilization levels. One exception is other medical transportation, where one site is offering a car service benefit for a $4 copayment.

It should be noted that some SHMO medical services have not been included in the table. These include audiology, radiology, optometry, Medicare dental, foot care, and durable medical equipment and prosthetic devices. These are not major cost items, and it is difficult to isolate them in reports and capitation estimates in a way that allows consistent analysis.

Copays and Deductibles. The challenge sponsors face with cost sharing is to achieve a balance in a number of areas, including: revenue (is it needed?); utilization (discouraging "unnecessary" but not "necessary use"); and collection costs. Another goal here is to minimize annoyance to members. Table 6–5 shows that the SHMO sites plan to require higher levels of direct cost sharing than have the HMO Medicare programs, even on services that are not part of long-term care. Copays are planned on a variety of these services at the various sites as was detailed in table 3–1. Highlights are the following: outpatient physician ($2 per visit at one site); emergency room without hospitalization ($15 per visit at one site); prescription drugs ($1 to $3.50 each at all sites); eyeglasses ($10 per set at one site, 50 percent copay at another); and hearing aids ($40 to $50 copay at 2 sites, 50 percent copay at another). Copays on long-term care services are used at all sites, accounting for revenues of $5 to $11 PMPM (about 2.5 percent to 4 percent of capitation).

Out-of-Plan and Administrative Costs. The major issues in predicting costs for out-of-area and out-of-plan emergency services are (1) What are the strategies to minimize them? and (2) Will nonreferred, nonemergency claims be paid? Kaiser, for example, experienced a number of large nonreferred, out-of-plan claims in the early months of Medicare Plus I. Kaiser chose to pay these claims even though it was not required to do so. See chapter 5 for strategies to reduce these claims, which can, if left unchecked, become a large problem in terms of costs and membership relations.

A major issue concerning administrative costs is whether free-standing SHMOs on the scale envisioned in the Demonstration are too "top-heavy." Can models like Elderplan and SHP pay their overhead, or do they need to tap the economies of scale of an HMO in such areas as marketing, membership accounting, and billing. Table 6–5 shows that per member costs of plan administration in SHMOs are projected to be considerably higher than such costs in the HMOs. In part, this is because of the costs of case management in the SHMO. These costs have been broken out in table 6–5, and they do not account entirely for the differences in administrative costs. Concerning methodology, sites with HMO partners have predicted administrative costs in part through the ACR. Budgetary methodologies were used to estimate all administrative costs at non-HMO sites and some administrative costs at HMO sites.

Reserves and Special Funds. Because of the many unknown factors involved in cost and revenue estimation for the initial period and also because of the small size of some of the sponsors, most of the sites have proposed setting aside special funds in the capitation. The rationales and uses of the funds at various sites will be described in more detail in chapter 7. In general, the funds exist either to offset potential future losses or to stabilize benefits in the future.

Making Cost and Utilization Estimates in the Chronic Care Area

The foregoing characterization of the chronic care benefit as a residual is an exaggeration. The intent is to dramatize the limits on benefits for Medicare-only members. In fact, other benefits and some revenues can be slightly altered to allocate more (or less) resources to long-term care. For Medicaid members, the chronic care benefit is not a residual at all. Their full long-term care costs can be prepaid in the SHMO, as is the case at three of the four sites.

Because of the difference in the flow of funds for the two types of members, sites face the problem of estimating the costs of both *full* and *limited* long-term care benefits. There are some similarities in making the two estimates, but also some differences. The key difference stems from the fact that the plan's exposure with limited benefits is capped by the dollar maximum. This makes accuracy in estimating utilization much less important than accuracy in estimating the number of users. Also, benefit structure issues (such as coinsurance and renewability) are especially important when funds for benefits are very limited. Site planners need to work harder to stretch benefits, and consciously manipulating structural variables is one way to do so.

The analysis that follows is meant to help sponsors work through these issues. It begins with an analysis of potential costs of a full chronic care benefit, first through a discussion of the key variables that need to be considered and then through an examination of available program data in light of these variables. It continues with a review of the issues involved in structuring and estimating costs for limited benefits. In both sections, examples of site choices are included.

Estimating the Full Need for and Utilization of Chronic Care Services. Estimating full long-term care benefit costs is probably the prime example of using the "best-guess" methodology. The accuracy of estimates depends heavily on several case-mix and resource allocation variables. As was seen in chapters 4 and 5, these variables can be identified and described, but they are not yet subject to good controls. It is important to review these variables prior to analyzing the available chronic care utilization data, because the data can be interpreted only to the extent there is information available on the variables.

The first step in estimating chronic care costs (whether for full or limited benefits) is to predict who will enroll. Enrollment is partly determined by marketing and luck, but sponsors can and should consciously choose the populations they want to serve. They may choose to seek relatively representative populations, as the Demonstration sites have, or they may enroll only Medicaid members, or select other options. They should then try to characterize the kinds and levels of need in these populations using available data and such accepted indicators as ADL and IADL levels. Sponsors should also think about other population factors that can affect need and utilization, such as geography, transportation, housing types, attitudes of members toward accepting formal assistance, and most important, the availability of informal care.

The second step is to lay out the chronic care benefits that may be offered and carefully think through the financial impacts and rationales for offering each of them. Planners should be sure about why they are offering a particular service: its attractiveness to consumers, because of clinical need, because the service will be a cost-effective substitute for a more expensive service. These assumptions may turn out to be wrong, but they should be specified at the outset so that they can be studied. The structure of coinsurance and renewability for benefits will also have obvious effects on cost estimates.

The third step, with population and benefits established, is for sponsors to decide and specify how they will respond to the estimated need. All the chronic care needs of all the elderly cannot be met in the SHMO, and program planners must decide how to allocate and ration resources. As was seen in chapter 4, there are two levels of decisions to be made when allocating resources among members. First, the program must devise eligibility and targeting guidelines. Depending on philosophy and goals, defensible arguments can be made for various targeting decisions, ranging from serving only the most impaired who are at imminent risk of entering nursing homes to also serving the mildly and moderately impaired with preventive services. Second, the program must develop a style (if not a set of specific guidelines) for prescribing services to eligible members. Norms of practice for chronic care similar to those used by physicians in acute care are yet to be developed. As was seen in chapter 4, these norms must take into account not only clinical functioning but also social (especially informal care), environmental, and even economic issues.

With these variables in mind, planners can turn to data collection and interpretation. Regrettably, data on chronic care utilization are scarce, inconsistent, and difficult to interpret, in large part because information on the key variables is often not available. To complicate the problem, data must be analyzed for both home- and community-based services and for institutional services. These will be dealt with in turn below.[14]

Data and reports from all significant home- and community-based demonstration programs were examined as background for making estimates for the SHMO. However, only a few of these programs reported data in a useful form—that is, in units of utilization of particular services per active clients per specific time period. The data in table 6–6 are from MJGC's Nursing Home Without Walls; Triage, in Connecticut; and a program in Manitoba, Canada; they are the best data on home- and community-based services that the Demonstration has been able to locate, but they still leave much to be desired. All programs had similar services, and all had relatively deep coverage (that is, clients could receive home care as long as these costs were less than 75 to 100 percent of alternative institutional costs).

While these programs offer helpful information on service utilization, there is no information available on prescription practices or the use of informal care. There is information, however, on the various eligibility and population issues, which is useful even though this information differs across programs. First, the three programs used different criteria to determine eligibility for program services. Nursing Home Without Walls and Manitoba had rather strict criteria. Nursing Home Without Walls accepted only those who met New York State nursing home preadmission standards (see the Elderplan site description in chapter 4 for details). In Winnipeg, Manitoba, the program's services were available to those "at risk" of institutionalization. It is difficult to tell which of the two sets of criteria is stricter or whether the criteria affect different groups (such as those with informal supports) in different ways. The utilization levels are dramatically different, but it is difficult to know whether to attribute the difference to population or other factors. When Abt Associates completes its evaluation of Nursing Home Without Walls, some of these questions may be answered.

Triage I had loose eligibility criteria: The program served any elderly person in the target area who "needed" services. However, data made available to Brandeis allowed an analysis of utilization by impairment level.

Table 6–6
Populations Served and Utilization Experience from Three Community-Based Long-Term Care Programs[a]

	(1) MJGC (Nursing Home Without Walls)	(2) Manitoba (Winnipeg-LTC)	(3) Triage (Home Health Group)	(4) Triage (Homemaker Group)
Definition of group	Nursing home certifiable at SNF level	At risk of hospitalization or placement in nursing home or other facility	Requires help with bathing, dressing, toilet, transfer, and/or eating; or is incontinent	Requires help with phoning, medications, money management, preparing meals, and/or mobility (no ADL needs)
Service use (units per group member per month)				
Nursing	3.4 visits	2.2 visits	1.1 visits	0.5 visit
Therapies	0.9 visits	0.1 visit	0.5 visit	0.1 visit
Home help[b]	17.9 visits[c]	15.5 hours	24.4 hours	6.6 hours
Chore	2.8 visits[c]	—	0.7 hours	1.0 hours
Orderly	—	1.4 hours	—	—
Meals	6.0 meals	—	3.2 meals	6.3 meals
Day hospital, respite, EARS	$145 month	—	—	—

a. The Nursing Home Without Walls Program is operated by MJGC in Brooklyn, New York. MGJC is a site in New York State's Long-Term Home Health Care Program. The program serves Medicaid beneficiaries who are found to qualify for SNF or ICF care according to the state's DMS-1 assessment instrument. The service utilization data were derived from the Elderplan initial capitation estimate for the severely impaired, which was based on Nursing Home Without Walls experience.

The Canadian Province of Manitoba offers a fully insured home care program to all residents who are at risk of institutional placement. The data here are from the City of Winnipeg and include only clients in nonacute, non–hospital-based programs.

Data on Connecticut's Triage Long-Term Care Demonstration Program were analyzed by Leonard Gruenberg at Brandeis. Assessment data were used to classify clients according to level of impairment, and utilization data were tabulated according to these levels.

b. Includes personal care worker, home health aide, homemaker, and (in Manitoba) chore.

c. Approximately 3 to 4 hours per visit for MJGC.

The figures in table 6–6 show that elderly with ADL limitations used similar amounts of services as did the Winnipeg clients, while those with only IADL problems used much less—especially in terms of personal care. Regrettably, no data are available on the ADL or IADL characteristics of clients in the other two programs.

Since all the programs in table 6–6 served only impaired clients, SHMOs had to take a second step in using these data. This was to estimate the proportions of chronic care utilizers in the SHMO population and, in turn, to use data such as those in table 6–6 to calculate service utilization per 1,000 members and PMPM costs. Some guides were available. First, the population served in Winnipeg represented 7.1 percent of the elderly there. Second, Brandeis analyses of national surveys show that the Triage "home health" group might represent between 3 to 6 percent of the local population, while the "homemaker" group might represent another 8 percent to 12 percent (Gruenberg and Leutz 1983). It is important for sponsors to remember that Medicaid eligibles are significantly more impaired than are other elderly persons, and separate calculations should be made for each group.

Once population assumptions were set (and all the other issues of population and program were considered), sponsors simply used the actuarial method to calculate average service utilization for the membership as a whole. For example, a sponsor who decided to follow Winnipeg exactly would estimate 1,848 chronic care nursing visits per 1,000 members per year (2.2 visits times 12 months times .07 of membership times 1,000).

To summarize: In estimating the number of long-term care users that a SHMO might find in its membership, a sponsor has some latitude in its choices—but probably within a rather narrow range. Overall, the sites estimated that between 5 and 14 percent of enrollees would use long-term care benefits at any one time, depending in large part on the stringency of eligibility and prescription criteria (see chapter 4). It was assumed that Medicaid utilization would be higher than average and that Medicare-only would be lower. In making service utilization estimates, sites tended to rely on the figures in columns 1 and 4 of table 6–6. However, the Nursing Home Without Walls data were reduced by at least 10 percent, owing to savings expected in a risk-based program, and the Triage "homemaker" group data were applied to only about a third of the estimated 12 percent moderately impaired membership, since most are not expected to qualify for benefits.

The estimate for chronic care nursing home utilization should be made in conjunction with the community care estimate, but additional data and assumptions are required. The estimate is largely dependent on two variables: first, the line drawn between Medicare-type and chronic care stays; and second, the proportion of members who will have long-term nursing home admissions. The first variable has been discussed above. To estimate the second, sites used their own program experience as well as national and regional data on utilization of institutional services. Elderplan used its experience in Nursing Home Without Walls, which shows that about 40 percent of the applicants to that program cannot be maintained in the community at less than 75 percent of alternative institutional costs—and may therefore need to enter nursing homes. The utilization of the Medicare Partners "long-stay" portion of the nursing home benefit was patterned after the work of Keeler, Kane, and Solomon (1981), using calculus once assumptions were made about local admissions rates and the distribution of lengths of stay. Kaiser did not make any specific assumptions about chronic nursing home utilization. While it may seem odd not to make such an important estimate, it should be remembered that Kaiser did not include a full long-term care benefit in its rate proposal to Medicaid. Making an accurate estimate of community-based and institutional utilization is not terribly important when the benefit is limited.

Structuring the Chronic Care Benefit for Private-Pay Members: Allocating Limited Long-Term Care Resources. Once a sponsor has an estimate of the capitation funds available for chronic care for Medicare-only members, planners must weigh the cost implications of various benefit structures. In chapter 4 it was shown that chronic care benefits can be consciously structured along the following dimensions:

Cost-sharing levels and mechanisms;

Allocation of funds into institutional versus community-based benefits;

Definition of the benefit period and the renewability of the benefit.

It is not necessary to repeat here the details of the various options or the implications of alternative structures for the allocation of long-term care resources to different types of members (such as the more or the less impaired, the low-income members or those with more resources). Nor will site choices be described again—these are shown in table 4–1. Rather, a series of summary statements will be made to indicate the impact of decisions along these dimensions on cost and utilization estimates. The following financial relationships should be kept in mind when making choices.

The higher the cost-sharing requirements in the SHMO, the more conservative the utilization data in table 6–6 become as estimates of SHMO experience. This is because these programs did not require cost sharing.

A cost-sharing structure that uses a large deductible and then free care will likely inhibit utilization for the moderately impaired, but it will not inhibit utilization once the deductible is met by the higher users of services.

Fully renewable nursing home benefits increase the importance of making an accurate estimate of rates of entry into nursing homes as well as lengths of stay. Long-term liability must be factored into financial estimates.

Nonrenewable nursing home benefits enable SHMOs to offer deeper coverage of home- and community-based services, and they therefore make it more important to accurately estimate utilization levels for such services.

Tight targeting and eligibility guidelines for chronic care will lead to higher average needs per eligible person than loose guidelines will, but tight guidelines will also mean that more benefit dollars will be available per eligible person.

Defining chronic care benefits in terms of a "benefit year" (that is, from the time a member becomes eligible for chronic care) rather than a "contract year" (from the time the member first joined the program) may increase the complexity of benefits management, but it should allow for richer benefit levels. This is because a contract-year structure allows some members to use a full year's benefits in less than a year's time and still be eligible for a new benefit at the anniversary of their enrollment.

Defining the chronic care benefit for home- and community-based services in terms of a monthly rather than an annual entitlement should moderate potential fluctuations in the plan's spending on these benefits (which could arise if initial eligibility is concentrated in particular months). Such a definition will also allow for marginally richer benefits (because more members will die or disenroll before their full year's benefits are used).

It is important to note that while these financial considerations are important in making decisions on benefit structures and allocation of resources, the clinical, marketing, and equity considerations discussed in chapters 4 and 5 should receive equal if not greater weight. In any case, internal consistency should be a common element among chronic care cost estimate assumptions, targeting and prescription guidelines, marketing strategies, and case-mix targets. It is also important to stress that all of these benefit structure issues are new. Therefore, no attempt was made to lock the plans into one approach. The variations and their associated impacts will form important research issues for the coming years, since benefit structure is a key ingredient in comprehensive chronic care insurance.

Conclusion

In conclusion, it is important to emphasize the iterative nature of the process of making financial estimates for the SHMO. Each site repeatedly reviewed revenue and cost assumptions and reconsidered its decisions on such issues as premium levels, long-term care benefit structures, utilization assumptions, eligibility criteria and related case-mix assumptions.

As the sites move through their first year of operations, the accuracy of the various assumptions will be tested, and in making their second round of financial estimates, planners will have the benefit of some experience. Accuracy and confidence in the estimates should increase substantially, and some changes (hopefully increases) in chronic care benefits may be indicated. The increased confidence in financial estimates should also allow sponsors to take greater financial risk in later years. Issues and choices regarding risk are the topic of the next chapter.

Notes

1. It should be noted that other public parties could participate in SHMO financing; most important would be agencies that finance home care services for the elderly (such as Title XX Block Grant Funds or Title VI of the Older Americans Act). In fact, the Medicare Partners site has obtained such funding. Since this is at this point a unique case, it will be discussed separately below.

2. It should be noted that HCFA is currently reviewing alternatives to the formula. It is not expected that the current SHMO Demonstration will be affected by any alteration in the formula, since negotiations have been conducted on the basis of the current formula. Of course, future SHMO sponsors should determine early which formula applies to them.

3. That is, 95 percent of the community beneficiaries will be reimbursed at 95 percent of current AAPCC factors, and 5 percent will be reimbursed at 200 percent of current factors: $(.95 \times .95) + (.05 \times 2) = 1$.

4. As was seen in chapter 4, most sites are projecting higher proportions of NHC members for purposes of service delivery and cost estimates. In estimating revenues based on smaller proportions, sites are being conservative. The 5 percent limit on the proportion of NHC members should, therefore, help the sites' bottom lines, but possibly at the expense of frail elderly who might have been enrolled without the limit. (See note, page 135.)

5. This is commonly called the "K" adjustment, which factors the estimated county per capita spending according to the weight of the county population on the AAPCC underwriting factors.

6. Readers unfamiliar with the techniques that HMOs use to "build up" rates may want to first read the cost estimate section of the chapter and then return to this section.

7. California pays OnLok for a full range of services on a risk basis, but the program enrolls only nursing home certifiable beneficiaries (Zawadski 1983).

8. Some of the concepts and terms in this section require knowledge of the basic types of cost estimate methodologies discussed in the next section of this chapter. If this section is difficult to follow, skip to the next and return.

9. The rate shown in table 6–4 is actually a compromise between the site proposal, which was 8 percent higher, and a state proposal, which was 14 percent lower.

10. Of course, dual eligibles should not lose current coverage of chronic care if the chronic care benefit is exceeded. The Kaiser-Oregon negotiations over including long-term care in year 2 will need to resolve this.

11. The 5 percent limit on the proportion of NHC members (see note, page 135) is very difficult to reconcile with this agreement not to queue Medicaid applicants. A site–state request for exemption from the limit was denied by HCFA. As of this writing, it is not known how the site and state will resolve the issues.

12. *Actuarial* is somewhat of a misnomer, since the basic method does not require the complex skills and training of an actuary.

13. It should also be noted that the draft regulations for implementing the TEFRA legislation require HMOs to use a very detailed series of ACR factors. This ACR requirement, as well as the requirement that at least 50 percent of plan members be neither in Medicare nor Medicaid, were waived for the Demonstration. However, they pose long-term survival issues for non-HMO sponsors in the Demonstration.

14. For additional useful background on chronic care home health services and institutional services, see Gruenberg 1981a, 1981b.

7
Managing Risk and Uncertainty

One of the integral features of the SHMO Demonstration from its conception has been that providers should be put at financial risk for delivering the full range of acute and chronic care services. In its purest form, being *at risk* means that the provider's revenues per member are set in advance.[1] The provider is then responsible for serving the membership according to contracted benefits, and, at year's end, it can keep any surplus but must absorb any loss.

There are a number of rationales for tying risk to prepaid capitated reimbursement. Most fundamentally, the practice is meant to foster efficiency. The lure of a surplus (profit) and the fear of a loss are incentives for providers to use human and material resources economically. Providers do so by making appropriate "substitutions" of nurse practitioners for physicians, for example, or by substituting nursing home care for acute hospital care, or by promoting preventive treatment. If providers know they can keep some of the savings generated by such efficiency, they will try to maximize it. Practically speaking, the need for coupling risk with prepayment can be dramatized when one imagines a prepaid capitated system *without* risk. Providers would be paid in advance for expected costs, but they would also be paid later (without penalty) for any excess costs above the capitation. Such a system contains incentives for providers to increase costs—and the means for them to do so.

A second basic rationale for provider risk is that responsibility for costs should be tied to ability to control them (Zelten 1981; Leighton 1979). The SHMO system is designed to allow providers to coordinate and manage a broad range of services. It is therefore appropriate that risk for a broad range of services should go hand in hand with this broader control.

Finally, predictability is a feature of prepaid, at-risk contracts that is attractive to all concerned. Providers can better predict revenue levels and flows, and the government and private individuals can better predict expenditures. Budgeting can be improved at all levels.

These arguments for provider risk are compelling and are central features of the SHMO. But although the concept is attractive, its implementation has been a challenge. The SHMO has so many new and untested features in organizational design, service system, marketing, and finance, that it was difficult even to identify the major variables much less to quantify them. Furthermore, most of the sponsors are relatively small, nonprofit organizations without the capital to gamble heavily on the program. Nor were they offered large start-up loans similar to those the government formerly gave to HMOs. Because of the number of unknowns and the sponsors' limited finances, the possibility of putting the sites at full risk to start was never seriously entertained in the Demonstration. The policy initially accepted by all parties called for partial risk to start, with the eventual goal of full risk. However, as the Demonstration neared implementation, the national political environment changed, and HCFA mandated that sites must assume full risk in the third year of operations. A full-risk requirement is also contained in the SHMO legislation. While the sponsors have accepted the requirement, its wisdom is debatable from the perspectives of both the providers and the government.

Sponsors and third parties should be aware of both the types of risks and unknowns in the model, and the financial magnitude of these risks. The first section below addresses these issues. Next, in order to share risk, sponsors and third parties need models. The models must be understood by all and must also accommodate the major needs of each party. The second section below describes some models that were considered, as well as those adopted at the sites. Finally, a concluding section discusses the functions of risk in the model, and the advisability of various ways of allocating risk among the participants. It also delves further into the dangers of moving to full risk too soon.

Areas of Risk and Uncertainty in the SHMO

In discussing risk, it is important to distinguish between the concepts of *risk* and *uncertainty* (Knight 1921). The concept of risk can be applied to outcomes that have a known probability of occurrence. In contrast, the concept of uncertainty can be applied to outcomes for which the probability of occurrence is not known; and in some cases, uncertainty implies that the range of potential outcomes is not even clearly understood. At this stage, the concept of uncertainty is probably more applicable to the most important financial unknowns in the SHMO than is the concept of risk. In most areas, however, the potential ranges of outcomes are thought to be known: What is unknown is how to assign probabilities to them.

This section will expand on the areas of risk listed in chapter 2. That discussion mentioned risks associated with fluctuations in unit costs, utilization, contract mix, age–sex–impairment characteristics of members, and enrollment pace. The intent here is to focus more closely on the areas in which the SHMO model creates new risks and uncertainties and also intensifies prior existing ones.

Selection Bias

If those who join the program are more or less "healthy" (that is, more or less costly) than the hypothetical population on whom the program rates are based, the program will have experienced what is called biased selection. Avoiding biased selection is important to providers as well as to the government, and each party obviously worries about a different bias: The provider's favorable selection is the government's unfavorable selection, and vice versa.

Two options were considered in the Demonstration to control for selection bias, and both are being used: (1) underwriting formulas that adjust third-party reimbursement according to health-related characteristics of members and (2) queuing (creating waiting lists) of applicants by health status. How reliable are these arrangements? The primary way in which reimbursement formulas such as the Medicare AAPCC adjust for selection bias is through underwriting—that is, paying more for some individuals than others on the basis of individual characteristics with known statistical relationships to costs. The AAPCC, for example, adjusts reimbursement according to four characteristics (age, sex, institutional status, and welfare status). There are both uncertainties and risks associated with the implementation of such a formula. For example, there is the chance that cost variations *within* underwriting cells are biased. That is, members may be systematically different from nonmembers in terms of a cost-related characteristic not included in the formula. For example, some researchers (Eggers 1980; Eggers and Prihoda 1982) argue that enrollees in two of three HMO Medicare demonstrations studied (Kaiser and Fallon) had lower prior-year utilization and costs than did a set of local nonenrollees matched according to the AAPCC factors. The third HMO (Marshfield) showed no significant difference in terms of prior utilization. Marshfield argued that unfavorable selection was a major factor in the losses experienced by their program.[2]

In addition to uncertainties concerning selection bias, there are identifiable risks due to purely random error in applying formulas such as the AAPCC. Gruenberg's (1982a) analysis of 1977 Current Medicare Survey (CMS) data indicates that a very small portion of beneficiaries account for a very significant proportion of total costs. This skew in the distribution of costs is only marginally identified by the AAPCC underwriting factors (Anderson, Resnick, and Gertman 1982). An internal Brandeis analysis of 1977 CMS data shows that because of this skew there is still a 5 percent risk that costs will turn out to be 5 percent higher or lower than predicted for an enrolled population of 5,000, even if selection is random.

In addition to facing selection bias uncertainty and risk vis-à-vis acute care utilization, SHMO planners must worry about bias regarding enrollees who will require long-term care services. The NHC modification of the AAPCC is intended to adjust Medicare reimbursement to protect against biased selection on impairment status, but it is important to remember that the purpose of the adjustment is to cover the higher acute care costs of the severely impaired. Even with the NHC factor, Medicare reimbursement does not directly cover the costs of long-term care services. Rather, these services are primarily financed through a pooling of savings on hospital costs and extra premiums from a balanced population of enrollees, the great majority of whom, it is assumed will not use these services.

The uncertainty about biased selection in the area of high chronic care needs is a major issue in the SHMO. The proportion of long-term care benefit users is expected to be small at all sites (between 5 percent and 12 percent of membership). Thus even small variations from predictions in actual enrollment will place programs in some financial jeopardy and also strain the service delivery system. Because the proportions of expected users are small and their costs are very high, and because individuals with current chronic care needs are fairly identifiable, most sites devised and adopted the direct approach of controlling for selection bias through queuing (see chapter 5). It is important to note, however, that this methodology is untried. While queuing is intended to control uncertainty, how effectively it will do so is itself uncertain.

Aging of the Enrolled Population

An initial analysis performed by Leonard Gruenberg (1982b) of Brandeis indicates that annual cost increases due to aging of the population might be three to four times higher for the long-term care costs of a given enrolled population than for their acute care costs. The implications of this are that the financial viability of the SHMO depends not only on enrolling the predicted population, but also on maintaining a viable risk pool in its membership over time. It should be pointed out that these estimated differences in cost increases are based on *full* expected long-term care costs. Thus, the manner in which a SHMO limits and structures its long-term care benefit (such as by making institutional benefits nonrenewable) will modify the extent of the difference (see chapters 4 and 6).

It is not likely that during the limited term of the Demonstration much light will be shed on the actual extent of cost increases due to an aging membership. Still, the cost implications of aging can at least be addressed through the concept of risk rather than uncertainty. As the initial Brandeis analysis shows, there are data on which to base projections, and although the financial implications are significant, they can be managed in the long run. To be a viable model, the SHMO will need to identify the limits of a workable insurance risk pool, be able to predict how its current membership will evolve, and find ways to recruit new members who fill out the risk pool according to desired targets. HMOs also must work to maintain a balance in their risk pools, but the issue is even more important in SHMOs, since the increased costs per age gradient are much higher for an older population using chronic care services. Therefore, SHMOs may need to manage case-mix more directly through mechanisms such as queuing.

Uncertainties in the Delivery System

Each of the SHMO sites is developing at least one new major service component in its model, and some are developing more than one. Each is also putting together this delivery system for the first time. While sites have made predictions about how effectively these new systems will function in terms of controlling costs and managing utilization, these assumptions are untested in many service areas. Thus, aside from possibly having to face excess utilization from unfavorable selection, sites may have problems meeting their utilization and cost predictions because of the incapacity of their service systems to perform as predicted. This type of uncertainty should be reduced considerably in later years of the Demonstration, but any new sponsor will need to face it initially.

New Benefits

There is considerable uncertainty in offering the SHMO's new long-term care benefit package. There were only scanty data on which sites could base their estimates of the proportions of users in the population as well as their levels of utilization. Many untested assumptions had to be made. Partial safeguards against the unknowns of chronic care were devised in benefit structures: Sites protected themselves against the risk of excess utilization by placing dollar caps on the benefit levels. Since such caps can be adjusted up or down, this model could be accommodated to a full range of benefit levels.

Maintaining the Participation of Informal Caregivers

The background analysis in chapter 1 indicated that informal caregivers (especially family members of the impaired person) provide about twice as much care to the elderly population as does the entire formal long-term care system. It is essential to the survival of the SHMO as a viable policy initiative, and as a sound financial entity, that the involvement of these informal caregivers be maintained.

There is no intention in the Demonstration of denying formal services to elderly members who currently have good informal supports. In fact, it is hoped that the SHMO can enhance the contributions of informal caregivers by coordinating formal and informal approaches and by relieving pressures through such services as respite care. It is known that the great majority of informal caregivers are both willing and able to maintain their helping roles toward their loved ones. In recognition of these relationships, it has been seen in chapter 4 that each site developed plans to maintain and improve informal care where appropriate. It is also known, however, that informal caregiving is a significant and unwanted burden to some people, and that they may try to shift the burden to the program. It is impossible at present to predict the extent to which such shiftig will occur, since the problem must be resolved on a case-by-case basis at each site. Suffice it to say that this area poses real uncertainties and that any significant shifting of responsibility toward the SHMO may upset financial plans.

Risk-Sharing Models for the SHMO Demonstration

One of the most difficult challenges in the development of the SHMO Demonstration was to devise models for sharing financial risk among provider entities, Medicare, and Medicaid. HCFA required the models to include all three parties and mandated that the circumstances be clearly stated under which the risk-sharing responsibilities of one ends and another begins. HCFA allowed the SHMO sponsors to specify a maximum risk level beyond which they would no longer be responsible for losses. Given the many risks and uncertainties that sponsors faced in undertaking the project, this loss limit represented a very important and supportive policy on HCFA's part.

Within this framework, what issues faced participants in designing risk-sharing models? Not surprisingly, some of the issues were very similar to those in the area of reimbursement. The first task was to establish the basis for determining each party's share of the risk. This was not difficult in a general sense. The only approach really considered for third parties was for each to be responsible for the utilization and costs of the services it covered and for the enrollees it supported. While the general approach was clear, planners considered a variety of specific ways to figure each party's share in the risk pool. The Brandeis recommendation and the general preference of sites was for the SHMO entity to be responsible for the areas of cost and utilization not covered by third parties, up to the specified maximum risk level. After that, the third parties would share risk in approximate proportions to their shares of services and enrollees.

Given this basic approach, Brandeis explored two models for implementing it: (1) through tracking utilization and costs by enrollee type and by service area, and (2) through pooling the funds, costs, and risks across service areas and enrollee type (that is, bottom-line risk sharing). Kaiser chose the former approach, while MJGC and Ebenezer–Group Health chose the latter. The fourth site, SCAN, chose to supplement bottom-line risk sharing with a proposal for "individual stop-loss" coverage, a form of reinsurance that is common in HMOs. The next section explores the tracking and bottom-line risk-pooling models, and then the SCAN proposal is discussed along with other risk-management mechanisms commonly used in HMOs.

The Tracking Model

There are two basic difficulties in devising and implementing tracking models for risk sharing. The first is operational. Medicaid and Medicare currently pay for many of the same services for their beneficiaries, but they pay for them under different circumstances. In the current system, the service overlap is managed by program eligibility and coverage guidelines that state where the responsibility of each party begins and ends. In order to manage the overlap in the SHMO, staff must develop and follow similar guidelines for defining responsibilities. The SHMO must define who pays for what portion of each service and must define the circumstances under which each payer is responsible. These definition and decision requirements are an operational burden. However, in order to manage chronic care benefits the Demonstration sites must track the most difficult of these factors anyway—that is, the distinction between postacute type and chronic-type nursing home and home health care.

A second difficulty with the tracking model is that the SHMO's incentives to deliver the proper balance of services most cost-effectively could be disturbed if risk-sharing arrangements were more advantageous with one third party than with the other—or if particular services in the package were covered by risk sharing more completely than others were. For example, if Medicaid were to assume a greater proportion of risk on its nursing home and home health responsibilities than were Medicare, the SHMO would face incentives to define Medicaid enrollee utilization as falling into the Medicaid arena. Or, to draw an example of the other eventuality, if either Medicare or Medicaid shared risk on some services (such as nursing home care) and not on others (such as home health care), the SHMO's incentives would be to overutilize the former, even when the latter might be more appropriate.

To address these issues, Brandeis recommended that these tracking models of risk-sharing incorporate two characteristics. First, risk sharing should cover general areas of the service package rather than specific services—for example, the entire long-term care benefit rather than the nursing home or home health care services within it. Second, the proportions of risk covered by each third party should be the same, so that no incentive exists to shift costs from one to the other.

Kaiser proposed a risk-sharing arrangement that is a variant of the tracking model. Kaiser and Oregon Medicaid were not able to agree on the inclusion of chronic care services for Medicaid beneficiaries in the first year of the SHMO. Still, the proposal is worth discussing as an example and since some of its components have been retained. One part of the proposal that still stands is that Kaiser will take full risk in Medicare Plus II for services currently covered under Medicare Plus, that is, all Medicare part A and B services plus additional medical benefits. Kaiser proposed that excess costs for new long-term care benefits should be entirely the responsibility of HCFA and Medicaid. Medicaid was asked to assume responsibility for Kaiser's losses in serving Medicaid enrollees' long-term care needs by supporting a risk stabilization fund at a level of $20 per Medicaid member per month. In turn, HCFA would be asked to assume full responsibility for excess long-term care costs for Medicare-only members (the other part of the proposal still in effect), as well as full costs for Medicaid members if their excess costs exceeded $20 per member per month.

While the proposed arrangement clearly gives Kaiser greater incentives to economize on acute care services than on long-term care services, these incentives are also clearly in the "right" direction. Incentives will be maximized to substitute skilled nursing care and home health care for acute institutional care. The model's only possible flaw here is that there will be no clear incentive in the initial year to economize on long-term care service utilization. Since Kaiser hopes to take full risk for these services during the second contract period, it could be argued that there is some incentive to "pad" initial utilization so that operation under full risk has a better chance of showing a surplus. There is no reason, however, to believe that Kaiser intends to do so or will in fact do so. Furthermore, if long-term care costs are high, Medicaid officials may well decide not to sign a contract for these services in year 2, thinking they could obtain better value in the fee-for-service system. Thus, it is expected that Kaiser will implement its long-term care component as if it were at risk for these services, and in a manner that tries to economize. Furthermore, it should be noted that the Research Center staff preferred the second model of risk sharing (funds pooling), but as was explained in chapter 2, Kaiser management was not willing to assume initial risk on the long-term care benefit package.

The Funds-Pooling Model

Brandeis's recommended approach to risk sharing uses a pooled-risk mechanism. In this model, each third party and the SHMO entity take risk for a proportion of "bottom-line" losses, according to the proportions of their funds and covered services in the SHMO capitation. This model defines risk shares prospectively, rather than retrospectively (that is, on the basis of actual service utilization by particular categories of enrollees).

It is easiest to explain this model through an illustration, using the Elderplan risk-sharing proposal. Elderplan's initial proposal was as follows:

HCFA's initial risk exposure would equal the proportion of the total program budget that is composed of Medicare part A and part B service costs (about 53 percent).

Medicaid's initial risk exposure would be for that proportion of the total program budget composed of Medicaid-covered services, including payments both for the core package and the supplemental acute and chronic coverage (about 18 percent).

Elderplan's initial risk exposure would be for the remaining proportion of the total program budget (29 percent), up to a maximum of $150,000.

Above this initial loss corridor (that is, about $521,000) Medicare and Medicaid will share in the risk according to the portion of third-party revenues they produce (that is, Medicare, 80 percent; Medicaid, 20 percent).

Actual utilization of particular services by particular types of enrollees does not enter into the reconciliation process in this risk-sharing model. In other words, both Medicare and Medicaid agree not to base their responsibilities on the utilization of "their" services by their enrollees. This arrangement should afford the SHMO maximum flexibility in devising the most cost-effective mix of services for each enrollee, in all covered service areas. Furthermore, it provides the SHMO with incentives to devise a fully integrated and economical service delivery system. It also maintains incentives for Elderplan to economize up to a relatively high level of total plan losses ($521,000), an arrangement that is also desirable.

Medicare Partners has arranged a bottom-line agreement with HCFA and Medicaid very similar to Elderplan's, but with a total first-year loss limit of $250,000. Also, before staff calculate responsibilities under the bottom-line agreement, they must first calculate responsibilities under the state's risk-sharing arrangement for Medicaid members (see chapter 6).

To conclude the discussion of the tracking and pooling risk-sharing models, it is important also to discuss arrangements for sharing surpluses.

Both HCFA and most Medicaid agencies made it clear that if a program is to assume only partial risk for loss, the program should alternatively be able to keep only a portion of any surplus realized during the contract period. This contention is certainly reasonable. Neither HCFA nor any Medicaid agency has yet stipulated that the risk-sharing corridor on the surplus side must be the same as that on the loss side. Indeed, a defensible policy might be to make the SHMO sponsor's opportunity for gain greater than its liability for losses. This would enhance incentives to economize, without exposing the program to unbearable levels of risk. The Elderplan proposal did not take this approach but rather set forth surplus corridors that mirror the risk corridors on the loss side. Kaiser plans to return any surplus to members through the benefit stabilization fund.

Other Risk-Sharing Models

Other risk-sharing models are available to sponsors, and during Demonstration planning several were explored by Brandeis, HCFA, and the sites. Most prominent among the models explored were more traditional risk-sharing and reinsurance arrangements used by HMOs, including "aggregate stop-loss" and "individual stop-loss." These models allow the provider to protect itself against particular kinds of risk (Leutz and Hannon 1981; Miller 1981).

Aggregate stop-loss coverage was obtained from Blue Cross by Fallon Clinic in the HMO Medicare Demonstration. The coverage protected the project against excess utilization of hospital services by the entire membership. The risk-sharing arrangement stated that the parties would share costs in specific proportions if average utilization or costs exceeded stated levels. Although such comprehensive coverage is rather unusual, Blue Cross was willing to offer it because it planned to enter the elderly HMO market.

A more common type of risk-sharing arrangement in HMOs is "individual stop-loss coverage." This arrangement protects the program against extremely high utilization levels by individuals. Some HMOs carry this in relation to hospital utilization, and levels of coverage often range between $15,000 to $30,000 per individual per year. Such coverage is attractive, since it protects against adverse selection, whether biased or random. Since prospective reimbursement formulas are not very effective when used to identify and compensate programs for extremely high utilizers, it may be advisable for programs assuming larger amounts of risk to obtain this other type of coverage. A "bad" selection of high utilizers could easily wipe out any economies realized in the operation of the program as a whole.

These advantages of individual stop-loss protection were very attractive to the SCAN site, which has obtained both bottom-line and individual stop-loss coverage from HCFA and which has coordinated individual stop-loss coverage from Medicaid. Medicaid will pay the plan on a fee-for-service basis for all Medicaid-covered services that exceed $15,000 per year for any Medicaid member. HCFA will pay on a fee-for-service basis for hospital costs of any member that exceed $50,000 per year. Premiums for these coverages were calculated by analyzing Medicaid and Medicare reimbursement tapes, and premiums were fixed at actual expected costs. Medicaid premiums vary by client types. Costs for the most common clients are $1.25 PMPM for categorically needy aged and $21.37 PMPM for nursing home certifiable aged. Medicare premiums are $1 PMPM. It is interesting to note that SCAN tried to obtain individual hospital stop-loss coverage privately and was quoted a premium of $7.37 PMPM for a $50,000 policy.

Individual stop-loss meshes with the site's plan to take a considerable bottom-line risk in the first year (on the order of $800,000). Individual stop-loss is also important to their internal risk sharing arrangement. It was shown in chapter 2 that SHP is departing somewhat from the other sites by setting up quite substantial levels of internal risk sharing in particular service areas. The individual provider partners are concerned about their exposure, and they want protection on hospital and medical utilization. Having this coverage makes them considerably more willing to assume large risk for the bottom line. SHP will integrate individual stop-loss coverage with the bottom-line risk-sharing arrangement with HCFA through a specific sequence of calculations. That is, stop-loss arrangements with third parties will be calculated before internal arrangements among partners, which will be calculated before bottom-line arrangements.

SHP must be very careful in structuring the incentives created by its internal and external risk-sharing arrangements. Since in many areas the SHMO Demonstration faces more uncertainty than risk, there are dangers in singling out particular kinds of risk, or types of members, for more protection in the initial period. Differential protection could give undesirable service-substitution incentives. But SHP may be pointing the way toward future risk-sharing models that are simpler to administer than the cumbersome bottom-line arrangement, with all its audits and potential disputes over accuracy of reporting. As providers gain experience with the capacity of their service systems to control costs, they may be able to relax the need for protection in some areas, while maintaining it in others. Once the workings of the mature SHMO are better understood, it may be possible to set performance standards in particular service areas, without worrying that the incentives created might militate against the efficient functioning of the entire system.

Funded Reserves

To supplement these external arrangements for protection against financial risk, most sites are creating special funds through the capitation to buffer potential losses. As was noted in chapter 6, the contribution rates of these funds range between about $6 and $10 PMPM; thus, in the eighteen-month first "year" of operations, accumulations should be between $300,000 and $500,000. As will be seen presently, the specific rationales and applications of these funds vary somewhat across sites, but there are two similarities. First, the sites see the funds as mechanisms both to protect against current-year shortfalls and to accumulate reserves for future years, when risk increases. This is an important consideration for relatively small sponsoring organizations without substantial reserves or endowments of their own on which to fall back. A second cross-site similarity among the reserve arrangements is that HCFA has required (with one small exception at Elderplan to be described below) that all funded reserves be applied to current-year losses *before* external risk sharing goes into effect. In other words, reserves will not be funded if plans run at a loss (unless that loss is less than the reserve level).

The government's rationale for this policy is that the reserve funds are benefit dollars that come out of "savings" on the AAPCC. If there are not sufficient savings to fund the reserves (that is, if a plan is running at a loss), then the reserves should not be funded. If plans were allowed to fund reserves regardless of losses, and were then allowed to apply the reserves as the provider's increased share of risk, the concept of provider risk could lose its meaning.

While this position is reasonable, it makes the reserve mechanism less useful to sites as a buffer against future risk and as a means to establish the financial independence of the SHMO. Some sites argued that they should be able to fund their reserves, regardless of bottom-line losses or gains. They drew a parallel to HMOs' setting aside funds to pay off start-up loans.

There may be some very difficult decisions down the road for smaller sponsors. A site that runs at a loss in the first year will need to obtain assurance from its corporate sponsor that it can meet the substantially increased second-year risk-sharing obligation. If a second-year loss follows, even a large sponsor might balk at the prospect of a third year at full risk. Not surprisingly, the three sites that have established significant special funds are those whose sponsors have the least capital to risk—that is, the long-term care agencies.

Medicare Partners will create two funds of equal size: a contingency fund and risk stabilization fund. The rationale for the former is to protect against the possibility of higher future costs that might arise from such sources as: the aging of the enrolled population, higher utilization when members become increasingly familiar with using the system, or simply having a bad year due to random variance in members' health care needs that is to be expected in a population this small. The purpose of the risk-stabilization fund is to maintain or possibly improve benefit levels for members and/or to reduce member costs. To avoid large fluctuations in benefit and premium levels, stabilization funds will be applied fifty-fifty in the two subsequent years.

Elderplan has also established two funds: a medical group incentive fund and a contingency reserve. The purpose of the medical group incentive fund is to reward the physicians' group for holding hospital and medical costs below projected capitation levels. It is funded at rates considerably lower than the contingency fund. Rationales for the contingency fund are similar to those at Medicare Partners. Furthermore, state insurance laws require Elderplan to set aside reserves to cover insolvency. The state reserve-funding requirements constitute HCFA's one exception to its policy of funding reserves only in the case of surplus. However, the funding level allowed by the state is $1.50 PMPM, which is less than a third of Elderplan's contingency funding, and, with Elderplan's small membership, not enough to meet the state's total reserve requirements by the end of the Demonstration.

SCAN Health Plan has the simplest reserve scheme, with only one contingency fund. Accumulations are meant to support a base for future operations and reserves. There is also a provision for applying any surpluses beyond the fund to enrich benefits and/or to lower member premiums.

In contrast to the other sites, Kaiser did not propose creating a reserve fund out of the general capitation. Kaiser will continue the benefit stabilization fund begun in Medicare Plus I, but this fund is more limited in purpose and scale than the funds at the other sites. It is maintained solely for the purpose of managing retroactive fluctuations in the calculation of the AAPCC ratebook that come from Kaiser's need to have a fixed, year-long prospective rate (Greenlick et al. 1983). However, as was described in the previous section, Kaiser did propose a risk stabilization fund to be financed through the Medicaid capitation. This fund would have been somewhat similar to the other sites' contingency funds, except that it would have covered costs only on specific services and members, and it was designed to be of a stable size rather than to grow from year to year.

Future Risk-Sharing Arrangements

If SHP individual stop-loss arrangements with HCFA and Medicaid prove to be workable and effective, they might be used by other sites to move more quickly to full bottom-line risk. The idea of aggregate stop-loss may provide another workable model, as long as standards of performance are mutually acceptable to providers and insurers.

Individual stop-loss coverage in the long-term care service area is probably not necessary in the SHMO as currently formulated, since individual benefit levels are already capped. Even for a SHMO operating at full risk for long-term care costs—both community-based and institutional—

individual stop-loss coverage probably does not make sense. While costs for an individual could become high ($45,000 a year for a skilled nursing bed at MJGC), these costs do not approach the astronomical levels of acute care. Furthermore, chronic illness is more predictable than is acute illness. It is possible to predict a certain number of such individuals in a capitation based on carry-overs from the previous year. Thus it is easier to plan for them financially. Some type of aggregate stop-loss coverage on nursing home care would probably be more advisable.

Another question that must be addressed in relation to both individual and aggregate stop-loss coverage is, Who should share in this risk? To a large extent, the answer depends on the service to be covered rather than on the eligibility status of the member. For example, both Medicare and Medicaid currently incur very high costs for individuals who undergo long hospital stays. Medicare might appropriately share in aggregate hospital stop-loss coverage, while both Medicare and Medicaid might appropriately share in stop-loss coverage of individual utilization. It is important to note that Medicaid's responsibility for individual stop-loss coverage should extend to SHMO members who are not Medicaid-sponsored, since it is safe to assume that many of these individuals would have spent down to Medicaid eligibility levels during a long hospitalization. Aggregate stop-loss protection for long-term nursing home stays would be more appropriately covered by Medicaid, again for at least a proportion of the costs generated by non-Medicaid enrollees.

For the initial period of the Demonstration, private reinsurers consider the SHMO too risky a venture to extend coverage to it, especially in the area of long-term care services. Therefore, sites turned to government funders to share the risk by reinsuring against the aggregate cost of the program and particular sections of program services. This arrangement may continue for some time—certainly in the long-term care area. As long as private reinsurers include a relatively high risk factor in their premiums, SHMO sponsors and the government may find it advisable to continue to arrange reinsurance coverage through government third parties. Premium levels for such coverage can be actuarially derived from third-party spending data. These data are comprehensive and reliable for Medicare services. Such reinsurance arrangements could pave the way for turning this business over to the private sector if and when the SHMO establishes itself as a viable system.

Conclusion

To conclude, it is appropriate to reflect on the role of provider risk in the SHMO model. There are really two separate reasons for provider risk. The first is to encourage providers to be efficient in the use of health care resources—that is, providers at risk will seek ways to save money and increase benefits. The second reason concerns the streamlining of the regulatory and reimbursement apparatus; that is, systems for such processes as claims review, utilization review, billing, and cost audits are simplified. Perhaps most important, with full risk the budgeting and financial management processes are better controlled. The government and the member can fix their spending levels in advance, and the provider knows what its revenues will be.

Obviously, a key test of the model will be how well both of these rationales hold up in practice. However, it must be decided which rationale is the more important and feasible to test in an initial demonstration project. Perhaps most important, we must ask whether sites really need pursue the "ultimate" test of the second rationale—full risk—in order to demonstrate the validity of either rationale. Might premature pursuit of full risk create undesirable outcomes in the delivery system, especially in the appropriateness and quality of patient care?

Degrees of Risk, Responsibility, and Control

It was argued above that some risk is essential to a prepaid, capitated system of reimbursement. Thus, the issue should not be whether there will be risk but rather how much risk there will be, and how fast it will increase. If one accepts the basic principle that responsibility should flow from control, then the principle behind full risk is that the provider is ready to control the new SHMO system in a manner that both assures financial stability and achieves, within the context of the system, the best possible care for members. A parallel assumption is that the government's roles are to (1) pay the SHMO a fair price for its services (but not too high a price) and (2) ensure that the program can deliver care to beneficiaries that is appropriate, of high quality, and, one hopes, a significant improvement in terms of benefits.

This book makes it plain that achieving these conditions will require a great deal of developmental work, experimentation, and research, both by the government and by providers. Reimbursement arrangements with Medicare and especially with Medicaid are untested first approximations. The assessment, reassessment, certification, and verification processes are also untried. The ability to control the risk pool through marketing and queuing is unknown. The potential efficiencies and inefficiencies of a consolidated delivery system have not been demonstrated.

The list could go on. If the Demonstration can significantly improve understanding, practice, and policy in all of these areas, it will have made a contribution. It is an open question whether the sites will have well-oiled machines ready to head into a third year of operations at full risk. The more important point is whether a reimbursement and regulatory system can be devised that will *at some point* allow sufficient control to support full risk.

Risk and the Service System

It must be remembered that the complex arrangements in finance, risk sharing, and corporate organization are all established to create a service delivery system that will increase both efficiency and effectiveness. Of course, financial incentives are important in encouraging efficiency among providers, but these incentives are not really at the heart of the SHMO's promise to improve the system or even to save money. Rather, the model should achieve efficiency primarily by improving effectiveness, appropriateness and, it is hoped, the quality of care.

For example, well-targeted home care should save on nursing home costs. Good primary care in institutional and noninstitutional long-term settings should cut hospitalization rates. Subacute nursing home units and highly skilled home care should cut lengths of hospital stays. In other words, the successful consolidation of the delivery system, because it appropriately manages levels of care, should at the same time lead to efficiency and cost savings. A great deal of risk is not needed to assure that providers work together to create the procedures, communications systems, and new divisions of labor that lead to efficient and effective care. Nor is great deal of risk needed to encourage provider partners to devise compatible corporate relationships and implement workable management and administrative systems.

In fact, undesirable effects may result from putting too much risk on these systems too soon. Pressures on both agencies and staff could create negative outcomes. If the provider partners take full responsibility before they feel they are in full control, they might end up safeguarding their own interests rather than those of the overall cooperative venture. Such self-interest might be reflected in internal rate negotiations, which could become confrontational. Provider partners might be tempted to exaggerate their costs in order to create a hidden surplus and cover feared losses. If full risk comes too soon, the SHMO system as a whole could become extremely conservative in its marketing, covered benefits, and financial projections. Of course, such self-protective behavior could also lead to large profits, which from the business point of view are the only legitimate justification for taking a large risk. While there may eventually be room for profit in SHMOs, it probably makes sense to limit providers' profits and losses until the difference between efficient and effective performance can be distinguished from mere profitability.

The pressures for savings would also be felt by professionals. While physicians might be able to withstand the pressure, case managers might not. As was shown in chapter 4, they will be in a very different position than that of physicians in the SHMO, for two reasons. First, unlike physicians, case managers are responsible for care that is strictly limited in dollar terms per member. Thus, they will often need to ration resources that may be insufficient to meet full levels of need. This makes the second difference between these two kinds of practitioners all the more important. Case managers will be creating and testing key elements of their practice for the first time in the SHMO, including assessment instruments and protocols to determine whether members are eligible to receive services. They will be developing new standards to assure quality of care and to allocate resources among members who need long-term care, taking into account the key factor of informal supports. They will be working with professionals in the acute care sector to establish the conditions under which patients are transferred across levels of care.

If the SHMO takes on too high a level of risk before case managers have adequate control over these systems, the possibility of improving professional practice in long-term care may be compromised. At each of the sites, case managers will be officially employed by the SHMO entity. Will they be able to resist pressure from administrators to give less than the patient needs and is eligible to receive? Will the ideas of prevention and enhancement of life be discarded before they have a chance to be tested? In short, might long-term care practice in the SHMO develop into a system for "bare bones" care because the pressures for savings are too great from the outset?

To put these questions into some perspective, it is important to remember that HMOs came into being only *after* medical practice was well-established. Physicians already had autonomous control over who needed their services and how much service they needed. A system was already established to pay for the bulk of these services. Thus, physicians entered HMO practice in the context of a "fat" system in which to achieve their economies and a set of professional standards that did not really need to be compromised to insure delivery of high-quality care. Yet some still question the wisdom of mixing financial incentives with the physician's capacity to exercise judgment about what is best for the patient.

Compare this to the position of the case manager. Case managers will come to the SHMO with professional training and experience in determining need and providing services, but their autonomy will be limited by resource constraints and eligibility guidelines not of their own making. Within this context, they will need to develop autonomy and also advocate for changes in benefits, eligibility, and resource allocation based on their professional judgment. Decisions about who receives long-term care and how much care they receive must obviously be made in the context of resource and eligibility constraints, but too much risk could create an atmosphere in which program managers cannot afford to listen to the judgments of other professionals. If this happens, the Demonstration will have squandered one of its most important opportunities. Long-term care practice needs the chance to develop into an independent professional force with standards of service and quality that can be trusted. Until this type of practice is established, it is probably not a good idea to put providers at a great deal of risk for these services.

In conclusion, it is important to remember that the SHMO is a demonstration project—perhaps the most complex demonstration ever tried in the health services area. Its planning and start-up have taken much longer than was initially anticipated, and it may also take more time than we would like to make the SHMO work well. Risk sharing may be neither a practical nor even a desirable policy for future SHMOs, but it is certainly the right course to take until we determine the true potential of the model.

Notes

1. Within the fluctuations of underwriting formulas' adjustments and of copays with utilization.

2. They also argued that the calculation of county costs was biased against them, since it did not adequately adjust for a large new hospital that was recently built to serve their area.

References

Abrahams, R., and W. Leutz. 1983. "The Consolidated Model of Case Management and Service Provision to the Elderly," *Pride Institute Journal* 2(4)(Fall).

American Association of PSROs. 1980. Untitled nationwide study of hospitalizations carried out on September 4.

Anderson, J., A. Resnick, and P. Gertman. 1983. *Prediction of Subsequent Year Reimbursement Using the Medicare History File: II. A Comparison of Several Models*, UHPC Background Paper. Boston: Boston University.

Austin, C.D. 1983. "Case Management in Long Term Care: Options and Opportunities," *Health and Social Work* 8 (1)(February).

Austin, C.D. 1981. "Client Assessment in Context," *Social Work Research and Abstracts* 17(1)(Spring).

Austin, C.D., and F.W. Seidl. 1981. "Validating Professional Judgement in a Home Care Agency," *Health and Social Work* 6(February).

Baxter, R., J. Callahan, S. Day, et al. 1983. *Initial Evaluation of the National Long-Term Care Demonstration* (Draft version). Waltham, Mass.: Brandeis University.

Bishop, C. 1981. "A Compulsory National LTC Insurance Program," in J. Callahan and S. Wallack, eds., *Reforming the LTC System*. Lexington, Mass.: Lexington Books.

Boyd, L., L. Miller, R. Pruger, et al. 1980. *Equity and Efficiency Project: First Year Report*. Berkeley: University of California, School of Social Welfare, January.

Burnet, J.J., and R.E. Wilkes. 1980. "Fear Appeals to Segments Only," *Journal of Advertising Research* (October).

Callahan, J. 1981. "Single Agency Option for Long-Term Care," in J. Callahan and S. Wallack, Eds., *Reforming the Long-Term Care System*. Lexington, Mass.: Lexington Books.

Callahan, J., L. Diamond, J. Giele, and R. Morris. 1980. "Responsibility of Families for Their Severely Disabled Elders," *Health Care Financing Review* 1(3)(Winter).

Callahan, J., and S. Wallack, eds. 1981. *Reforming the Long-Term Care System*. Lexington, Mass.: Lexington Books.

Carter, A., and E. Kennedy. 1983. "Ebenezer Society: An Interdependent Caring Community," *Pride Institute Journal* 2(4)(Fall).

Cohen, J. 1983. *Public Programs Financing Long-Term Care*. Washington, D.C.: Urban Institute.

Donobedian, A. 1966. "Evaluating the Quality of Medical Care," *Milbank Memorial Fund Quarterly* 44.

Eggers, P. 1980. "Risk Differential between Medicare Beneficiaries Enrolled and Not Enrolled in an HMO," *Health Care Financing Review* 1(3)(Winter).

Eggers, P., and R. Prihoda. 1982. "Pre-Enrollment Patterns of Medicare Beneficiaries Enrolled in "At-Risk" HMOs," *Health Care Financing Review* 4(1)(September).

Eustis, N., J. Greenberg, and S. Patten. 1984. *Long-Term Care: A Policy Approach*, Monterey, Calif.: Brooks Cole.

Fallon Community Health Plan. 1981 and 1982. *Alternative Models for Prepaid Capitation Financing of Health Care Services for Medicare/Medicaid Recipients.* Worcester, Mass.: Fallon Clinic, Annual Reports.

Fischer, C. 1980. "Differences by Age Groups in Health Care Spending," *Health Care Financing Review* 1(4)(Spring).

Flexner, W., C. McLaughlin, and J. Littlefield. 1977. "Discovering What the Health Consumer Really Wants," *HMC Review* (Fall).

Fullerton, W. 1981. "Finding the Money and Paying for Long-Term Care Services," in J. Melzer, F. Farrow, and H. Richmond, eds., *Policy Options in Long-Term Care.* Chicago: University of Chicago.

Galblum, T., and S. Trieger. 1982. "Demonstrations of Alternative Delivery Systems Under Medicare and Medicaid," *Health Care Financing Review* 3(3)(March).

Galblum, T. 1982. "Review of the Marketing and Enrollment Experience in Medicare HMO Demonstrations," Baltimore: HCFA, July 12.

GAO. 1982. *The Elderly Should Benefit from Expanded Home Health Care but Increasing These Services Will Not Insure Cost Reductions*, Washington, D.C.: U.S. Government Accounting Office.

GAO. 1979. *Entering a Nursing Home: Costly Implications for Medicaid and the Elderly*, Washington, D.C.: U.S. Government Accounting Office.

Garrick, M.A., and W.L. Moore. 1979. "The Application of Uniform Assessment and Standards on Aged and Disabled Recipients of Social and Health Care Support Systems," in R.A. Solen et al., eds., *Community-Based Care Systems for the Functionally Disabled: A Project in Independent Living.* Olympia, Wash.: State of Washington, Department of Social and Health Services.

Glazer, E., and C.A. Snyder. 1983. "State of the Art for Self-Care for the Elderly," Report for the F.V. Burden Foundation, Elderplan, Inc., Brooklyn, New York, January.

Glazer, E., C. Snyder, and D. Kodner. 1985. "Aging Populations and the Emergence of Prepaid Health Plans: A Unique Opportunity for Health Promotion," *Journal of Family and Community Health* (February).

Greenberg, J. 1983a. *A Guide to Developing Marketing Strategies for Social/HMOs*, Paper prepared for Social/HMO Demonstration Project. Waltham, Mass.: Brandeis Unviersity.

Greenberg, J. 1983b. "States Develop Alternative Long-Term Care Programs with Medicaid Waivers," *Business and Health* (December).

Greenberg, J., and D. Doth. 1982. "Minnesotan's Knowledge and Views about Long-Term Care: Preliminary Findings." Minneapolis: University of Minnesota.

Greenberg, J., D. Doth, and C. Austin. 1981. *A Comparative Study of Long-Term Demonstrations: Lessons for Future Inquiry.* Minneapolis: Center for Health Services Research.

Greenberg, J., and W. Leutz. 1984. "The Social/HMO and Its Role in Reforming the Long-Term Care System," in P. Feinstein, M. Gornick, and J. Greenberg, eds., *Long-Term Care Financing and Delivery Systems: Exploring Some Alternatives.* Baltimore: Health Care Financing Administration, June.

Greenberg, J., and W. Pollak. 1981. "Cost Estimation and Long-Term Care Policy," in F. Farrow, J. Meltzer, and H. Richman, eds., *Policy Options in Long-Term Care.* Chicago: University of Chicago Press.

Greenlick, M. 1983. "An Investigation of Selection Bias in an HMO Enrolled Experiment." *Health Journal*, 5(1), Fall, 1984.

Greenlick, M., S. Lamb, T. Carpenter, T. Fischer, S. Marks, and W. Cooper. 1983. "A Successful Medicare Prospective Payment Demonstration," *Health Care Financing Review* 4(4)(Summer).

Gruenberg, L. 1982a. "The AAPCC—A Preliminary Examination of the Issues," UHPC Working Paper. Waltham, Mass.: Brandeis University.

Gruenberg, L. 1982b. "The Effect of the Aging of the Enrolled Population on Utilization and Costs in the Social/HMO: Implications for Financing," UHPC Working Paper. Waltham, Mass.: Brandeis University.

Gruenberg, L. 1981a. "Home Health Services in the Social/HMO," UHPC Working Paper. Waltham, Mass.: Brandeis University.

Gruenberg, L. 1981b. "Nursing Home Utilization and Costs in the Social/HMO," UHPC Working Paper. Waltham, Mass.: Brandeis University.

Gruenberg, L., and W. Leutz. 1983. "Estimating Prospective Capitation Payments for Long-Term Care for the Social/HMO." Paper presented at the 111th Annual Meeting of APHA, Dallas, Texas, November 16.

Gruenberg, L., and N. Stuart. 1983. "An Analysis of Factors Related to Variations in the Proportion of Elderly in the Community Using Medicaid," UHPC Working Paper. Waltham, Mass.: Brandeis University.

Gruenberg, L., and N. Stuart. 1982a. "A Health Status-Based AAPCC: The Disability Level Approach," UHPC Working Paper. Waltham, Mass.: Brandeis University.

Gruenberg, L., and N. Stuart. 1982b. "Variations in the Distribution of Severely Impaired Elderly: An Analysis of 1977 Health Interview Survey Data," UHPC Working Paper. Waltham, Mass.: Brandeis University.

Haley. 1968. "Benefit Segmentation: A Decision-Oriented Research Tool," *Journal of Marketing* (July).

Harrington, C., R. Newcomer, and C. Newacheck. 1982. *Prepaid LTC Health Plans: A Policy Option for California's MediCal Program*. San Francisco: University of California Aging Health Policy Center.

HCFA. 1982. *Evaluation of Coordinated Community-Oriented Long-Term Care Demonstration Projects*, Preliminary Report, HCFA Contract No. 500–80–0073, October, Baltimore, Md.

HCFA. 1981. *Long-Term Care: Background and Future Directions*, Baltimore, Md.: Health Care Financing Administration.

Health Interview Survey. 1977, 1979. Washington, D.C. USDHEW, National Center for Health Statistics.

Hughes, G.D. 1978. *Marketing Management: A Planning Approach*. Reading, Mass.: Addison-Wesley.

InterStudy. 1981. "Survey Analysis of Callers to the HMO/Medicare Program," Minneapolis: InterStudy, Inc., mimeo.

Kane, R., et al. 1982. "Predicting the Course of Nursing Home Patients: A Progress Report," *NCHSR* (January).

Kane, R.A., and R.S. Kane. 1981. *Assessing the Elderly: A Practical Guide to Measurement*, Lexington, Mass.: Lexington Books.

Keeler, E., R. Kane, and D. Solomon. 1981. "Short- and Long-Stay Residents of Nursing Homes," *Medical Care* 19(3)(March).

Knight, F. 1921. *Risk, Uncertainty, and Profit*, New York: Houghton Mifflin Co.

Kodner, D. 1984. "MJGC: From Multi-Level Long-Term Care Institution to Social/HMO," in R. Bennet et al., eds., *Coordinated Service Delivery Systems for the Elderly: New Approaches to Care and Referral in New York State. Advanced Models and Practice in Aged Care*, #2, New York: V.T. Hayworth Press.

Kodner, D. 1981. "Who's S/HMO," *Home Health Care Services Quarterly* 2(4)(Winter).

Kodner, D., W. Mossey, and R. Dapello. 1983. "New York's Nursing Home Without Walls: A Provider-Based Community Care Program for the Elderly," in R. Zawadski, ed., *Community-Based Systems of Long-Term Care*, A Special Issue of *Home Health Services Quarterly* 4(3–4)(Fall–Winter).

Kotler, P. 1976. *Marketing for Non-Profit Organizations*. Englewood Cliffs, N.J.: Prentice-Hall.

Kunkel, S., and C. Powell. 1981. "The AAPCC under Risk Contracts with Providers of Health Care," *Transactions* 33.

Lambert, Z.V. 1980. "Elderly Consumers' Knowledge Related to Medigap Protection Needs," *Journal of Consumer Affairs* (Winter):434–57.

Leighton, R. 1979. "Selective Risk-Sharing: A New Reimbursement Alternative," in *Perspectives on Medicare and Medicaid Management*. Baltimore: Health Care Financing Administration.

Leonard, D. 1975. "Can Focus Group Interviews Survive," *Marketing News* (October 10).

Leutz, W. 1982. "Recommended Reimbursement and Risk Sharing Arrangements for the Social/HMO Demonstration," UHPC Working Paper. Waltham, Mass.: Brandeis University.

Leutz, W., and F. Hannon. 1981. "Capitation Finance in the Social/HMO," UHPC Working Paper. Waltham, Mass.: Brandeis University.

Luft, H.S. 1978. "How Do HMOs Achieve Their Savings?," *New England Journal of Medicine* 298(24)(June 15).

Manning, W.G., A. Liebowitz, G. Goldberg et al. 1984. "A Controlled Trial of the Effect of a Prepaid Group Practice on Use of Services," *New England Journal of Medicine* 310(23)(June 7).

Marks, S. 1983. "Going at Risk for Durable Medical Equipment." *Group Health Journal*, 5(1), Fall, 1984.

Master, R.J., et al. 1980. "A Continuum of Care for the Inner City," *New England Journal of Medicine* 302(June).

McAuliff, W. 1979. "Measuring the Quality of Medical Care: Process Versus Outcome," *Milbank Memorial Fund Quarterly* 57(1)(Winter).

McHolland, G. 1982. *Prepaid Health Plan Rate Development: Fiscal Year 1981/1982 Rates*. Sacramento, Calif: State of California.

Meiners, M. 1982. "The State-of-the-Art in Long-Term Care Insurance." Washington, D.C.: National Center for Health Services Research.

Miller, S. 1981. "Reinsurance in an S/HMO Environment," UHPC Working Paper. Waltham, Mass.: Brandeis University.

Mindel, C. 1979. "Multigenerational Family Households: Recent Trends and Implications for the Future," *Gerontologist* 19(5).

Nagi, S. 1976. "An Epidemiology of Disability among Adults in the U.S." *Health and Society* (Fall).

Nelson, J. 1982. "Tax Subsidies for Elderly Care." Washington, D.C.: Center for the Study of Social Policy.

Pollak, W. 1973. "Federal Long-Term Care Strategy," Washington, D.C.: The Urban Institute Working Paper #970–04–01 (October).

Popko, K., and P. Laskey. 1982. "The Social/HMO: Is It Feasible in a Community Hospital Setting?," *Hospital Progress* (October).

Project PHRED. Undated. *Ratesetting Guide for Prepaid Medicaid Contracts,* HCFA R&D Series Report Number 7. Baltimore, Md.: Health Care Financing Administration.

Quinn, J.L. 1982. *Triage II: Final Report,* vol. I. Wethersfield, Conn.: Triage, February.

Rand Corp. 1981. "Cost-Sharing and National Health Insurance." Discussion paper.

Sager, A. 1983. "A Proposal for Promoting More Adequate Long-Term Care for the Elderly," *Gerontologist* 23(1)(February).

Salisbury, P. 1983. "Elderplan Marketing Plan: Strategies, Plans, and Tactics for Marketing a Social/HMO," Elderplan Internal Planning Paper, January.

Sapienza, A. 1980. "Psychographic Profiles—Aide to Health Care Marketing," *HCM Review* (Fall).

Schneider, D. 1980. *Patient/Client Assessment in New York State,* vol. I. Troy, N.Y.: Schneider and Associates.

Scholen, K., and Y. Chen, eds., 1980. *Unlocking Home Equity for the Elderly.* Cambridge, Mass.: Ballinger.

Scott, W.R. 1982. "Managing Professional Work: Three Models of Control for Health Organizations," *Health Services Research* 17(3)(Fall).

Shen, J., and R. Zawadski. 1981. *Long-Term Care Costs in a Consolidated Model.* San Francisco: OnLoc Senior Health Services, Technical Report Number 302.

Smits, H., J. Feder, and W. Scanlon. 1982. "Medicare's Nursing Home Benefit: Variations in Interpretation," *New England Journal of Medicine* 14:955–62.

Soldo, B. 1983. "In-Home Services for the Dependent Elderly: Determinants of Current Use and Implications for Future Demand." Washington, D.C.: Urban Institute, May.

Titus, S.L. 1981. "Barriers to the HMO Option for Those Over Age 65," Minneapolis: University of Minnesota, Center for Health Services Research, August.

Trieger, S., T. Galblum, and G. Riley. 1981. *HMOs: Issues and Alternatives for Medicare and Medicaid.* Baltimore: Health Care Financing Administration.

USDHEW. 1973. *Financial Planning Manual.* Washington, D.C.: Office of HMOs.

Wallack, S., and J. Greenberg. 1983. "Public Financing of Long-Term Care: Its Relationship to Delivery Systems and Private Sector Initiatives." Waltham, Mass.: University Health Policy Consortium.

Wecksler, M.E., S. Durmaskin, and D. Kodner. 1983. "New Goals for Education in Geriatric Medicine," *Annals of Medicine* 96(6)(December).

Willemain, T. 1980. "Beyond the GAO Cleveland Study: Client Selection for Home Care Services," *Home Health Care Services Quarterly* 1(3)(Fall).

Wolfson, D., and L. Diamond. 1981. "Developing a Marketing Strategy for an S/HMO." Waltham, Mass.: Brandeis University.

Wood, K. 1978. "Casework Effectiveness: A New Look at the Research Evidence," *Social Casework* (November).

Woodson et al. 1981. *Long-Term Care: Guidelines for Quality.* Denver: University of Colorado Health Sciences Center, Center for Health Services Research.

Zawadski, R., ed. 1983. *Community Based Systems of Long-Term Care,* A special issue of *Home Health Services Quarterly* 4(3/4)(Fall–Winter).

Zelten, R. 1981. "Provider Reimbursement Alternatives and the Placement of Financial Risk: A Framework for Analysis," *Topics in Health Care Financing* (Winter).

Zimbalist, J. 1983. "The Design and Development of a Model Geriatric Practice," Elderplan Internal Report, December. Brooklyn, N.Y.

Index

About the Authors

Walter Leutz is a research associate at Brandeis University's Florence Heller Graduate School and associate director of the Social Health Maintenance Organization demonstration project. His professional interests have recently focused on health and employment issues in aging. He has worked on the Social Health Maintenance Organization project since 1981, where his primary responsibilities have been to develop cost estimates, benefit structures, and reimbursement models. His other experience in the social welfare field includes community organizing, addiction treatment, labor process analysis, and teaching.

Jay Greenberg is associate director for research at the Heller School's Health Policy Center. He coordinates the Center's research activities and is the director of the Social Health Maintenance Organization demonstration project. His recent professional activities have focused on the needs of the elderly and the problems confronted by state and federal government in developing effective forms of delivery for health and community-based support services. Dr. Greenberg has served as a consultant to numerous federal, state, and local governments. His extensive research activities have included studies in the housing and service needs of the elderly, a comparison of in-home and nursing home care, and the development of a model for coordinating long-term care services in Minnesota.

Ruby Abrahams, M.A., M.S.W., is currently a research associate at the Health Policy Center, Brandeis University, working primarily on service delivery and case management aspects of the Social Health Maintenance Organization project. Prior experience includes research, planning and program development in areas of aging, discharge planning, community services for the elderly, mutual help programs, community mental health, and ambulatory care. Publications include chapters in books concerning community mental health and mutual support systems, journal articles on case management, mental health of the elderly, mutual help programs, and ambulatory care planning.

Jeffrey Prottas has a long-term professional interest in the organization of service delivery agencies and the management of not-for-profit organizations. His most recent work has been on health care programs offering managed care, the evaluation of the nation's organ procurement agencies, and the impact of technical innovations on a mass transit authority. Dr. Prottas is the author of numerous articles on these and other organizational issues.

Larry Diamond is a senior research associate at the Heller School, where he has worked on the SHMO project, on deinstitutionalization policies and programs, and on retiree health benefit plans. Previously, Dr. Diamond was affiliated with the Center for Health Planning at Boston University. He is adjunct assistant professor at the Boston University School of Medicine and the New England Gerontology Center at the University of New Hampshire.

Leonard Gruenberg is a senior research associate at the Heller School. He has been involved with the SHMO demonstration since its inception and currently directs research on the project. His research interests center on reimbursement and delivery systems for long-term care. He worked previously at the Hebrew Rehabilitation Center for the Aged in Boston.

About the Brandeis University Health Policy Center

The Health Policy Center (HPC) at Brandeis University's Heller Graduate School was established in 1978 for the purpose of encouraging interdisciplinary and inter-institutional collaboration in health services research, policy analysis, and education and training. Since its inception, the staff at the HPC has focused on the design, development, implementation, and evaluation of innovative financing and delivery systems. Through the Health Policy Research Consortium established in 1984 (in cooperation with Boston University, the Center for Health Economics Research and the Urban Institute) the HPC also functions as the Health Care Financing Administration's major research and policy organization, focusing on such topics as hospital and physician prospective payment, uncompensated care, prospective payment systems, and long-term care policy. HPC education and training programs include an intense two-year doctoral program jointly offered by Brandeis and Boston Universities and a part-time training program designed to assist communities in developing health care cost-containment strategies.